ADVANCES
IN CHILD DEVELOPMENT
AND BEHAVIOR

Volume 19

Contributors to This Volume

Martin S. Banks

Cynthia A. Berg

Francine C. Blumberg

Arthur P. Ginsburg

Marc Marschark

Lynn Nall

Mary J. Naus

Stuart I. Offenbach

Peter A. Ornstein

Daniel S. P. Schubert

Herman J. P. Schubert

Robert J. Sternberg

Mazie Earle Wagner

ADVANCES
IN
CHILD DEVELOPMENT
AND
BEHAVIOR

edited by

Hayne W. Reese
Department of Psychology
West Virginia University
Morgantown, West Virginia

Volume 19

 1985

ACADEMIC PRESS, INC.
Harcourt Brace Jovanovich, Publishers

Orlando • San Diego • New York • Austin
London • Montreal • Sydney • Tokyo • Toronto

BF721
A45
Vol. 19

ACADEMIC PRESS, INC.
Orlando, Florida 32887

United Kingdom Edition published by
ACADEMIC PRESS INC. (LONDON) LTD.
24–28 Oval Road, London NW1 7DX

LIBRARY OF CONGRESS CATALOG CARD NUMBER: 63-23237

ISBN 0–12–009719–2

PRINTED IN THE UNITED STATES OF AMERICA

85 86 87 88   9 8 7 6 5 4 3 2 1

Contents

Contributors

Numbers in parentheses indicate the pages on which the authors' contributions begin.

MARTIN S. BANKS
Department of Physiological Optics, School of Optometry, University of California, Berkeley, Berkeley, California 94720 (207)

CYNTHIA A. BERG
Department of Psychology, Yale University, New Haven, Connecticut 06520 (1)

FRANCINE C. BLUMBERG
Department of Psychological Sciences, Purdue University, West Lafayette, Indiana 47907[1] (83)

ARTHUR P. GINSBURG
Aviation Vision Laboratory, Aerospace Medical Laboratories, Wright-Patterson Air Force Base, Ohio 45433 (207)

MARC MARSCHARK
Department of Psychology, University of North Carolina at Greensboro, Greensboro, North Carolina 27412 (49)

LYNN NALL
Department of Psychology, University of North Carolina at Greensboro, Greensboro, North Carolina 27412 (49)

MARY J. NAUS
Department of Psychology, University of Houston—University Park, Houston, Texas 77004 (113)

STUART I. OFFENBACH
Department of Psychological Sciences, Purdue University, West Lafayette, Indiana 47907 (83)

PETER A. ORNSTEIN
Department of Psychology, University of North Carolina at Chapel Hill, Chapel Hill, North Carolina 27514 (113)

DANIEL S. P. SCHUBERT
Case Western Reserve University School of Medicine, and Department of Psychiatry, Cleveland Metropolitan General Hospital, Cleveland, Ohio 44109 (149)

HERMAN J. P. SCHUBERT
Buffalo, New York 14221 (149)

[1]Present address: National Asssessment of Educational Progress/Educational Testing Service, Princeton, New Jersey 08541.

vii

ROBERT J. STERNBERG
*Department of Psychology, Yale University, New Haven, Connecticut
  06520 (1)*
MAZIE EARLE WAGNER
Buffalo, New York 14221 (149)

Preface

The amount of research and theoretical discussion in the field of child development and behavior is so vast that researchers, instructors, and students are confronted with a formidable task in keeping abreast of new developments within their areas of specialization through the use of primary sources, as well as being knowledgeable in areas peripheral to their primary focus of interest. Moreover, journal space is often simply too limited to permit publication of more speculative kinds of analyses that might spark expanded interest in a problem area or stimulate new modes of attack on a problem.

The serial publication *Advances in Child Development and Behavior* is intended to ease the burden by providing scholarly technical articles serving as reference material and by providing a place for publication of scholarly speculation. In these documented critical reviews, recent advances in the field are summarized and integrated, complexities are exposed, and fresh viewpoints are offered. They should be useful not only to the expert in the area but also to the general reader.

No attempt is made to organize each volume around a particular theme or topic, nor is the series intended to reflect the development of new fads. Manuscripts are solicited from investigators conducting programmatic work on problems of current and significant interest. The editor often encourages the preparation of critical syntheses dealing intensively with topics of relatively narrow scope but of considerable potential interest to the scientific community. Contributors are encouraged to criticize, integrate, and stimulate, but always within a framework of high scholarship. Although appearance in the volumes is ordinarily by invitation, unsolicited manuscripts will be accepted for review if submitted first in outline form to the editor. All papers—whether invited or submitted—receive careful editorial scrutiny. Invited papers are automatically accepted for publication in principle, but may require revision before final acceptance. Submitted papers receive the same treatment except that they are not automatically accepted for publication even in principle, and may be rejected. The *Advances* series is usually not a suitable place of publication for reports of a single study, or a short series of studies, even if the report is necessarily long because of the nature of the research.

The use of sexist language, such as ''he'' or ''she,'' as the general singular pronoun in contributions to the *Advances* series is strongly discouraged. The use of ''he or she'' (or the like) is acceptable; it is widespread and no longer seems cumbersome or self-conscious.

I wish to acknowledge with gratitude the aid of my home institution, West Virginia University, which generously provided time and facilities for the preparation of this volume. I also wish to thank Drs. Earl C. Butterfield, Andrew Ortony, Willis F. Overton, Scott G. Paris, and Stella Vosniadou for their editorial assistance, and Mrs. Ann Davis for her excellent secretarial services.

Hayne W. Reese

RESPONSE TO NOVELTY: CONTINUITY VERSUS DISCONTINUITY IN THE DEVELOPMENTAL COURSE OF INTELLIGENCE

Cynthia A. Berg and Robert J. Sternberg

DEPARTMENT OF PSYCHOLOGY
YALE UNIVERSITY
NEW HAVEN, CONNECTICUT

1

I. Introduction

Theorists and researchers of cognitive development have for decades perceived their task to be the description and explanation of continuities, discontinuities, stabilities, and instabilities of mental processes throughout human development. Their theoretical and empirical research has culminated, for the most part, in proposing qualitative, stage-like periods of intellectual development throughout the life span, and little stability of individual differences in intellectual development from infancy to later childhood (e.g., McCall, 1979a,b; Piaget, 1950, 1952; Wohlwill, 1973, 1980). Research in habituation of infant visual information processing, recognition memory, and certain aspects of infant temperament has, however, demonstrated stability of individual differences in some information processes (e.g., Bornstein, 1984; Campos, Barrett, Lamb, Goldsmith, & Stenberg, 1983; Fagan & Singer, 1983; Lewis & Brooks-Gunn, 1981) in the early years of life. We interpret this research as suggestive of one element of continuity in intellectual functions throughout development and as a potential means whereby the nature of intelligence can be understood. This element is the individual's response to novelty.

Why nominate one's response to novelty, rather than some other cognitive function, as a major element of individual differences in intelligence across the life span? Many theorists and researchers investigating intelligence throughout the history of psychology have either implicitly or explicitly, or both, included in their definition of intelligence the ability to deal with novelty of a variety of kinds. Two of the past theorists who were most explicit about the role of novelty in intellectual functioning are Stern and Pintner. For example, Stern (1914/1977, p. 3) defined intelligence as "a general capacity of an individual consciously to adjust his thinking to new requirements: it is general mental adaptability to new problems and conditions of life." In a study of experts' conceptions of intelligence in 1921, conducted by the editors of the *Journal of Educational Psychology* ("Intelligence and Its Measurement," 1921), Pintner offered the following definition of intelligence: "The ability of the individual to adapt himself adequately to relatively new situations in life" (p. 139).

We find that the ability to deal with novel tasks and situations occupies a similar prominent place in the theoretical work of Piaget (1950, 1952). Piaget identified intelligence as involving a process of adaptation whereby the cognitive system of the individual strives for maximal control over its environment. Adaptation involves the operation of two complementary processes, assimilation and accommodation. Assimilation refers to the process of adapting external stimuli to one's own internal mental structures, whereas accommodation refers to the complementary process of adapting these mental structures to the organization of the environment. Equilibration was posited as the mechanism of cognitive change and served to explain how it is possible for humans to construct new and increasingly powerful systems of cognitive structures from old cognitive structures (Piaget, 1967). An external disturbing event (i.e., a novel stimulus) places a current cognitive structure in disequilibrium, which is compensated for by virtue of the responses of the subject to these intrusions, through the process of equilibration.

Psychometric theorists also recognize the importance of dealing with novelty in their theories of intelligence. For example, Cattell and Horn (e.g., Cattell, 1971; Horn, 1968) have proposed that intelligence is of at least two different kinds, fluid and crystallized. Vernon (1971) has made a similar argument. Fluid intelligence is best measured by tasks that require adaptation to new situations and for which prior learning provides relatively little advantage; crystallized intelligence is best measured by tasks in which the problem solving of the task has been learned as a result of education, acculturation, or both.

Researchers in artificial intelligence also recognize one's response to novel tasks and situations as an important element of intelligence. Schank (1980), for instance, identified intelligence as "what people do in brand new situations. . . . the ability to make generalizations from completely new situations that are useful for future needs" (p. 13).

The ability to deal with novel task demands occupies one subtheory, the experiential subtheory, of a recent theory of human intelligence, the triarchic theory of human intelligence and its development (Berg & Sternberg, 1985a; Sternberg, 1985). The experiential subtheory relates intelligence to the level of experience one has with a task or situation. Tasks are held to be more apt measures of intelligence as they approach the point on an individual's continuum of experience at which they are quite novel, but at which the individual still has some prior knowledge to guide him or her in task solution. We will later review some literature that seems to support this subtheory of the work of Sternberg and colleagues.

Finally, the notion that dealing with novelty is an important component of intelligence is evident not only in the theorizing of researchers and theorists who study intelligence (i.e., in explicit theories of intelligence), but also in the notions that laypersons hold about intelligence (i.e., in implicit theories of intelligence). Berg and Sternberg (1985b) investigated peoples' notions of what intelligence consists of at various points in adult intellectual development. Young, middle-aged, and older adults were asked to rate the likelihood that individuals of average and exceptional intelligence at 30, 50, and 70 years of age would engage in a subset of behaviors that were identified in earlier experiments to be important in characterizing intelligent individuals at these ages. Although the results indicated that slightly different characteristics underlie people's notions of intelligence at different points in young, middle, and older age, the ability to deal with novel task demands and situations was viewed as an important characteristic of intelligence at all ages. This ability to deal with novelty included behaviors such as "is able to perceive and store new information," "is able to analyze new topics in new and original ways," and "is able to learn and reason with new kinds of concepts."

In this article we examine the evidence for regarding intelligence as, in part, deriving from one's response to novelty. We further consider the type of synthesis our position might bring to the study of the development of intelligence throughout the life span. Research and theorizing are reviewed in diverse domains, such as infant visual information processing, infant recognition memory, selected aspects of infant temperament (e.g., task persistence and attention span), psychometric intelligence, Piagetian intelligence, and cognitive psychology, in order to demonstrate the idea that one's response to novel tasks and situations is intimately involved in the construct of intelligence. An organizing framework is provided for conceptualizing intelligence as, in part, a response to novelty. This framework comprises two major aspects: a motivational aspect, according to which one's interest in, curiosity about, and preference for novelty are involved in intelligent functioning; and an information-extraction aspect, which involves identification of those component processes that are involved in the acquisition of novel information. We argue that viewing intelligence as involving one's response to novelty, of a variety of kinds, may provide theorists a means for understanding at least one source of continuity in the nature of intelligence across the life span. In turn, this continuity may suggest a relatively stable source of individual differences in intellectual development.

II. Distinguishing Two Types of Continuity

Two potentially independent types of continuity should be differentiated, although they have often been misconstrued to be the same entity and have both been used as evidence for assertions regarding the continuity or discontinuity of intellectual and cognitive functions across the life span (Appelbaum & McCall, 1983; McCall, 1979a,b).

The first type of continuity can be thought of as the continuity in the fundamental nature of the attribute under study, here, intelligence. McCall (1979a,b) stated that to determine whether a given attribute is continuous or discontinuous, one must examine the developmental function of that attribute (i.e., view the measured value of the attribute under study plotted across age). This developmental function is said to be continuous when changes across age in the attribute are quantitative, and discontinuous when changes in the attribute over age are qualitative. A plot of weight over age would be continuous because the fundamental character of weight is the same at every age. In contrast, intelligence, as defined at least within the Piagetian perspective (e.g., Piaget 1950, 1952), would represent a discontinuous developmental function because the actual nature of intelligence is said to undergo qualitative changes across time, resulting in stages of cognitive development such as sensorimotor intelligence and formal operations.

The adoption of such a stringent criterion for the existence of continuity of a particular trait, namely, that changes over age are quantitative, not qualitative in nature, which implies that intelligence be measured in precisely the same manner at each of various ages, seems to preclude the demonstration of any continuity in a construct such as intelligence over the course of intellectual development. Given the limitations in the response capabilities of the infant, relatively few behaviors are measurable during this time of intellectual development that can be compared to the same behaviors at later points in life. Even if researchers were to compare those behaviors that are exhibited during early infancy with the same behaviors at some later points in development, such a comparison would be inappropriate for addressing questions regarding continuity in the nature of intelligence and stability of individual differences in intelligence. The behavior in infancy would almost certainly measure a different construct than the same behavior in childhood and adulthood. Thus, perhaps a more appropriate test for the continuity in the nature of a construct such as intelligence is whether or not the measures assess the same underlying processes involved in intelligence, that is, demonstrate construct validity, not whether or not our measurements are exactly the same at various points in intellectual development.

The second type of continuity may be better construed as relative stability, namely, the relative stability of individual differences on a given attribute at various ages (e.g., Appelbaum & McCall, 1983; McCall, 1979a,b). Typically, this type of continuity is approached by correlating scores on tests measuring the attribute of interest at two different ages. Some amount of stability of individual differences results when individuals maintain their relative rank ordering on a given attribute within a group at two different ages. Thus, the correlation between scores on tests reflective of the attribute at two different ages is significantly different from zero. Instability of individual differences results when an individual's score on an attribute is not predictable from knowledge of his or her previous score, and thus is reflected in a nonsignificant correlation between scores on tests measuring this attribute at the two times of interest. For example, components of hyperactive behavior have been found to be longitudinally stable over a 5-year period in children varying in age from 2.5 to 7.5 years (Halverson & Waldrop, 1976). Scores on tasks designed to measure intelligence, in contrast, have typically shown little stability of individual differences, particularly during the developmental period between early infancy and later childhood. For instance, McCall (1979b) reported a median correlation, based on several studies, of .09 between test scores at 1–6 months and 5–7 years.

As one might sense from the preceding examples, little evidence is available for either of these two types of continuity. Theorists have speculated that the developmental function of intelligence exhibits little continuity. Major stage theorists, such as Baldwin (1906–1915), Piaget (1952), and H. Werner (1948), have posited that the actual nature of intelligence changes as one moves from infancy to adulthood. In particular, cognitive development is said to consist of invariant sequences of qualitative change and growth in mental functioning, resulting in various semi-distinct stages noted for their own particular organizations, structures, and processes. Thus, Baldwin (1906–1915) identified separate modes or levels of consciousness, that is, different ways in which a child comes to learn about his or her world: prelogical, quasilogical, logical, and hyperlogical. Analogously, Piaget (1952) divided intellectual development into four major periods: sensorimotor, preoperational, concrete–operational, and formal–operational. These assertions regarding the qualitative difference between intelligence as manifested in infancy and in early adulthood have been said to be based far less on data pertaining to the theory than on careful conjecture and the evolutionary thinking of the time (S. White, 1983). Piaget's stage theory of cognitive development, with clear and visible roots in the work of Baldwin (e.g., Cahan, 1984; Cairns, 1983; Ross & Kerst, 1978), can be said to be more dependent on empirical research than was Baldwin's earlier work. However, those theoretical assertions regarding the abrupt qualitative distinctions between stages are those that have been most subject to empirical refutation (e.g., Brown & Desforges, 1979; Gelman & Baillargeon, 1983; Siegel & Brainerd, 1978).

Empirical attempts to provide support for the discontinuity of the developmental function of intelligence in the early infant and childhood years have come from reanalyses of the Fels Longitudinal Study (McCall, Hogarty, & Hurlburt, 1972) and the Berkeley Growth Study (McCall, Eichorn, & Hogarty, 1977), conducted by McCall and colleagues. The Fels and Berkeley longitudinal studies involved administration of infant and childhood intelligence tests several times during the first years of life. For purposes of brevity we shall examine in more detail only the reanalysis of the

Fels study, as the results from the reanalysis of the Berkeley Growth Study are similar.

The Fels researchers administered the Gesell tests (Gesell & Amatruda, 1962) at 6, 12, 18, and 24 months of age, the Stanford–Binet at 3.5, 6, and 10 years, and the Wechsler Intelligence Scale for Children at 7 or 11 years or the Wechsler–Bellevue at 13 years. McCall *et al.* (1972) analyzed subjects' responses via principal component analyses for each of the ages at which the Gesell was administered. The first principal component that emerged from each of these four analyses was interpreted to represent the predominant character underlying intelligence at that age. Changes over age in the item composition of the first component were examined to reflect discontinuities in the developmental function of intelligence. Items that loaded on the first principal component at 6 and at 12 months of age contained behaviors characteristic of gross and fine motor movement, although at 12 months of age certain social behaviors also began to appear. The first principal component at 18 months of age contained items reflective of verbal behavior, namely, aspects of verbal production and verbal comprehension, this trend becoming even more predominant at 24 months of age.

McCall (1979a) argued on the basis of these data that the developmental function of intelligence is discontinuous with respect to these age ranges. We would like to argue that this discontinuity in the developmental function could largely be attributable to the different item composition that is involved on each of the tests at these ages. For example, the Gesell at 6 and 12 months is dominated by items related to motor behaviors and contains relatively few language items, whereas the Gesell at 18 and 24 months contains many fewer motor items and many more items related to vocabulary and language usage than at the earlier ages (e.g., Gesell & Amatruda, 1962). McNemar (1951) and others (e.g., Guilford, 1952) have noted that the factors that emerge from component analysis are heavily dependent on the selection of items that are used in the intercorrelation matrices that are analyzed. Thus, the differential frequency with which items are distributed in these various content areas on the Gesell (i.e., motor, adaptive, and personal–social) may largely account for the discontinuities that McCall and colleagues report.

Research on the stability or instability of individual differences in intelligence from infancy to early adulthood has revealed little stability in intelligence, particularly in the early childhood years, namely, using early infancy scores to predict later childhood scores. McCall (1979b) reported, on the basis of several studies, median correlations that ranged from a low of .06 between intelligence test scores at 1-6 months and 8-18 years to a high of .59 between intelligence test scores at 19-30 months and 3-4 years. When correlations between scores on tests of intelligence in early infancy and scores on tests of intelligence in later childhood are examined, two trends are apparent. First, correlations appear to increase with the age at which the infant test is administered, so that the later in infancy the intelligence test is given, the higher the correlation between scores on tests of intelligence in infancy and scores on tests of intelligence in childhood. Second, correlations appear to increase, the shorter the developmental period that is being predicted, such that correlations are highest when the amount of time between the infant test and the childhood test being predicted is shortest.

The research examining the relationship between early infant and later childhood mental performance has typically involved global, overall scores as measures of mental performance. Research suggests that when more specific abilities are assessed in early infancy, the stability coefficients are somewhat higher. For example, the work of Siegel (1979, 1981) has demonstrated that many of the subtests of the Uzgiris–Hunt Scale (Uzgiris & Hunt, 1975) and the Bayley Developmental Index (Bayley, 1969), administered at various points in the first 2 years of life, are predictive of later cognitive performance (as assessed by the Stanford–Binet at 36 months) and language abilities (as measured by the Reynell Language Scales at 36 months). The Bayley Mental Developmental Index was significantly related to the Stanford–Binet at 36 months when administered at 4 ($r = .35, p < .001$), 8 ($r = .27, p < .001$), 12 ($r = .38, p < .001$), 18 ($r = .57, p < .001$), and 24 ($r = .69, p < .001$) months of age. Schemes, a subtest of the Uzgiris–Hunt scales, assessing the type and number of different activities that a child demonstrates with familiar objects at 4 months of age, is significantly related to both Stanford–Binet performance at 36 months ($r = .42, p < .001$) and Reynell Language Comprehension at 36 months ($r = .31, p < .001$). These relationships, although significant, are modest, particularly between measures of intelligence in early infancy (4–8 months) and later childhood (3 years).

Correlations between scores on tests of infant intelligence and scores on tests of later childhood intelligence are thought to be higher for clinical groups (e.g., premature infants and fetal and neonatal infants at-risk) and for infants with mental deficiencies than for normal groups. However, in a recent review article, Kopp and McCall (1982) suggested that many of the high correlations predicting later mental performance from early mental performance for at-risk and handicapped infants may be explainable, in part, by statistical artifacts alone. For example, data derived from clinical samples and samples of mentally deficient infants are typically based on small sample sizes. Moreover, the infants are diagnosed via a variety of different clinical techniques and criteria. In any case, although these stability coefficients are higher for at-risk infants than for normal infants, they are still far from perfect.

The two types of continuity have been said to be potentially independent, in that continuity or discontinuity in the developmental function does not influence the stability or instability of individual differences (McCall, 1979a,b; Wohlwill, 1973, 1980). In actual practice, however, the two types of continuity may be quite interdependent. For example, research on the stability of individual differences in intelligence has involved tasks that theorists posit to be measures of intelligence. As was discussed above, theorists have typically assumed, through the influence of major theorists such as Baldwin and Piaget, that intellectual and cognitive development is characterized by a stage-like progression that entails qualitative rather than quantitative changes (e.g., Flavell, 1971; Piaget, 1950, 1952; Wohlwill, 1973). Thus, the tasks that are used to measure stability of individual differences throughout development, based upon such stage theories, have a qualitatively different nature in infancy than in early and later childhood (e.g., Bayley, 1969; Terman & Merrill, 1960; Uzgiris & Hunt, 1975). In particular, tasks that are used to measure intelligence in infancy, such as the Bayley (1969), tap simple sensory and motor skills; tasks used in later childhood, such as the Stanford–Binet (Terman & Merrill, 1960), tap the child's discrimination, encoding, memory, and vocabulary abilities, to name just a few. If the tasks that are used to measure intelligence in infancy were made more similar in kind to the tasks used to measure intelligence in early childhood, thereby increasing construct validity, perhaps predictive validity might be improved.

The current theoretical and empirical position on either type of continuity appears, then, to be that the developmental function is discontinuous and that individual differences in this developmental function are unstable in the early months and years of life (e.g., Bayley, 1970; Case, 1978; McCall, 1979a,b; Ulvund, 1984). Although this position may be the predominant view held by researchers in the field of developmental psychology, some investigators are still examining cognition in the early years for a common mechanism whereby cognitive development occurs (e.g., Keil, 1981; Sternberg, 1984b) and for stability of individual differences in intelligence (e.g., Bornstein & Ruddy, 1983; Fagan & McGrath, 1981; Lewis & Brooks-Gunn, 1981; Ruddy & Bornstein, 1982; Siegel, 1979, 1981). For example, the desire for a mechanism of cognitive development is evident in the work of Keil (1981, 1984), who has posited that cognitive development is guided by a set of constraints that guide the development of cognitive structures and processes. These constraints remain invariant throughout development. The interest in a mechanism of cognitive development is also apparent in a recent book whose authors specifically examine mechanisms of continuity in cognitive development (see Sternberg, 1984a).

Research on early infant visual habituation and visual recognition memory and later childhood intelligence (e.g., Bornstein, 1984; Fagan & McGrath, 1981; Lewis & Brooks-Gunn, 1981) suggests that continuity of individual differences in intelligence may exist when intelligence is defined as an individual's response to novelty. We shall now selectively review the research and theorizing that seem to support the contention that intelligence throughout the course of intellectual development can be construed, in part, as a response to dealing with novelty. The review is selective in two major respects. First, we concentrate on longitudinal research that examines the relationships between behaviors in early infancy and later childhood as this literature most directly addresses issues of stability of individual differences in intellectual development and continuity in the nature of intelligence. Second, we examine research that most explicitly examines the relationships between response to novelty and concurrent cognitive functioning in childhood and adulthood. Although almost any cognitive task can be seen, in some respects, to measure an individual's response to some type of novel stimulus and in fact the major goal of the development of our cognitive skills is to assimilate and accommodate to such tasks, we restrict our review of this second literature to those tasks that deal with the relations between a response to novelty and intelligence directly. We also consider the development of component operations that might underlie the ability to deal with novelty.

III. Relations between Infant Response to Novel Stimuli and Later Cognitive Development

Three areas of research, reviewed in this section, indicate that the response to novelty may be a source of stability in intellectual functions throughout the early years of life and may provide a way in which the nature of intelligence can be understood. Longitudinal research on infant habituation of attention, infant recognition memory, and two aspects of infant temperament, namely, attention span and task persistence, are reviewed because they share two things in common. First, unlike many other areas of research in early infancy, these three areas provide evidence for some stability of individual differences between infancy and childhood. Second, habituation, infant recognition memory, and temperament scales of attention span and task persistence purport to measure the infant's interest in and attention to novel stimuli in his or her environment.

A. INFANT HABITUATION OF ATTENTION

Habituation can be defined as the response decrement that occurs when a stimulus is repeatedly presented to an organism. For example, if a stimulus S_1 is either repeatedly presented or continuously presented, an infant will initially attend to S_1, but attention will decline over time. This decrement in attention is thought to represent the infant's increasing memory or knowledge of the stimulus, through the infant's construction of mental representations corresponding to the familiar stimulus. When a novel stimulus S_2 is presented to the infant subsequent to habituation to S_1, dishabituation occurs; that is, the infant's attention to the stimulus greatly increases. This increment in attention is thought to reflect the infant's discrimination that S_2 is discrepant from the mental representation that has been formed for S_1. Investigators have proposed (e.g., McCall & Kagan, 1967), and some empirical evidence suggests (McCall, Kennedy, & Appelbaum, 1977; McCall & McGhee, 1977), that moderate discrepancies between the novel and familiar stimulus will produce greater attention. A highly novel stimulus will not elicit the infant's attention because the stimulus is so different from the mental representation the infant has constructed that the infant is not sufficiently motivated to explore the stimulus.

Habituation of infant attention has been examined for several sensory modalities (e.g., auditory stimuli, olfactory stimuli, and visual stimuli) via a variety of response measures (e.g., nonnutritive sucking, heart rate, respiration, and galvanic skin response). Perhaps the most common modality-response pairing, at least in the work examining the relation between infant habituation of attention and later cognitive development, is the visual stimulus–visual response pairing, often referred to as the visual attention paradigm (e.g., Bornstein, 1984). We will restrict our selective review to empirical work conducted within the visual attention paradigm via the fixed-trials procedure. The fixed-trials procedure involves presenting stimuli to infants for a fixed number of trials, in which the presentation of the stimuli is controlled by the experimenter (e.g., Fantz, 1964). Within this paradigm alone, habituation has been used to investigate a wide variety of processes. For example, the visual attention paradigm has been used to examine attention, memory, discrimination, categorization, concept formation, and individual differences in cognitive development. (For a complete review of the habituation literature see Bornstein, 1984; Cohen, DeLoache, & Strauss, 1979; Kessen, Haith, & Salapatek, 1970; Olson & Sherman, 1983; J. Werner & Perlmutter, 1979.)

One methodological concern must be raised before we examine the empirical research in this area. Demonstrating a response decrement to repeated visual stimuli cannot, by itself, be interpreted as evidence for habituation. This response decrement could be attributable to sensory accommodation, effector fatigue, or a change in the infant's state of arousal or alertness. Various control conditions have been developed to allow investigators to dismiss these alternative interpretations for the decrement in response and to be more confident that the response decrement truly represents habituation (e.g., Bornstein, 1984; Kessen *et al.*, 1970). One control condition involves presenting a novel stimulus following visual habituation. If the infant shows recovery of visual fixation to this novel stimulus in comparison to the level of fixation on the last trial of habituation, that is, if dishabituation occurs, then effector fatigue and change of state can be excluded as determinants of response decrement. A second control condition involves comparing fixation times to a pretest stimulus, different from the habituation stimulus, to a re-presentation of this stimulus after habituation has taken place. If the infant's fixation to the posttest stimulus is not significantly different in length from the infant's fixation to the pretest stimulus, it can be assumed that habituation has taken place, rather than effector fatigue or a change of state. Several studies that we shall review, on the relation between early infant habituation to visual information and later cognitive development, have involved these control conditions.

Two questions of interest arise when examining the relation of early infant habituation and cognitive performance. The first is whether a relationship exists between early infant habituation and concurrent cognitive functioning. The second is whether a relationship exists between early infant habituation and later childhood mental abilities. We shall examine the research addressed to each of these questions.

Research by Ruddy and Bornstein (1982) is addressed to both of these questions. They examined 20 full-term infants at 4 months and again when the infants were 12 months old. Infants were shown five vertical red bars for 15 trials via a fixed-trials procedure. A pretest/posttest control condition was used, giving infants two trials with faces prior to the habituation trials and four trials repeating the faces after habituation trials. Two response variables were used: the amount of habituation (i.e., the percentage decline in the amount of time the infant fixates to the first presentation of the stimulus, first-look length, from the initial two trials of the habituation series to the final two trials) and the rate of habituation (i.e., the first pair of consecutive trials for which the average first look declined to 80% or less of the average for the initial two trials without a subsequent rebound to over 90%). Approximately 1 week prior to the habituation session, infants were given the Bayley Scales in their home. In addition, the home visit included observations of various infant and mother behaviors. At 12 months of age, the Bayley scales were again administered at home and observations were made with regard to the mother's attention and the speech to the child. Questionnaires were administered to the mothers to assess aspects of the child's speech. The dependent measures of the study were then correlated.

The results indicated that attention decrements could be credited to habituation and not to fatigue or some type of state change, in that the average first look at the faces after the habituation trials (6.8 seconds) was not significantly different from the average first look at the faces prior to the habituation trials (6.5 seconds). Little relationship between infant habituation and current cognitive performance was found, as evidenced by low and nonsignificant correlations between amount of habituation at 4 months and the Bayley score at 4 months ($r = .09$) and between the rate of habituation at 4 months and the Bayley score at 4 months ($r = .08$). Amount and rate of habituation were related to the observation of the infant's active manipulation of objects (e.g., squeezing, banging of objects) at 4 months ($r = .60, p < .01$ and $r = -.60, p < .01$, respectively). Thus, those infants who habituated more and faster at 4 months were those infants who were observed, at the same age, to be more active in their manipulation of objects. Amount of habituation and the rate of habituation at 4 months of age were also related to Bayley scores at 12 months of age ($r = .46, p < .05$ and $r = -.49, p < .05$, respectively), and to estimates of the infants' vocabularies at 12 months ($r = .52, p < .05$ and $r = -.39$, $p < .10$, respectively), indicating that infants who habituated more and faster at 4 months had higher Bayley scores and larger vocabularies at 12 months. Bayley scores at 4 months of age were also related to Bayley scores at 12 months of age ($r = .47, p < .05$). The degree to which mothers at 4 months encouraged the child's attention was significantly related to the infants' vocabularies at 12 months ($r = .55, p < .01$). Multiple regression analyses, conducted to determine the power of mother's encouraging attention and habituation amount in predicting 12-month vocabulary size, suggested that these two predictors were largely independent contributors to the infant's vocabulary size.

Three tentative conclusions can be drawn from this study. First, infant habituation to visual stimuli assessed at 4 months taps different processes from the Bayley Scales at 4 months. Second, individual differences in the amount and rate of habituation in infancy are predictive of later individual differences in mental performance. In fact, the amount and rate of habituation in infancy are as predictive of later Bayley performance as is the actual Bayley itself. Third, amount of habituation and rate of habituation may be relatively independent of environmental contributors to later cognitive functioning.

Further support for these conclusions comes from research by Lewis and Brooks-Gunn (1981). These investigators administered a visual attention task and the Escalona and Corman Scales of Sensori-Motor Development (Escalona & Corman, 1967) at 3 months and the Bayley Test of Infant Development (Bayley, 1969) at both 3 months and 24 months of age to two samples of infants. The first sample, including 22 infants, was tested on visual habituation both for form and for color; the second sample, including 57 infants, was tested only on habituation for form. The measures included the amount of habituation that occurred with repeated presentations of a visual stimulus and the amount of dishabituation that occurred to a novel stimulus. These measures were then intercorrelated. No significant correlations were found between Bayley scores or Escalona–Corman scales at 3 months of age and either amount of habituation or amount of dishabituation. Again, infant visual attention appears to be measuring something different from the sensorimotor abilities that the Bayley and the Escalona–Corman assess. The amount of habituation at 3 months was highly related to later intelligence in the first sample ($r = .61, p < .01$) and unrelated to later intelligence in the second sample ($r = -.18$). Quite large and significant correlations did exist, however, between amounts of dishabituation and the Bayley scores at 24 months for both samples ($r = .52$, $p < .05$ and $r = .40, p < .01$), suggesting that infants who recovered better from habituation had higher Bayley scores at 24 months. In this study, Bayley scores at 3 months did not predict Bayley scores at 24 months, although the visual attention measures did. Thus, individual differences in the amount of habituation and dishabituation in infancy were more predictive of later Bayley performance than the actual Bayley itself.

Some research also suggests that a relationship exists between habituation performance in infancy and cognitive performance in later childhood. Lewis and colleagues (Lewis, Goldberg, & Campbell, 1969) reported that response decrement to a visual stimulus at 12 months predicted intelligence as measured by the Stanford–Binet at 44 months ($r = .46$ for girls, $r = .50$ for boys; $p < .05$ for each). Caution must be exercised in interpreting these results, for habituation may not have been demonstrated in these studies, as dishabituation to the novel stimulus did not occur. The response decrement that occurred could be attributable to either effector fatigue or stage changes.

In sum, research on habituation of visual information processing seems to indicate that measures of infant habituation are unrelated to measures of concurrent intellectual performance (i.e., tests that tap simple motor and sensory abilities such as the Bayley) but are predictive of later intellectual performance on tasks that measure more cognitive abilities.

B. INFANT RECOGNITION MEMORY

A hypothesis generating a great deal of research in infant recognition memory is that the infant's ability to recognize a previously seen stimulus may involve processes similar to those tapped on later intelligence tests and may be reflective of early intelligence (e.g., Fagan & Singer, 1983). One of the first studies of infant recognition memory and later intelligence was conducted by Yarrow, Klein, Lomonaco, and Morgan (1975). These investigators examined 39 lower-class black infants at 6 months and at 3.5 years. At 6 months, the infants were assessed on several cognitive–motivational variables. One of these variables, manipulation of novel objects, involved allowing an infant to handle and become used to a bell, the familiar object. Following this period of familiarization, the bell was paired with 10 novel objects, presented one at a time. Recognition was assessed as the amount of time the infant spent handling the novel objects. The amount of time spent handling the novel objects was significantly related to scores on the Stanford–Binet Intelligence Test measured at 3.5 years of age ($r = .35$, $p < .05$).

Further research investigating infant recognition memory and later intelligence has also indicated that continuities may exist between the infant's ability to recognize previously seen information and performance on later intelligence tests. Fagan and McGrath (1981) tested 93 children on their recognition of previously seen targets for the relationship this recognition had to later vocabulary tasks. The paradigm was a modification of one used by Fantz (1967) and is as follows. Infants were presented identical pairs of picture stimuli (e.g., a face or an abstract pattern). Following this period of initial familiarization with the stimuli, the familiar stimulus and a novel stimulus were presented to the infant simultaneously. Recognition memory was defined as the mean percentage of total fixation to novel targets. Thus, a score of 50% would indicate that the infant fixated an equal amount of time to the novel and the familiar stimulus, indicating no evidence of recognition memory. A score sufficiently above 50% would be taken as evidence that the familiar stimulus had been remembered. Early infant recognition memory scores, measured at either 5 or 7 months, were then correlated with later vocabulary tests of intelligence, measured at either 4 or 7 years. The correlation between early infant recognition memory scores averaged over 5 and 7 months and vocabulary scores at 4 years of age was .37 ($p < .01$) and at 7 years was .57 ($p < .01$).

Let us compare these correlations to those obtained in typical studies predicting later childhood cognitive performance from early infancy intelligence tests. McCall (1979b) reported, on the basis of several studies, me-

dian correlations of .21 between infant intelligence test scores at 1–6 months
and childhood intelligence test scores at 3–4 years, .32 between infant intelligence test scores at 7–12 months and childhood intelligence test scores
at 3–4 years, .09 between infant intelligence test scores at 1–6 months and
childhood intelligence test scores at 5–7 years, and .20 between infant intelligence test scores at 7–12 months and childhood intelligence test scores
at 5–7 years. The correlations obtained by Fagan and McGrath (1981) between infant recognition memory scores and vocabulary items at 4 years
are slightly above those reported by McCall, and the correlations between
infant recognition memory scores and vocabulary items at 7 years are greatly
beyond those reported by McCall for this age range.

Further support for the utility of infant recognition memory as a predictor of later individual differences in intelligence comes from a study by
Fagan (1981, reported in Fagan & Singer, 1983). Fifty-two white infants and
16 black infants, living in the same neighborhood, were tested at 7 months
of age for recognition memory and were given the Peabody Picture Vocabulary Test and the picture vocabulary and naming portion of the Stanford–
Binet Intelligence Test at 3 years of age. Each infant's mother was also given
a vocabulary test. Recognition memory was assessed as in the Fagan and
McGrath (1981) research. A significant relationship obtained between recognition scores at 7 months and vocabulary performance at 3 years of age
($r = .36, p < .01$). Recognition memory was unrelated to race, birth order,
mother's vocabulary, or parental education. Infant recognition memory appears, then, to be relatively unaffected by early environmental influences.
Scores on the Peabody Picture Vocabulary Test were, however, related to
race, birth order, and mother's vocabulary, such that white children scored
higher than did black children, mothers with better vocabularies had children with better picture vocabulary scores, and children of earlier birth order scored better than did children of later birth order. Multiple regression
analyses indicated that the best model predicting later Peabody Picture Performance included only two variables, namely, the recognition score in infancy and one's birth order, accounting for 51% of the total variance.
Similar results were obtained when Fagan reanalyzed the data from the Fagan and McGrath (1981) study.

Thus, it would appear that individual differences in visual recognition
ability in infancy are predictive of later individual differences in verbal intelligence. Further research by Fagan (1984a) suggests that infant recognition memory is a better predictor of later intellectual functioning than are
traditional sensorimotor measures of infant intelligence, such as the Bayley.

Research on differences in recognition memory between children who are
known to differ in their measured intelligence represents a different tack at
examining the relationship between individual differences in infant recog-

nition memory and intelligence. Miranda and Fantz (1974), using the same paradigm as that of Fagan and McGrath (1981), examined differences in infant recognition memory between normal and Down's Syndrome infants at 8–16, 17–29, and 30–40 weeks. They found significant differences between these two groups of infants on various recognition tasks: abstract patterns differing along a variety of dimensions, abstract patterns differing in their arrangement of elements, and photos of an infant's versus a woman's face. In general, normal infants were better able to recognize familiar stimuli than were Down's Syndrome infants as evidenced by larger memory recognition scores and larger difference scores between fixation to novel versus familiar stimuli. Down's Syndrome infants did, however, show some recognition.

Confirmation of this decreased ability of Down's Syndrome infants to recognize previously seen information comes from research by Cohen (1981), who used the visual attention habituation paradigm discussed earlier. Cohen used response recovery, that is, the amount of dishabituation, as the measure of decrement in attention. Down's Syndrome infants were compared to normal infants at 19, 23, and 28 weeks. The results indicated that normal infants exhibited dishabituation at all ages, although Down's Syndrome infants did not evidence dishabituation until 28 weeks.

In sum, research with the recognition memory paradigm has demonstrated that individual differences in visual recognition ability in infancy are more predictive of later individual differences in tested intelligence than are individual differences in the traditional sensorimotor measures of infant intelligence. In addition, differences in visual recognition ability have been demonstrated between groups of infants who are thought to differ in their measured intelligence. Results are also suggestive that measures of infant recognition memory are relatively unaffected by early environmental influences.

C. TWO ASPECTS OF INFANT TEMPERAMENT: TASK
PERSISTENCE AND ATTENTION SPAN

Two key concepts guide much of the theoretical and empirical work on temperament. First, temperament is said to be closely intertwined with the mood, affect, and the emotional character of the infant (e.g., Campos *et al.*, 1983; Goldsmith & Campos, 1982; Rothbart & Derryberry, 1982). Second, individual differences in temperament are thought to be stable over the infant's lifetime, to be consistent over different situations, and to be largely determined by constitutional make-up (e.g., Buss & Plomin, 1975; Campos *et al.*, 1983). Although these two key concepts guide much of the theoretical and empirical work on temperament, great variability exists in the types of behaviors assessed in reference to temperament. For example, the Bayley Infant Behavioral Record (Bayley, 1969) assesses aspects of the infant's interpersonal and affective behavior (e.g., social orientation, general emotional tone, fearfulness), motivational variables (e.g., goal directedness, attention span, endurance), and various interests in specific aspects of his or her sensory experience (e.g., manipulating objects, mouthing or sucking toys, and body motion). We will concentrate, in our selective review, on the literature on those aspects of infant temperament that are most closely related to concurrent and later cognitive performance.

To include a discussion of the temperamental behavioral characteristics of the infant in an article dealing with intelligence and one's response to novelty may seem inappropriate. We argue, however, that the inclusion is appropriate for two reasons. First, certain aspects of infant temperament, namely, attention span and task persistence, seem to be highly related to concurrent and later cognitive functioning. On the surface, this demonstration of continuity between early infant temperament and later intellectual abilities may seem unrelated to the element of continuity that is the topic of this article, one's response to novelty. However, and this is our second reason for including a section on temperament, theorists and researchers assert that the temperamental behaviors, attention span and task persistence, represent the infant's "duration of interest given a new stimulus" (Campos *et al.,* 1983, p. 835; Goldsmith & Campos, 1982). Although this attentional response is not measured in the same behavioral units as recognition memory and habituation, both measured in terms of the infant's length of fixation, these three domains of research (i.e., infant habituation, infant recognition memory, and aspects of infant temperament) seem to reflect a similar underlying process, the infant's response to a novel stimulus, and particularly his or her attentional response. We will discuss further in Section III,D (on Explanatory Mechanisms) how infant habituation, infant recognition memory, and aspects of infant temperament measure the infant's response to novelty and how this response may be the mediating link between these three areas of research and later intellectual performance. First, let us selectively review the research that demonstrates a relation between aspects of early infant temperament and concurrent and later mental functioning.

Matheny, Dolan, and Wilson (1974) examined ratings on the Bayley Infant Behavior Record and test scores from the Bayley Mental Scale for 55 pairs of twins at 6, 12, 18, and 24 months of age, selected from the larger population of twins in the Louisville Twin Study. Only children who had been tested at each of these ages were included in the study. Two behavioral composites were formed from the 25 separate rating scales measured by the Bayley Infant Behavioral Record, based on prior research (Dolan, Matheny, & Wilson, 1974; Matheny & Brown, 1971) that had indicated high intercorrelations among these behaviors: primary cognition (ratings of the infant's object orientation, goal-directedness, attention span, reactivity, vocalization, gross motor movement, and fine motor coordination) and extraversion (ratings of the infant's social orientation to the experimenter, cooperation, and emotional tone).

Scores on these two composite measures were then correlated with the Bayley Mental Test Scores measured at each of the ages. Scores on the Primary Cognition composite were significantly related to concurrent performance on the Bayley Mental Tests at all ages for both males and females. (Separate correlations are reported herein for males and females because the authors did not report overall correlations.) For example, at 6 months, scores on the Primary Cognition composite were correlated with scores on the Bayley Mental Test with $r = .77$ ($p < .05$) for females and $r = .86$ ($p < .05$) for males. At 24 months, scores on the Primary Cognition composite were correlated with scores on the Bayley Mental Test with $r = .52$ ($p < .05$) for females and $r = .66$ ($p < .05$) for males. Scores on the Extraversion composite were related to concurrent scores on the Bayley Mental Tests for females, although the relationship was less strong than for Primary Cognition, and for males only at 24 months. For example, the correlations between scores on the Extraversion composite and scores on the Bayley Mental Test for females ranged from a low of .33 ($p < .05$) at 6 months to a high of .43 ($p < .05$) at 12 months. For males, the only significant correlation between scores on the Extraversion composite and scores on the Bayley Mental Test was at 24 months ($r = .40, p < .05$).

Relationships between these behavioral composites and subsequent Bayley Mental Test Scores were also examined. Significant relationships obtained between early Primary Cognition scores and later scores on the Bayley Mental Tests at nearly all ages for males. For females, these relationships were somewhat lower, with only two correlations reaching significance. For males, correlations between Primary Cognition scores at 6 months of age were highly correlated with later scores on Bayley Mental tests at 12 months ($r = .48, p < .05$), 18 months ($r = .57, p < .05$), and 24 months ($r = .43, p < .05$). For females, the correlation between Primary Cognition scores at 6 months and later Bayley Mental Test scores reached significance only for the 18-month Bayley ($r = .43, p < .05$). The correlations between early Extraversion scores and later scores on the Bayley Mental Tests were low and nonsignificant at all ages and for both sexes. Thus, behaviors reflecting task orientation, motivation, and attention span were related to both concurrent and later cognitive functioning, but behaviors reflective of the infant's sociability were only somewhat related to concurrent cognitive functioning and were unrelated to later cognitive functioning.

Results from another large twin study, the longitudinal Collaborative Perinatal Project, also indicate that aspects of infant temperament may be related to later cognitive functioning (Goldsmith & Gottesman, 1981). Goldsmith and Gottesman (1981) assessed several behavioral dimensions, similar to the 25 behaviors from the Infant Behavioral Record (Bayley, 1969), and aspects of intellectual functioning for 504 twin pairs at 8 months, 4 years, and 7 years of age. The various behaviors from the Infant Behavioral Record were factor analyzed, separately for each age. Factor scores on a vigorous, persistent activity factor (e.g., speed of response and active manipulation) at 8 months were related to concurrent assessments of mental development with r in the range of .5–.6. These factor scores were also somewhat related to intelligence as measured at 4 years of age ($r = .31$ for males and $r = .12$ for females). The task persistence factor scores at 4 years of age (e.g., attention span and goal orientation) were correlated significantly with concurrently assessed intelligence both for males ($r = .57$) and for females ($r = .60$). Data were not reported for the relationships between task persistence at 7 years of age and concurrent assessments of intelligence.

Because this study involved the examination of both identical and fraternal twins, estimates of hereditary and environmental influences on aspects of temperament could be examined for both the individual behaviors from the Infant Behavioral Record and for the factors that were discussed above by examining differences between monozygotic (MZ) and dizygotic (DZ) concordance. Of particular interest are the co-twin similarity estimates for the particular behaviors and factors that were most highly related to concurrent and later cognitive performance. For the vigorous persistent activity factor at 8 months, the difference between MZ and DZ concordance was .22 ($p < .01$), indicating a substantial genetic origin. The factor of task persistence at 4 years yielded a difference score between MZ and DZ concordance of .31 ($p < .001$), again indicating a large constitutional origin. It might appear, then, that those aspects of temperament that are predictive of later intelligence are those that are largely genetic in origin.

To conclude, task persistence and attention span appear to be two temperamental characteristics that are often related to both concurrent and later cognitive functioning. These two aspects of temperament, like visual habituation and recognition memory, may have a large genetic contribution.

D. EXPLANATORY MECHANISMS

We have selectively reviewed the literature on the relationship between infant habituation of attention, infant recognition memory, and various aspects of infant temperament, on the one hand, and concurrent and later cognitive functioning, on the other. Although we have implied throughout our presentation of this literature what researchers view to be the explanatory or causal mechanisms underlying these relationships, we now explicitly outline these mechanisms. We argue that although these explanations may at first seem quite disparate in content, nevertheless they may actually indicate an element of continuity between early infant behavior and later intelligence, namely, the infant's response to novelty of various kinds.

First, how do researchers explain, on the one hand, the lack of relationship between various measures of infant habituation to visual stimuli and early scores on infant tests of intelligence, and on the other hand, the existence of a relationship between measures of infant habituation and scores on tests of intelligence later in childhood? Although no fully articulated accounts of these relationships, or lack thereof, exist, accounts of what habituation entails and speculations on what the relationship is between habituation and concurrent and later mental functioning do exist.

Visual attention is said to be the beginning of information processing (Bornstein, 1984). The observed behavior to explain is an infant's decline in visual attention as a stimulus is repeatedly presented. Many models of the decline in visual attention, which signifies habituation, suggest underlying processes of mental construction and comparison, analogous to Piaget's processes of assimilation and accommodation (Bornstein, 1984; Kessen *et al.*, 1970; Sokolov, 1960, 1963). The infant is said to encode and store information about the stimulus, during which time the infant is constructing some type of trace of the stimulus—a memory trace, a neural trace, a schema, etc. A complementary process to this construction process exists, namely, comparison, whereby new stimuli are continually being compared with the existing mental representation that has been previously constructed. Visual attention is maintained so long as the visual stimulus and the mental construction are not isomorphic. This visual attention is said to represent the period of time during which the trace of the stimulus is being refined to a more accurate and fully articulated representation of the stimulus. Visual attention declines as the stimulus and the trace of the stimulus become more similar. Thus, habituation represents component processes in the acquisition of information. Indices of habituation, such as the rate and amount of habituation, indicate how fast and how completely infants encode a stimulus, construct an accurate trace of a stimulus, and distinguish this trace from other stimuli in their environment.

Infant habituation of visual information processing is said to be unrelated to concurrent cognitive functioning because the motor requirements of many early infant tests of intelligence (Bayley, 1969) are not a factor in the tests of habituation of infant visual attention. In fact, this lack of motor functions in the measurement of infant habituation is precisely why measures of habituation of infant visual information processing are thought to be related to later childhood measures of intelligence, and measures of infant intelligence are typically not. Infant habituation of attention involves processes that are precursors of individual differences in perhaps all tests of later intelligence, such as encoding, comparison, and attentional distribution. Infant perceptual–motor tests may involve fewer such precursors of intellectual individual differences in the later years of childhood. Lewis and Brooks-Gunn (1981) interpreted the relationship between early infant habituation and later cognitive functioning as indicating that one of the earliest components of intellectual functioning that has predictive value for later cognitive functioning is individual differences in attentional ability.

Second, what is the mechanism whereby an infant's longer fixation to a novel stimulus, namely, the infant's recognition of the stimulus, is related to later intellectual functions? As in the case of infant habituation of attention, fully worked out theories of the relationship between recognition memory and later intelligence do not exist, although models of recognition memory exist and various hypotheses have been drawn to explain the relation between early recognition memory and later intelligence.

Models of infant recognition memory are fairly similar to the model of visual attention presented above. For example, schema models of memory, heavily influenced by the theoretical work of Bartlett (1932), have been used to interpret the empirical work on infant recognition memory. Analogous to the model presented previously for visual attention, complementary processes of mental construction and comparison are posited to occur with regard to incoming stimuli. The differential amount of time infants fixate on novel as opposed to familiar targets is said to represent an orienting reaction that facilitates processing of the new stimulus. Thus, those infants who display better recognition memory are faster, more thorough, or both in aspects of the mental construction process, such as encoding, comparison, and other information-extraction processes. Some researchers have interpreted individual differences in infant recognition memory as attributable to differences in the encoding processes that underlie tests of recognition memory and that are similar to processes that are involved in later intelligence and cognitive tests (Fagan & McGrath, 1981; J. Werner & Perlmutter, 1979). Both Siegler (1984) and Sternberg (1984b) have stressed the key role of encoding in the continuity of intellectual development, and Sternberg (1984b) has stressed the importance of comparison as well.

Fagan (1984b) posits that the basis of continuity for the relationship between infant recognition memory and later measures of intelligence consists in a set of knowledge-acquisition processes that underlie the general factor of intelligence. These processes include the ability to detect similarities and differences among stimuli, the ability to detect invariants across stimuli, the ability to abstract prototypes from particular individual stimuli, and other processes involved in abstraction. Individual differences in intelligence are considered to reflect individual differences in the speed of the operation of the processes involved in knowledge acquisition.

The recognition memory scores found in infancy seem to measure, in part, the infant's preference for novelty (Sternberg, 1981b). In other words, the infant indicates greater interest in novel, rather than familiar stimuli. This preference seems almost motivational in nature. The need to seek out novelty is highly dependent on the schemes that are available to the infant (Mischel, 1971). That is, if an external event is highly discrepant from, or too familiar to, the existing schema, the infant is less interested than if the stimuli presents a more moderate degree of discrepancy from the schema (McCall & McGhee, 1977). This preference for novel stimuli leads to better and more finely tuned abilities in the component processes of recognition memory. For example, the discrimination abilities that are involved in determining whether two stimuli are the same or different are component processes involved in memory recognition that become more efficient, the more one looks at novel stimuli. Those infants who have a motivational style or preference for novelty may spend more time during their early years gazing at novel, rather than at familiar, stimuli in their environment. This novelty-seeking behavior of the infant, then, may reveal processes that are precursors of individual differences in later tests of intelligence.

Third, how do researchers explain the relationship between selected aspects of infant temperament and concurrent and later cognitive functioning? Few fully adequate models of the mechanisms involved in how early task persistence and attention span are related to concurrent and later mental functioning (Campos *et al.,* 1983) exist and thus the explanation that follows is as much our construction as it is a representation of the thinking of other researchers and theorists.

The temperamental characteristics that are most related to concurrent and later cognitive functioning, such as attention span and task persistence, have been interpreted to represent the infant's duration of *attention* and *interest* in a *new* stimulus (Campos *et al.,* 1983; Goldsmith & Campos, 1982). Let us examine, in turn, these three words in this interpretation of attention and task persistence and the explanatory mechanisms offered above for the relation between infant habituation and infant recognition memory on the one hand, and concurrent and later cognitive functioning on the other.

First, the infant's attention to novel stimuli, indicated by the infant's scoring highly on temperamental scales of attentiveness and task persistence, is similar to the precursor of individual differences in intelligence that

was postulated above for infant habituation of visual information processing (Lewis & Brooks-Gunn, 1981) and for infant recognition memory. Second, the infant's interest in novel stimuli, again indicated by the infant's
scoring highly on temperamental scales of attentiveness and task persistence, is similar to the second mechanism offered for the relation found
between infant recognition memory and later intelligence, namely, the infant's preference for novelty. This preference for, and interest in novel as
opposed to familiar stimuli, is translated into the infant's spending more
of his or her time viewing novel stimuli. Extreme amounts of attention and
task persistence may interfere with the processes of knowledge acquisition
that are required on tasks of habituation and recognition memory. For example, the infant whose attention is held for long periods of time in the
task of viewing a mobile may be less interested in viewing other objects,
thereby decreasing the amount of information that can be acquired about
other stimuli in the environment. However, concentrated attention and task
persistence are necessary for acquiring information in many situations (see
Lerner & Lerner, 1983). The infant who is easily distracted by stimuli other
than the ones to which he is to habituate or to recognize will be at a disadvantage in constructing a representation of the stimulus as compared with
the infant whose attention is concentrated on the stimuli. New knowledge
is best acquired when attention and interest are focused on the stimuli to
be acquired (e.g., Berg & Sternberg, 1985a; Kagan, 1984; Sternberg, 1985).
Infants who demonstrate more task persistence and are more alert may be
better able to extract information from the stimuli around them, through
facilitation in a variety of information processes (see Lerner & Lerner, 1983).

  We must point out that these two aspects of temperament, attention span
and task persistence, do not tap the same identical processes that are tapped
by habituation of visual information processing and infant recognition
memory. Recall that these two aspects of temperament were significantly
related to concurrent infant intelligence, as measured by the Bayley. Measures of infant habituation of visual attention and recognition memory were
not, however, significantly related to Bayley scores in infancy. In addition,
measures of infant recognition memory may not be perfectly related to measures of infant visual information processing. Further research is needed to
determine the relationships between infant temperament, infant habituation
of attention, and recognition memory. However, a common element appears to exist between the relationships that have been reported for infant
habituation of attention, recognition memory, and infant temperament and
later tested intelligence, namely, the infant's response to novelty and the
component processes (e.g., encoding, allocation of attention, and comparison) that accompany this response.

IV. Relations between Response to Novelty and Concurrent Cognitive Functioning in Childhood

Although rather convincing evidence suggests that the ability to deal with novelty is an important element of continuity in intellectual abilities between early infancy and later childhood, little research has been explicitly addressed to the response to novelty in the school years. We will restrict our review in this section to literature that demonstrates that the ability to deal with novelty is related to concurrent measures of intelligence. We are unaware of any longitudinal research on the relationship between the response to novelty and later intellectual functioning in adulthood.

Research by Harter and Zigler (1974) suggests that the preference for novel visual stimuli can discriminate between children of normal intellect, noninstitutionalized retarded children, and institutionalized retarded children, matched for mental age. The normal children were first and second graders divided into those of lower mental age (mean mental age = 6.3, mean chronological age = 6.6) and those of higher mental age (mean mental age = 8.4, mean chronological age = 7.7). The noninstitutionalized retarded children were attending special education classes in the same public school district as the normal children and were also divided into those of lower mental age (mean mental age = 6.1, mean chronological age = 10.2) and those of higher mental age (mean mental age = 8.2, mean chronological age = 11.9). The institutionalized retarded children were residents of state schools for the mentally retarded and were divided into those of lower mental age (mean mental age = 6.1, mean chronological age = 12.1) and those of higher mental age (mean mental age = 8.4, mean chronological age = 14.5). The task used to tap the children's interest in novel stimuli was a set of cardboard boxes. Children were presented cardboard houses, on the front of which were two doors. On the outside of one door was a picture; behind the door was the identical picture. The outside of the other door was blank and behind it was a novel picture. The measure of curiosity or interest in novelty was the number of trials the child chose the blank, as opposed to the other door.

Results suggested that normal children chose the unknown picture much more often than did noninstitutionalized retarded children, who in turn made more choices of the unknown picture than did institutionalized retarded children. Those normal children with a higher mental age and higher intelligence chose the unknown picture more often than did normal children of lower mental age and lower intelligence. Thus, the preference for novel stimuli not only distinguished mentally retarded children from children of normal intellect, but also distinguished between children of higher and lower intellect (or between older and younger children) within the normal range of intelligence.

Bransford and colleagues have examined how the response to novelty is related to educational success, rather than to intelligence per se. They examined how students differing in academic success approach the problem of learning new facts and factual relationships. For example, Franks, Vye, Auble, Mezynski, Perfetto, Bransford, Stein, and Littlefield (1982) compared academically more and less successful fifth graders on passages regarding two types of robots and two types of field trips. An explicit and an implicit version of each type of passage was constructed, each containing a total of 18 facts to be remembered. The explicit version provided justifications for the various characteristics or facts to be remembered, but the implicit version merely stated the facts. For example, the explicit version might state that the robot "had a bucket on top of its head in order to carry paint"; the implicit version would state simply that the robot "had a bucket on top of its head" (p. 415). These items were chosen to be related to the problem of seeming arbitrariness that faces the novice when learning new information. For example, when first learning to play chess, the fact that a bishop makes certain moves that the knight is not allowed to make is arbitrary.

Subjects were then tested via a cued recall test. More successful students recalled the same mean number of items on explicit and implicit passages; less successful students recalled far fewer items from the implicit than from the explicit passages. This result was accompanied by the successful students spending much more time studying implicit than explicit passages; less successful students spent much more time studying the explicit than implicit passages. The less successful students were inefficient in their allocation of attentional resources, unaware that more study time was required for the implicit, rather than the explicit, passages. [This result is in agreement with research by Wagner and Sternberg (1983), who found that more able readers were more apt in adjusting their allocation of time and other resources in response to changing reading demands.] When less successful students were trained to activate knowledge that would make the characteristics of the robots in the implicit passages seem less arbitrary, performance greatly improved. In fact, less successful students with training performed at the level at which the more successful subjects had performed. The results suggest that less successful students are relatively unaware of the difficulty in learning arbitrary information. Although less successful students do not spontaneously elaborate novel information so as to facilitate memory, they can be trained to recognize the arbitrariness of information and to reduce this arbitrariness by making the appropriate elaborations.

Marr and Sternberg (1986) more explicitly investigated the role that the response to novelty plays in school success and in intellectual performance. They examined the extent to which gifted and nongifted students (in sixth, seventh, and eighth grades) differed in their response to various novel manipulations and problems. The task was a measure of how well students incorporated novel concepts into a familiar verbal analogical reasoning problem. The task comprised two parts. Part one consisted of verbal analogy items presented in a multiple-choice format. Part two consisted of comparable verbal analogy items preceded by a "precue" that was related to a term in the analogy and that varied on two dimensions, novelty (novel versus familiar information) and relevance (information relevant versus irrelevant to the analogy). Students were instructed to solve each analogy as if the precue statement was true. For instance, the following precue was novel and relevant to the solution of the analogy: "Lakes are dry" (the precue) was followed by the analogy item "Trail : Hike :: Lake : (a) swim, (b) walk, (c) water, (d) dust." The correct answer here is (b) walk. Students were also given the number series and verbal analogies subtests of the Thorndike–Hagen Cognitive Abilities Test and a test of mathematical insight. Teachers' ratings of intellectual ability were obtained for a subset of the students.

Results indicated that both response latencies and error rates were greater in the novel precue condition than in the familiar precue condition. Subjects also spent more time reading the novel precue information than the familiar precue information. Intellectually gifted and nongifted individuals did not differ greatly in their processing of familiar information, but did differ significantly in their processing of novel information. When the precue information was familiar, both gifted and nongifted students attended more to irrelevant than to relevant information. When the precue information was novel, however, gifted individuals attended nearly exclusively to the relevant information, whereas the nongifted students did not differentially attend to the relevant or irrelevant information.

The total number correct on the precued analogies predicted teachers' ratings of intellectual ability ($r = .42, p < .05$). The total number correct on the precued analogies was also related to the children's enrollment in a program for the gifted ($r = .31, p < .05$), and this relationship was slightly stronger than were other relationships between the traditional measures of cognitive ability and children's enrollment in this program. For example, number series scores were correlated by $r = .21$ ($p > .05$) and verbal analogy scores were correlated by $r = .27$ ($p < .05$) with enrollment in the program. The ability to deal with novelty appears to be related to measures of intelligence, although this ability goes beyond what is typically assessed on intelligence tests. For example, the total number correct on the precued analogies was only modestly correlated with the number series scores ($r = .30$, $p < .05$) and the verbal analogy scores ($r = .32$, $p < .05$).

The research of Marr and Sternberg (1986) tapped the ability to deal with novelty in both the comprehension of the task and in the solution of the task. Research of Davidson and Sternberg (1984) tapped the ability of individuals to deal with novelty in the solution of insight problems. An example of a mathematical insight problem is, "If you have black socks and brown socks in your drawer, mixed in the ratio of 4 to 5, how many socks will you have to take out to make sure of having a pair the same color?" Davidson and Sternberg (1984; Sternberg & Davidson, 1982) argued that three cognitive processes form the basis for insightful thinking when they are performed in a new and imaginative fashion: selective encoding, selective combination, and selective comparison. Selective encoding involves the insight that only some information is relevant to problem solution and entails sifting out relevant from irrelevant information. Selective combination consists of the insight of combining information that has previously seemed unrelated in a way that facilitates problem solution. Selective comparison occurs when one has an insight regarding a relationship between new information and previously acquired information. Davidson and Sternberg examined how these three cognitive processes are related to individual differences in intelligence.

First, children identified as intellectually gifted or nongifted in grades four through six were given verbal insight, mathematical insight, mystery, and inductive reasoning problems. Verbal insight problems required subjects to define unknown words embedded in a verbal passage. Mathematical insight problems were similar to the example provided above. The mystery stories also involved selective encoding, selective combination, and selective comparison, but required subjects to figure out how a detective knew the identity of the criminal in the story. The inductive reasoning problems were from Letter Sets, from the Kit of Reference Tests for Cognitive Factors (French, Ekstrom, & Price, 1963), and involved choosing a set of letters, from among five sets, that were based on a rule different from the other sets (e.g., WXYZ, ABCD, FGHI, PQRT, KLMN).

Gifted students were found to perform better than nongifted on all the problems. In a second study, gifted and nongifted individuals were compared on insight problems specifically designed to examine the selective encoding process by presenting insight problems in some of which the relevant information for problem solution was underlined. Children were instructed to attend to the underlined information and to ignore information that was not underlined, as it was irrelevant to problem solution. Again, gifted children outperformed the children of average intelligence. Performance was better when the relevant information was underlined than when it was not, and this cuing was more beneficial for average than for gifted children. Evidently, gifted children spontaneously engaged in successful selective encoding, and children of average intelligence had difficulty in selective encoding, but were helped by cues that could provide this insight.

Another study involved comparing gifted and nongifted children on insight problems designed specifically to examine the cognitive process of selective combination. In one condition, subjects were cued by giving them information on how to organize and combine elements of the problem in order to solve it. In the uncued condition, subjects were given regular insight problems. As in the second study, gifted individuals perfomed better on the insight problems than did nongifted individuals and all individuals performed better in the cued condition than in the uncued condition. But again, children of average intelligence benefited more than did gifted children when they were cued with the insight of selective combination. Again, gifted children seemed to utilize spontaneously the insight of selective combination; children of average intelligence did not. Similar results were found when individual differences in the cognitive process of selective comparison were examined. Thus, these three cognitive processes appear to tap elementary operations in the ability to deal with novelty in the solution of insight problems and seem to underlie individual differences in intelligence.

Dweck and Elliott (1983) have examined the development of children's theories of intelligence and the relationships these theories have to motivational patterns in new achievement situations. Their research suggests that children come to hold, by the end of grade school, one of two different theories of intelligence. According to the "entity" theory, intelligence consists of a global, stable trait, of which a person has a fixed amount and which is displayed and determined through performance on a variety of tasks and problems. According to the "instrumental–incremental" theory, intelligence consists of an expanding set of skills and behaviors that is enlarged by one's own efforts. In achievement settings, children who hold the entity theory appear to select tasks that will allow them to look smart, perform well, and avoid mistakes; children who hold the incremental–instrumental theory select tasks that will afford them opportunities for learning, viewing the opportunity to make mistakes as just one consequence of becoming more intelligent. The incremental–instrumental theorist, then, may have more interest in novel situations than the entity theorist and may respond to novel stimuli in a different fashion from the entity theorist. Prior to approximately second grade, children appear to favor the incremental–

instrumental view of intelligence. With development, they come to hold the more normative entity view of intelligence.

Although entity theorists and instrumental–incremental theorists do not differ in their measured intelligence, Dweck and Elliott (1983) speculated that holding the entity theory of intelligence may have several disadvantages for the child in a variety of achievement and learning situations. These two types of theorists differ in their learning goals and in their tolerance of only partial attainment of these goals. The learning goals of the entity theorist are normative and rigid, with partial attainment of the goals interpreted to be reflective of one's own failure. For the instrumental–incremental theorist, learning goals are long-term, flexible, and personal, with partial attainment of the goal interpreted as having considerable value as part of the learning process. An incremental–instrumental view of intelligence encourages greater feelings of perceived control over various aspects of task solution via the decreased reliance on the judgments and beliefs of others for the perception of one's own abilities.

Harter's research on intrinsic motivation (1981a, 1981b; Harter & Connell, 1984) is consistent with Dweck's work on entity and instrumental–incremental theorists. Harter's work has focused on the extent to which childrens' motivation in academic learning situations is determined by an intrinsic interest, preference, and curiosity for learning, in contrast with an extrinsic interest in pleasing the teacher and in earning good grades. Three dimensions of motivation have been examined that were defined by an intrinsic to extrinsic pole: a preference for challenging versus easy work, a desire to satisfy one's curiosity versus a desire to please one's teacher and earn good grades, and an interest in solving problems independently versus an interest in solving problems with the teacher. Through the examination of data sets consisting of large numbers of children from grades three through nine, an intrinsic to extrinsic shift was found across these ages (Harter, 1981b). Older children were less intrinsically motivated with regard to challenge, curiosity, and independent mastery than younger children. In both the elementary school years and the junior high school years, intrinsically motivated children perceived themselves as more competent cognitively than extrinsically motivated children (Harter & Connell, 1984). In addition, intrinsically motivated children were also actually more competent, as assessed through traditional achievement tests.

In sum, this selective review of research investigating children's responses to various aspects of novel problems and situations seems to suggest that individual differences in the response to novelty—interest in novel visual stimuli, ease in integrating novel information into one's own prior experience, ability to deal with novel component processes, and motivational response to novel situations—are related to individual differences in intelligence.

V. Relations between Response to Novelty and Concurrent Cognitive Functioning in Adulthood

Sternberg describes human intelligence as involving

> not merely the ability to learn and reason with new concepts but the ability to learn and reason with new kinds of concepts. Intelligence is not so much a person's ability to learn or think within conceptual systems that the person has already become familiar with as it is his or her ability to learn and think within new conceptual systems, which can then be brought to bear upon already existing knowledge structures. (Sternberg, 1981a, p. 4)

Sternberg (1982) examined adults' abilities to reason with novel concepts in a concept-projection task. The task was designed to permit separate observation of the effects of conceptual novelty (i.e., how unfamiliar concepts were) and conceptual complexity (i.e., the number of conceptual changes that were required to solve the problem). Consider one of the four variants that were used. The age of persons was described as presently perceived and as perceived in the year 2000. The age of the persons could be represented either by a small or large stick picture or by the words *plin* (meaning born a child and stays a child for 30 years), *kwef* (born an adult and stays an adult for 30 years), *balt* (born a child, but becomes an adult over the course of 30 years), or *pros* (born an adult, but becomes a child during a 30-year period). Subjects were given information about the age of the person in the present state and in the future state and were required to make inferences regarding these states. For example, a person might be described verbally as an "adult" in the present, and described pictorially as a "child" in the year 2000. One would infer that the person was a pros. Conceptual novelty represents the idea that problems which are consistent with our experience (i.e., children who change into adults) should be easiest to solve. Conceptual complexity refers to the notion that problems in which people do not change states (i.e., children remaining children and adults remaining adults) should be easiest to solve because they do not require additional mental transformations to deal with state changes. Latency and error rates were used as indices of the ease with which subjects solved the problems.

The results suggested that both conceptual novelty and conceptual complexity influence the ease of information processing, with conceptual complexity having a greater effect. An information-processing model of task performance accounted for an average of 92% of the variance in the reaction-time data. More importantly, those information-processing components that measured the ability to deal with novelty in this task (e.g., changing representational systems from pictorial to linguistic) were those that were most highly related to scores on induction tests; indeed, the relationships were higher than those typically found between cognitive task performance and psychometric measures of intelligence. Whether novelty was produced by the novelty of the concept or by the unfamiliarity of the linguistic term used to define the concept was unclear, given that they were confounded in the study.

Tetewsky and Sternberg (1985) disentangled these two aspects of novelty by examining college-aged students on a reasoning task in which the novelty of a concept and the familiarity of the name used to define the concept were orthogonally varied. In a familiar-concept condition, subjects were told that leaves change color with the seasons. In an unfamiliar-concept condition, subjects were told that rocks change color with the seasons. Either familiar names (spring, winter, summer, fall) or unfamiliar names (*soob, trit, blen, mave*) were used to identify the seasons. This experimental manipulation resulted in four different situations: (1) familiar season names describing a familiar concept, namely, leaves changing color with seasonal variations; (2) unfamiliar season names describing the seasonal changes in the color of the leaves; (3) familiar season names describing changes in the color of rocks; and (4) unfamiliar season names describing changes in the color of rocks. Subjects in each condition were given information about the color of the rocks or the color of the leaves at the beginning of the season, and were also given information about the state of events at the end of the season. Subjects were required to indicate what color these objects would be at the end of the season, based on the information contained in the problem. In addition to completing this concept-projection task, subjects were given several ability measures: geometric series completion, letter and number series, and deductive syllogisms.

Results indicated that neither the use of novel concepts with unfamiliar terms to identify these concepts nor the use of familiar concepts with familiar names to describe these concepts provided subjects with great difficulty, as measured by both reaction times taken to solve the problem and by error rates. Subjects did experience difficulty in this task when they were asked to use a familiar name to identify a novel concept or a novel name to identify a familiar concept. Thus, subjects had the most difficulty with problems in which some of the information contained in the problem related in some way to their prior knowledge, but in which other aspects of the problem were outside their range of experience. The difficulty was not in unfamiliarity of concepts or of language, but in integrating the familiar with the unfamiliar.

Raaheim's (1974, 1984) analysis of problem situations is consistent with the results described above in the work of Tetewsky and Sternberg (1985). Raaheim (1974) like Morgan (1941), posited that a problem situation involves some elements or conditions that are known and other elements that are unknown. A solution of the problem situation requires a discovery of how to deal with the unknown factors of the situation. Raaheim (1974) identified intelligence as "the ability to transform what are, at first glance, new or unknown situations, into familiar, more or less easily mastered situations" (p. 53). He argued that intelligence is most evident in problem situations in which a moderate degree of unfamiliarity is evident. Thus, if the problem situation is too familiar, that is, if it contains no unknown factors—no deviations from past experience—it is not a good measure of intelligence. In contrast, if the task is very unfamiliar and its performance is not facilitated by any prior experience of the individual, it is better solved by active exploration than by intelligent reflection. Consider an example of a problem situation in which the elements of the problem are very unfamiliar to the people endeavoring to solve the problem.

Raaheim uses the "hatrack problem" of Maier (1930) to measure the ability to deal with novelty. The problem presents to the subject three objects (a C-clamp and two sticks) for the task of constructing a hatrack. The best solution involves clamping the two sticks together, placing them between the floor and the ceiling, and using the clamp handle as the hook. Burke and Maier (1965) examined the performance of college students on this task and on 18 different tests of intelligence and personality. No relationship existed between success in solving the hatrack problem and performance on any of the intellectual and personality measures. Raaheim and Kaufmann (1972) conducted research using the hatrack problem but examined in more detail how subjects performed the task. They were particularly interested in how many attempts subjects made at a solution either before the correct solution was accomplished or before the time limit expired. Those subjects who were eventually successful in solving the problem made many more solution attempts, thereby exploring the details of the task, than did those who did not solve the task. Again, as in the Burke and Maier study, no differences between solvers and nonsolvers were demonstrated on a variety of ability measures.

Although Raaheim stated that the typical hatrack task is not a problem situation, as defined above, he has shown that it can be turned into a problem situation by providing subjects with some additional information. For example, if subjects are told that "the ceiling must somehow enter into the picture," success on the hatrack problem is then related to fairly standard measures of intellectual abilities. He argues that this hint does more than simply facilitate performance on the hatrack task. It turns the task into a problem situation and one that draws on one's intellectual abilities, because some of the elements of the problem are known and thus the unknown or deviating elements can be recognized and dealt with appropriately.

Raaheim argued that tasks are differentially appropriate for measuring an individual's intelligence, depending upon where they lie on the contin-

uum of novelty versus familiarity for the individual. The identification of
the boundaries of various tasks in their ability to tap intelligent functioning
must be done separately for each individual, according to Raaheim. Thus,
if groups of individuals are to be compared in their level of intelligence,
the tasks used must be shown to be at the same points on the continuum
of familiarity–unfamiliarity for each individual. This idea that intelligence
is best measured when task performance deals with an optimal level of novelty, and that intellectual abilities can be compared across individuals only
when task performance is equated for these individuals in terms of novelty,
is incorporated into the triarchic theory of human intelligence and its development (Berg & Sternberg, 1985a; Sternberg, 1985).

The vast literature investigating adult intellectual development within
Cattell and Horn's theory of fluid and crystallized intelligence (e.g., Cattell,
1971; Horn, 1968) suggests that the ability to deal with novelty remains an
integral component of intelligence throughout the adult life span. Fluid intelligence is tested, in part, by virtue of the novelty of tests for the population to which they are being administered; crystallized intelligence is tested
by virtue of the cultural familiarity of the tests being given for this population. Developmental studies have shown that scores on tests measuring
fluid intelligence begin to decline early in adulthood; scores on tests measuring crystallized intelligence show stability and in some cases increments
throughout the adult life span (Horn & Cattell, 1967). For example, the
Raven Progressive Matrices, a test of fluid intelligence, places novel demands on the examinee. Age differences, favoring young adults, have been
found on this task (Cunningham, Clayton, & Overton, 1975).

Research conducted by Cornelius (1984) has suggested that older adults
view tasks measuring fluid intelligence as less familiar, more difficult, more
effortful, and more highly speeded than do younger adults; in contrast,
measures of crystallized intelligence do not show any age-related differences
in perceived familiarity, difficulty, effort, or speed. Others have also speculated that a contributing factor to the declines with age in performance
on measures of fluid intelligence is that the tasks are less familiar for older
adults than for young adults (e.g., Botwinick, 1973; Eisdorfer, 1968; Murrell, 1970).

Intervention research with older adults has demonstrated that performance on tests of fluid intelligence can be improved with both practice and
training. For instance, Willis, Blieszner, and Baltes (1981) examined the effectiveness of both cognitive training and practice on older adults' performance of figural relations, a measure of fluid intelligence. Not only was
the cognitive training effective and the effects of this training maintained
over a 6-month period, but the training transferred to other measures of
fluid intelligence. The training and practice on measures of fluid intelligence

made these tasks less novel for the older individuals thereby producing positive effects on their performance.

The difficulty that older adults exhibit in dealing with novel tasks and stimuli does not seem to arise from the older adults' decreased interest in learning new things. Camp, Rodrigue, and Olson (1985) compared young, middle aged, and older individuals on the Ontario Test of Intrinsic Motivation, which allows for a separation of the traits of specific and diversive curiosity. Specific curiosity refers to the interest aroused by specific stimuli that are novel and complex; diversive curiosity refers to the interest aroused in the absence of specific stimuli and involves seeking out stimulation in response to boredom (Berlyne, 1960; Day, 1971). Camp *et al.* (1985) found no age differences in specific curiosity, however, age differences were found favoring younger adults in diversive curiosity. Thus, although no age differences were found in interest in learning new things about specific topics, young individuals did experience more interest in seeking out stimulation as a result of boredom. Further research is needed to clarify the role that intrinsic motivation and curiosity play in adults' ability to deal with novel stimuli.

In sum, this brief look at the literature on adults' responses to novel problems suggests that the response to novelty is an integral component of intelligent functioning. Throughout adulthood, moderate levels of novelty seem to be best for measuring intelligence.

VI. A Conceptual Framework for Viewing the Response to Novelty as an Integral Component of Intelligence throughout Development

First, let us consider an overview of the framework we will provide for conceptualizing intelligence as, in part, a response to novelty. This framework comprises two major aspects: a motivational aspect according to which one's interest in, curiosity about, and preference for novelty is involved in intelligent functioning; and an information-extraction aspect which identifies those component processes that are involved in the acquisition of novel information. Let us examine in greater detail these two aspects of intellectual development.

A. MOTIVATIONAL ASPECT

The motivational aspect deals with the energizing element of intellectual life, which involves one's interest in, curiosity about, and preference for novel stimuli, tasks, and environmental contexts. These elements of the motivational aspect are evident in one's response to novelty at all ages throughout development, although we shall discuss later how it is difficult to disentangle elements of the motivational aspect from the components of the information-extraction aspect at particular points during development. Our discussion of the motivational aspect and the relation between the motivational aspect and other notions of motivation will be necessarily scant, as a comprehensive review of the literature in this area is beyond the scope of this article.

The motivational aspect is deemed necessary in a discussion dealing with the response to novelty and intelligence in the way that Piaget (1981) believed that "there is no cognitive mechanism without affective elements" (p. 3) and that "affectivity play[s] the role of an energy source on which the functioning of intelligence depend[s]" (p. 5). Piaget states that there is an intrinsic need for cognitive structures to perpetuate themselves by more functioning. The source of this need is the realization that a discrepancy exists between one's schemas and the environment. Piaget speaks of an optimal range of environmental novelty, that which is neither too familiar nor too unfamiliar, which best attracts the child's interest.

The notion that an individual will be motivated to respond to a novel stimulus in relation to the degree of discrepancy between the stimulus and the individual's schemas has come to be known as the discrepancy hypothesis (e.g., McCall & Kagan, 1970; McCall & McGhee, 1977; Piaget, 1952). The idea that the motive to be interested in and to master novelty is related to later intellectual functioning has been evident in other work on motivational constructs in child psychology, such as mastery motivation (Yarrow, McQuiston, MacTurk, McCarthy, Klein, Vietze, 1983), effectance motivation (R. White, 1959; Zigler, 1971), intrinsic motivation (Harter, 1981a,b; Hunt, 1965) and diversive and specific curiosity (Berlyne, 1960). Although investigators examining this motive in infancy and early childhood have operationalized it in slightly different ways, research in this area has demonstrated that such a motive can be defined and measured, that this motive has some cross-age stability, and that the motive is predictive of later intelligence.

Yarrow and colleagues (Yarrow *et al.,* 1983) examined several components of mastery motivation during the infant's first year of life. These investigators have demonstrated that there are individual differences in the ways that infants as young as 6 months of age make contact with new tasks, explore them, and try to master them. These individual differences are moderately stable between 6 and 12 months of age. In fact, one component of mastery motivation, exploratory behavior, was not only stable from 6 to 12 months but was also significantly related to the mental and motor scales of the Bayley at 6 months ($r = .34, p < .01$ and $r = .34, p < .01$, respectively) and to the mental subscale of the Bayley at 12 months of age ($r = .40$, $p < .01$). The infant's exploration of and experimentation with objects, many of which will be novel, have been posited by Hunt (1965) as important energizing elements for intellectual growth that continue throughout life.

Individual differences in intrinsic motivation can be said to be related to individual differences in intelligence in a variety of ways (Haywood & Burke, 1977; McCall & McGhee, 1977). First, individuals may differ in the degree of discrepancy that is tolerated between the individual's existing schemas and the outside environment. Those individuals who tolerate larger degrees of discrepancy or incongruity between schemas and environment are those individuals who will be exposed to and adapt (assimilate and accommodate) to more complex and unfamiliar stimuli than will individuals who cannot tolerate such degrees of discrepancy. Thus, an individual's need or preference for novel stimulation is highly related to his or her endurance of discrepancies. Second, individuals who are attracted to novel stimuli, in part because of their tolerance of larger degrees of discrepancy, will be exposed over their lifetime to more complex stimuli and will have developed more advanced schemas for dealing with their environment. Individuals who are unwilling to expose themselves to novel experiences limit their opportunities for learning.

In addition, in later childhood, those individuals who remain more intrinsically motivated to deal with novelty will be less dependent on external rewards in motivating them to master new and challenging tasks, thereby facilitating their interaction with a larger number of tasks. Evidence for stability of individual differences in achievement behavior comes from the Fels Longitudinal Studies (Kagan & Moss, 1983). Achievement behavior, defined as the child's persistence and interest in challenging tasks (not so different than the definition of intrinsic motivation advanced by Harter as discussed above), as measured at 3 years and beyond was predictive of achievement behavior in later childhood, adolescence, and early adulthood. In addition, achievement behavior as measured at 3 years and beyond was highly related to intellectual competence in adulthood.

Evidence suggests that intrinsic motivation is influenced by both genetic and environmental influences. Recall that the two aspects of temperament reflecting the infant's interest in novel stimuli, namely attention span and task persistence, were found to have a substantial genetic origin. As the infant develops, intrinsic motivation appears to be quite malleable with regard to environmental influences. For example, a developmental shift may occur, coinciding with the onset of school, that decreases the child's intrinsic interest in novel stimuli (Dweck & Elliott, 1983; Harter, 1981). The research of Harter and Zigler (1974), reviewed above, and the theoretical work of Zigler (1971) also suggest the malleability of intrinsic motivation. Children with extremely deprived life histories, such as institutionalized retarded children, demonstrated much less intrinsic motivation than noninstitutionalized retarded children.

B.　INFORMATION-EXTRACTION ASPECT

The information-extraction aspect deals with the key information-processing components that are involved in assimilating novel information to prior experience. The information-extraction aspect comprises three component processes: deciding how to allocate attentional resources, encoding, and comparison (see also Davidson & Sternberg, 1984; Sternberg, 1984b). Let us consider these processes in more detail.

The first component involves the decision of how to allocate attentional resources to various aspects of the problem solution. Infants who decide to allocate a disproportionate amount of their attention to novel stimuli will spend more time refining the other three components of information extraction. Lewis and Brooks-Gunn (1981) interpreted the relationship between early infant habituation and later cognitive functioning as reflective of the predictive value of individual differences in attentional ability for later cognitive functioning. The research reviewed on infant temperament also demonstrated significant relationships between attention span and later measures of mental functioning. This component was evident in the work of Marr and Sternberg (1986), reviewed above, as intellectually gifted individuals allocated their attention to the most relevant information for problem solution, whereas individuals of average intelligence did not. This component was also apparent in the work of Bransford and colleagues, also reviewed above. This component was a key metacomponent in the triarchic theory of intelligence and its development (Berg & Sternberg, 1985a; Sternberg, 1985), and is of importance in Kahneman's (1973) work on attentional flexibility.

The encoding component involves the initial perception of information, the identification of the attributes of a stimulus, and the retrieval of relevant information about these attributes from working memory. With increasing amounts of practice and knowledge in the particular domain of interest, encoding components become more efficient by becoming more selective in encoding information, and in separating out relevant from irrelevant information. This information-extraction component has been posited to be the locus of individual differences in infant recognition memory and the element of continuity between infant recognition memory and later intellectual abilities (e.g., J. Werner & Perlmutter, 1979). The work of Davidson and Sternberg (1984), reviewed above, indicates the importance of selective encoding as a potential source of individual differences in intelligence. Theories of cognitive development have also emphasized the role of encoding in the continuity of intellectual development (Siegler, 1984; Sternberg, 1984b).

Once the elements of a problem have been encoded, these elements must be compared. Comparison is used to relate newly formed cognitive structures to old cognitive structures. As the encoding components become more selective with experience, the comparison components also become selective in that they are operating only on the relevant information passed to them from the encoding components. Comparison becomes more efficient with experience and knowledge, as larger numbers of old cognitive structures become available with which the new cognitive structures can be compared. Comparison was posited to be part of the mental construction process involved in the component behaviors of infant habituation of attention and recognition memory. Comparison has been identified as a critical individual difference variable in intellectual functioning and as a component that is integral to many mental tasks (Caruso & Sternberg, 1985). The work of Davidson and Sternberg (1984; Sternberg, 1985), reviewed above, also suggests the importance of comparison in the ability to deal with novelty and in intellectual functioning.

The development of the components of the information-extraction aspect involves not only repeated practice and tuning of these components, but also the automatization of such components (Sternberg, 1984b). Controlled information processing requires large amounts of attentional capacity, is facilitated by practice on the components of interest, and is under the voluntary control of the individual. Conversely, automatic information processing involves minimal amounts of attentional capacity, is relatively unaffected by further practice on the components in question, and is not under the voluntary control of the individual (Schneider & Shiffrin, 1977; Shiffrin & Schneider, 1977).

In processing information from new domains or domains in which expertise has yet to be acquired, the individual relies primarily upon controlled information processing. In processing information from old domains or domains in which one has gained expertise, the individual relies upon automatic information processing. When an individual first encounters a task, the ability to deal with novelty comes into play. More intelligent individuals will more quickly and fully be able to extract the relevant information from the novel situation. With continued exposure to and experience with a given novel situation, the more intelligent individual will more readily be able to begin to automatize component processes. Automatization frees processing resources for handling new, novel tasks (see Sternberg, 1984b).

C. DEVELOPMENT OF THE MOTIVATIONAL ASPECT
AND THE INFORMATION-EXTRACTION ASPECT

In early infancy, the motivational aspect and the information-extraction aspect appear to be inseparable. For example, the work of Matheny *et al.* (1974), reviewed above, indicates strong relationships between motivational aspects of the infant's behavior (e.g., goal-directedness) and concurrent mental functioning. Whether or not this seeming inseparability of motivational processes from cognitive processes in early infancy is attributable to a limitation in our theoretical work, our lack of empirical techniques for separating these two aspects, or real inseparability is as yet unclear. For Piaget (1952, 1981) as well as for others (see e.g., Ulvund, 1980; Yarrow & Messler, 1983), the motivation to explore, to have an interest in, and to solve and master novel stimuli is inseparable from cognitive processes involved in adapting to one's environment.

Beyond early life though, these two aspects appear to become differentiated so that assessments of aspects of motivation, such as interest in, preference for, and curiosity about novel stimuli, are no longer as interdependent as in early life on processes involved in information extraction. Piaget acknowledged (see Mischel, 1971) that this separation of affect and cognition is made possible by the emergence of language and the child's ability to represent things that are not present. This ability develops sometime in the second year of life. Although the motivational aspect and facets of the information-extraction aspect can be measured separately in early childhood, they appear to be highly related. Those individuals who have greater intrinsic motivation are the individuals who are more likely to become more experienced and better able to deal with the components of the information-extraction process.

VII. Summary and Conclusions

In this article, we have reviewed research in diverse domains that has provided evidence for the assertion that intelligence can be construed, in part, as a response to novelty. We began by distinguishing two types of continuities, namely, the continuity in the fundamental nature of intelligence throughout development and the relative stability of individual differences in intellectual abilities at various ages. Current empirical and theoretical work has culminated in a proposition that the actual nature of intelligence is discontinuous, at least in the early years of life, and that individual differences in intellectual functions are unstable (Bayley, 1970;

McCall, 1979a,b). Research on aspects of an infant's response to novelty and the relationship between this response and later intellectual functioning was examined and interpreted as reflective not only of one element of continuity in the actual nature of intelligence throughout development but also of a stable source of individual differences in intellectual development. Other literature reviewed suggested that the interest in and ability to deal with novelty remains an integral component of individual differences in intelligence throughout the life span.

A framework for conceptualizing intelligence as, in part, the response to novelty was offered to provide some synthesis to the literature we have reviewed on the relationship between one's response to novelty and intelligence across the life span. This framework comprises two major aspects: a motivational aspect, referring to interest in, curiosity about, and preference for novelty, and an information-extraction aspect, referring to component processes that are involved in the acquisition of novel information. These two aspects of dealing with novelty were evident in the literature that was reviewed above. They seem integral to intellectual development.

We are not alone in positing the importance of one's response to novelty as a major element of individual differences in intelligence across the life span. Other researchers and theorists from diverse disciplines within psychology, such as artificial intelligence, Piagetian psychology, and psychometric intelligence, as well as layperson's commonsense notions about intelligence, have also indicated the importance of the ability to deal with novelty in intelligent functioning. We view the motivational and information-processing response to novelty as a source of stability in intellectual functions across development and as an element of continuity in the actual nature of intelligence. This position stands in opposition to positions such as McCall's (1979a,b), according to which the developmental function of intelligence is discontinuous and individual differences in intelligence are unstable. The research examined here indicates that empirical evidence is mounting to suggest that intelligence can be construed as having an element of continuity throughout development. That element of continuity is response to novelty.

ACKNOWLEDGMENTS

This article was written while the first author was supported by a Yale University Graduate Fellowship. The first author also wishes to acknowledge several stimulating and helpful conversations with William Kessen on the topic of this article.

42   *Cynthia A. Berg and Robert J. Sternberg*

REFERENCES

Appelbaum, M. I., & McCall, R. B. (1983). Design and analysis in developmental psychology. In P. H. Mussen (Series Ed.) & W. Kessen (Vol. Ed.), *Handbook of child psychology* (Vol. 1, pp. 416–476). New York: Wiley.

Baldwin, J. M. (1906–1915). *Thought and things: A study in the development and meaning of thought, or, genetic logic* (4 Vols). New York: Macmillan, 1906–1911; New York: Putman, 1915 (reprinted by Arno Press, New York, 1974; by A.M.S. Press, New York, 1976; and by Scholarly Reprints, New York, 1976).

Bartlett, F. C. (1932). *Remembering: A study in experimental and social psychology.* London: Cambridge Univ. Press.

Bayley, N. (1969). *Bayley scales of infant development: Birth to two years.* New York: Psychological Corp.

Bayley, N. (1970). Development of mental abilities. In P. H. Mussen (Ed.), *Carmichael's manual of child psychology* (Vol. 1, pp. 1163–1209). New York: Wiley.

Berg, C. A., & Sternberg, R. J. (1985a). A triarchic theory of intellectual development during adulthood. *Developmental Review,* in press.

Berg, C. A., & Sternberg, R. J. (1985b). Implicit theories of intelligence across the adult lifespan. Submitted.

Berlyne, D. E. (1960). *Conflict, arousal, and curiosity.* New York: McGraw-Hill.

Bornstein, M. H. (1984). Habituation of attention as a measure of visual information processing in human infants: Summary, systematization, and synthesis. In G. Gottlieb & N. A. Krasnegor (Eds.), *Measurement of audition and vision in the first year of life: A methodological overview.* Norwood, NJ: Ablex.

Bornstein, M. H., & Ruddy, M. (1983). Infant attention, maternal stimulation, and early cognitive and linguistic development in singletons and twins. In H. Bouma & D. Bouwhuis (Eds.), *Attention and performance X.* Hillsdale, NJ: Erlbaum.

Botwinick, J. (1973). *Aging and behavior.* Berlin and New York: Springer-Verlag.

Brown, G., & Desforges, C. (1979). *Piaget's theory: A psychological critique.* Boston: Routledge & Kegan Paul.

Burke, R. J., & Maier, N. R. F. (1965). Attempts to predict success on an insight problem. *Psychological Reports,* **17**, 303–310.

Buss, A. H., & Plomin, R. (1975). *A temperamental theory of personality development.* New York: Wiley.

Cahan, E. D. (1984). The genetic psychologies of James Mark Baldwin and Jean Piaget. *Developmental Psychology,* **20**, 128–135.

Cairns, R. B. (1983). The emergence of developmental psychology. In P. H. Mussen (Series Ed.) & W. Kessen (Vol. Ed.), *Handbook of child psychology* (Vol. 1, pp. 41–102), New York: Wiley.

Camp, C. J., Rodrigue, J. R., & Olson, K. R. (1985). Curiosity in young, middle aged, and older adults. *Educational Gerontology,* in press.

Campos, J. J., Barrett, K. C., Lamb, M. E., Goldsmith, H. H., & Stenberg, C. (1983). Socioemotional development. In P. H. Mussen (Series Ed.) & M. M. Haith & J. J. Campos (Vol. Eds.), *Handbook of child psychology* (Vol. 2, pp. 783–917). New York: Wiley.

Caruso, D. R., & Sternberg, R. J. (1985). Toward an information-processing model of intellectual development. Submitted.

Case, R. (1978). Intellectual development from birth to adulthood: A Neo-Piagetian interpretation. In R. S. Siegler (Ed.), *Children's thinking: What develops?* (pp. 37–72). Hillsdale, NJ: Erlbaum.

Cattell, R. (1971). *Abilities: Their structure, growth, and action.* New York: Houghton Mifflin.

Cohen, L. B. (1981). Lags in the cognitive competence of prematurely born infants. In S. L. Friedman & M. Sigman (Eds.), *Preterm birth and psychological development.* New York: Academic Press.

Cohen, L. B., DeLoache, J. S. & Strauss, M. S. (1979). Infant visual perception. In J. D. Osofsky (Ed.), *Handbook of infant development* (pp. 393–438). New York: Wiley.

Cornelius, S. W. (1984). Classic pattern of intellectual aging: Test familiarity, difficulty, and performance. *Journal of Gerontology, 39,* 201–206.

Cunningham, W. R., Clayton, V., & Overton, W. (1975). Fluid and crystallized intelligence in young adulthood and old age. *Journal of Gerontology, 30,* 53–55.

Davidson, J. E., & Sternberg, R. J. (1984). The role of insight in intellectual giftedness. *Gifted Child Quarterly, 28,* 58–64.

Day, H. I. (1971). The measurement of specific curiosity. In H. I. Day, D. E. Berlyne, & D. E. Hunt (Eds.), *Intrinsic motivation: A new direction in education.* Toronto: Rinehart and Winston of Canada.

Dolan, A. B., Matheny, A. P., & Wilson, R. S. (1974). Bayley's infant behavior record: Age trends, sex differences, and behavioral correlates. *JSAS Catalog of Selected Documents in Psychology, 4,* 9–10.

Dweck, C. S., & Elliott, E. S. (1983). *Achievement motivation.* In P. H. Mussen (Series Ed.) & E. M. Hetherington (Vol. Ed.), *Handbook of child psychology* (Vol. 4, pp. 643–692). New York: Wiley.

Eisdorfer, C. (1968). Arousal and performance: Experiments in verbal learning and a tentative theory. In J. Talland (Ed.), *Human aging and behavior.* New York: Academic Press.

Escalona, S., & Corman, H. (1967). *Albert Einstein scales of sensori-motor development.* Unpublished manuscript.

Fagan, J. F. (1981). *Infant memory and the prediction of intelligence.* Paper presented at the meeting of the Society for Research in Child Development, Boston, April.

Fagan, J. F. (1984a). *Infants' attention to visual novelty and the prediction of later intellectual deficit.* Paper presented at the International Conference on Infant Studies, April.

Fagan, J. F. (1984b). The intelligent infant: Theoretical implications. *Intelligence, 8,* 1–9.

Fagan, J. F., & McGrath, S. K. (1981). Infant recognition memory and later intelligence. *Intelligence, 5,* 121–130.

Fagan, J. F., & Singer, L. T. (1983). Infant recognition memory as a measure of intelligence. In L. P. Lipsitt (Ed.), *Advances in infancy research* (Vol. 2, pp. 31–78). Norwood, NJ: Ablex.

Fantz, R. L. (1964). Visual experience in infants: Decreased attention to familiar patterns relative to novel ones. *Science, 146,* 668–670.

Fantz, R. L. (1967). Visual perception and experience in early infancy: A look at the hidden side of behavior development. In H. W. Stevenson, E. H. Hess, & H. L. Rheingold (Eds.), *Early behavior: Comparative and developmental approaches.* New York: Wiley.

Flavell, J. H. (1971). Stage-related properties of cognitive development. *Cognitive Psychology, 2,* 421–453.

Franks, J. J., Vye, N. J., Auble, P. M., Mezynski, K. J., Perfetto, G. A., Bransford, J. D., Stein, B. S., & Littlefield, J. (1982). Learning from explicit versus implicit texts. *Journal of Experimental Psychology: General, 111,* 414–422.

French, J. W., Ekstrom, R. B., & Price, I. A. (1963). *Kit of reference tests for cognitive factors.* Princeton, NJ: Educational Testing Service.

Gelman, R., & Baillargeon, R. (1983). A review of some Piagetian concepts. In P. H. Mussen

(Series Ed.), & J. Flavell & E. M. Markman (Vol. Eds.), *Handbook of child psychology* (Vol. 3, pp. 167–230). New York: Wiley.

Gesell, A., & Amatruda, C. (1962). *Developmental diagnosis: Normal and abnormal child development, clinical methods and practical applications.* (3rd ed.). New York: Harper.

Goldsmith, H. H., & Campos, J. J. (1982). Toward a theory of infant temperament. In R. N. Emde & R. J. Harmon (Eds.), *The development of attachment and affiliative systems: Psychobiological aspects* (pp. 161–193). New York: Plenum.

Goldsmith, H. H., & Gottesman, I. I. (1981). Origins of variation in behavioral style: A longitudinal study of temperament in young twins. *Child Development, 52,* 91–103.

Guilford, J. P. (1952). When not to factor analyze. *Psychological Bulletin, 49,* 26–37.

Halverson, C. F., & Waldrop, M. F. (1976). The relations between preschool activity and aspects of intellectual and social behavior at age 7.5. *Developmental Psychology, 12,* 107–112.

Harter, S. (1981a). A model of mastery motivation in children: Individual differences and developmental change. In W. A. Collins (Ed.), *Minnesota symposium on child psychology* (Vol. 14, pp. 215–254). Hillsdale, NJ: Erlbaum.

Harter, S. (1981b). A new self-report scale of intrinsic versus extrinsic orientation in the classroom: Motivation and informational components. *Developmental Psychology, 17,* 300–312.

Harter, S., & Connell, J. P. (1984). A model of children's achievement and related self-perceptions of competence, control, and motivation orientation. *Advances in Motivation and Achievement, 3,* 219–250.

Harter, S., & Zigler, E. (1974). The assessment of effectance motivation in normal and retarded children. *Developmental Psychology, 10,* 169–180.

Haywood, H. C., & Burke, W. P. (1977). Development of individual differences in intrinsic motivation. In I. C. Uzgiris & F. Weizmann (Eds.), *The structuring of experience* (pp. 179–210). New York: Plenum.

Horn, J. L. (1968). Organization of abilities and the development of intelligence. *Psychological Review, 75,* 242–259.

Horn, J. L., & Cattell, R. B. (1967). Age differences in fluid and crystallized intelligence. *Acta Psychologica, 26,* 107–129.

Hunt, J. McV. (1965). Intrinsic motivation and its role in psychological development. In D. Levine (Ed.), *Nebraska symposium on motivation* (Vol. 13, pp. 189–282). Lincoln: Univ. of Nebraska Press.

Intelligence and its measurement: A symposium (1921). *Journal of Educational Psychology, 12,* 123–147, 195–216, 271–275.

Kagan, J. (1984). *The nature of the child.* New York: Basic Books.

Kagan, J., & Moss, H. A. (1983). *Birth to maturity: A study in psychological development.* New Haven: Yale University Press.

Kahneman, D. (1973). *Attention and effort.* New York: Prentice-Hall.

Keil, F. C. (1981). Constraints on knowledge and cognitive development. *Psychological Review, 88,* 197–227.

Keil, F. C. (1984). Mechanisms of cognitive development and the structure of knowledge. In R. J. Sternberg (Ed.), *Mechanisms of cognitive development* (pp. 81–100). San Francisco: Freeman.

Kessen, W., Haith, M. M., & Salapatek, P. H. (1970). Human infancy: A bibliography and guide. In P. H. Mussen (Ed.), *Carmichael's manual of child psychology* (Vol. 1, pp. 287–445). New York: Wiley.

Kopp, C. B., & McCall, R. B. (1982). Stability and instability in mental performance among normal, at-risk, and handicapped infants and children. In P. B. Baltes & O. G. Brim, Jr.

(Eds.), *Life-span development and behavior* (Vol. 4, pp. 33-61). New York: Academic Press.

Lerner, R. M., & Lerner, J. V. (1983). Temperament-intelligence reciprocities in early childhood: A contextual model. In M. Lewis (Ed.), *Origins of intelligence* (pp. 399-421). New York: Plenum.

Lewis, M., & Brooks-Gunn, J. (1981). Visual attention at three months as a predictor of cognitive functioning at two years of age. *Intelligence, 5,* 131-140.

Lewis, M., Goldberg, S., & Campbell, H. (1969). A developmental study of information processing within the first three years of life: Response decrement to a redundant signal. *Monographs of the Society for Research in Child Development,* 34(9, Serial No. 133).

Maier, N. R. F. (1930). Reasoning in humans. 1. On direction. *Journal of Comparative Psychology,* 10, 115-143.

Marr, D., & Sternberg, R. J. (1986). Analogical reasoning with nonentrenched concepts: Effects of conceptual novelty on gifted and nongifted students. *Cognitive Development,* in press.

Matheny, A. P., & Brown, A. (1971). Activity, motor coordination and attention: Individual differences in twins. *Perceptual and Motor Skills,* 32, 151-158.

Matheny, A. P., Jr., Dolan, A. B., & Wilson, R. S. (1974). Bayley's infant behavior record: Relations between behaviors and mental test scores. *Developmental Psychology,* 10, 696-702.

McCall, R. B. (1979a). Qualitative transitions in behavioral development in the first two years of life. In M. H. Bornstein & W. Kessen (Eds.), *Psychological development from infancy: Image to intention* (pp. 183-224). New York: Wiley.

McCall, R. B. (1979b). The development of intellectual functioning in infancy and the prediction of later IQ. In J. D. Osofsky (Ed.), *Handbook of infant development* (pp. 707-741). New York: Wiley.

McCall, R. B., Eichorn, D. H., & Hogarty, P. S. (1977). Transitions in early mental development. *Monographs of the Society for Research in Child Development,* 42(Serial No. 171).

McCall, R. B., Hogarty, P. S., & Hurlburt, N. (1972). Transitions in infant sensorimotor development and the prediction of childhood IQ. *American Psychologist,* 27, 728-748.

McCall, R. B., & Kagan, J. (1967). Stimulus-schema discrepancy and attention in the infant. *Journal of Experimental Child Psychology,* 5, 381-390.

McCall, R. B., & Kagan, J. (1970). Individual differences in the infant's distribution of attention to stimulus discrepancy. *Developmental Psychology,* 2, 90-98.

McCall, R. B., Kennedy, C. B., & Appelbaum, M. I. (1977). Magnitude of discrepancy and the distribution of attention in infants. *Child Development,* 48, 772-785.

McCall, R. B., & McGhee, P. E. (1977). The discrepancy hypothesis of attention and affect in infants. In I. C. Uzgiris & F. Weizmann (Eds.), *The structuring of experience* (pp. 179-210). New York: Plenum.

McNemar, Q. (1951). The factors in factoring behavior. *Psychometrika,* 16, 353-359.

Miranda, S. B., & Fantz, R. L. (1974). Recognition memory in Down's Syndrome and normal infants. *Child Development,* 45, 651-660.

Mischel, T. (1971). Piaget: Cognitive conflict and the motivation of thought. In T. Mischel (Ed.), *Cognitive development and epistemology* (pp. 311-351). New York: Academic Press.

Morgan, J. J. B. (1941). *Psychology.* New York: Farrar & Rinehart.

Murrell, K. F. H. (1970). The effects of extensive practice on differences in reaction time. *Journal of Gerontology,* 25, 268-274.

Olson, G. M., & Sherman, T. (1983). Attention, learning, and memory in infants. In P. H. Mussen (Series Ed.) & M. M. Haith & J. J. Campos (Vol. Eds.), *Handbook of child psychology* (Vol. 2, pp. 1001-1008). New York: Wiley.

Cynthia A. Berg and Robert J. Sternberg

Piaget, J. (1950). *The psychology of intelligence.* New York: Harcourt.
Piaget, J. (1952). *The origins of intelligence in children.* (M. Cook, Trans.). New York: International Universities Press.
Piaget, J. (1967). *Six psychological studies* (D. Elkind, Ed.). New York: Random House.
Piaget, J. (1981). *Intelligence and affectivity: Their relationship during child development.* Palo Alto, CA: Annual Reviews.
Raaheim, K. (1974). *Problem solving and intelligence.* Oslo: Universitetsforlaget.
Raaheim, K. (1984). *Why intelligence is not enough.* Soreidgrend: Sigma Forlag.
Raaheim, K., & Kaufmann, G. (1972). Level of activity and success in solving an unfamiliar task. *Psychological Reports,* **30,** 271–274.
Ross, B. M., & Kerst, S. M. (1978). Developmental memory theories: Baldwin and Piaget. In H. W. Reese & L. P. Lipsitt (Eds.), *Advances in child development and behavior* (Vol. 12, pp. 183–229). New York: Academic Press.
Rothbart, M. K., & Derryberry, D. (1982). Development of individual differences in temperament. In M. E. Lamb & A. L. Brown (Eds.), *Advances in developmental psychology* (Vol. 1). Hillsdale, NJ: Erlbaum.
Ruddy, M., & Bornstein, M. H. (1982). Cognitive correlates of infant attention and maternal stimulation over the first year of life. *Child Development,* **53,** 183–188.
Schank, R. C. (1980). How much intelligence is there in artificial intelligence? *Intelligence,* **4,** 1–14.
Schneider, W., & Shiffrin, R. M. (1977). Controlled and automatic human information processing: I. Detection, search, and attention. *Psychological Review,* **84,** 1–66.
Shiffrin, R. M., & Schneider, W. (1977). Controlled and automatic human information processing: II. Perceptual learning, automatic attending, and a general theory. *Psychological Review,* **84,** 127–190.
Siegel, L. S. (1979). Infant perceptual, cognitive, and motor behaviours as predictors of subsequent cognitive and language development. *Canadian Journal of Psychology,* **33,** 382–395.
Siegel, L. S. (1981). Infant tests as predictors of cognitive and language development at two years. *Child Development,* **52,** 545–557.
Siegel, L. S., & Brainerd, C. J. (Eds.). (1978). *Alternatives to Piaget: Critical essays on the theory.* New York: Academic Press.
Siegler, R. S. (1984). Mechanisms of cognitive growth: Variation and selection. In R. J. Sternberg (Ed.), *Mechanisms of cognitive development* (pp. 141–162). San Francisco: Freeman.
Sokolov, E. N. (1960). Neuronal models and the orienting reflex. In M. A. B. Brazier (Ed.), *The central nervous system and behavior.* New York: Josiah Macy, Jr. Foundation.
Sokolov, E. N. (1963). *Perception and the conditioned reflex.* Oxford: Pergamon.
Stern, W. (1977). The psychological methods of testing intelligence. In D. N. Robinson (Ed.), *Significant contributions to the history of psychology 1750–1920* (Series B, pp. 1–144). Washington, DC: University Publications of America (original work published 1914).
Sternberg, R. J. (1981a). Intelligence and nonentrenchment. *Journal of Educational Psychology,* **73,** 1–16.
Sternberg, R. J. (1981b). Novelty-seeking, novelty-finding, and the developmental continuity of intelligence. *Intelligence,* **5,** 149–155.
Sternberg, R. J. (1982). Natural, unnatural, and supernatural concepts. *Cognitive Psychology,* **14,** 451–488.
Sternberg, R. J. (Ed.). (1984a). *Mechanisms of cognitive development.* San Francisco: Freeman.
Sternberg, R. J. (1984b). Mechanisms of cognitive development: A componential approach. In R. J. Sternberg (Ed.), *Mechanisms of cognitive development* (pp. 163–186). San Francisco: Freeman.

Sternberg, R. J. (1985). *Beyond IQ: A triarchic theory of human intelligence.* New York: Cambridge University Press.

Sternberg, R. J., & Davidson, J. E. (1982). The mind of the puzzler. *Psychology Today,* **June,** 37–44.

Terman, L. M., & Merrill, M. A. (1960). *Stanford-Binet intelligence scale.* Cambridge, MA: Riverside.

Tetewsky, S., & Sternberg, R. J. (1985). Conceptual and linguistic determinants of nonentrenched thinking. Submitted.

Ulvund, S. E. (1980). Cognition and motivation in early infancy: An interactionist approach. *Human Development,* **23,** 17–32.

Ulvund, S. E. (1984). Predictive validity of assessments of early cognitive competence in light of some current issues in developmental psychology. *Human Development,* **27,** 76–83.

Uzgiris, I., & Hunt, J. McV. (1975). *Assessment in infancy: Ordinal scales of psychological development.* Urbana: Univ. of Illinois Press.

Vernon, P. E. (1971). *The structure of human abilities.* London: Methuen.

Wagner, R. K., & Sternberg, R. J. (1983). *Executive control of reading.* Unpublished manuscript, Yale University, Department of Psychology, New Haven, CT.

Werner, H. (1948). *Comparative psychology of mental development* (rev. ed.). Chicago: Follett.

Werner, J. S., & Perlmutter, M. (1979). Development of visual memory in infants. In H. W. Reese & L. P. Lipsitt (Eds.), *Advances in child development and behavior* (Vol. 14, pp. 1–56). New York: Academic Press.

White, R. W. (1959). Motivation reconsidered: The concept of competence. *Psychological Review,* **66,** 297–333.

White, S. H. (1983). The idea of development in developmental psychology. In R. M. Lerner (Ed.), *Developmental psychology: Historical and philosophical perspectives* (pp. 55–77). Hillsdale, NJ: Erlbaum.

Willis, S. L., Blieszner, R., & Baltes, P. B. (1981). Intellectual training research in aging: Modification of performance on the fluid ability of figural relations. *Journal of Educational Psychology,* **73,** 41–50.

Wohlwill, J. F. (1973). *The study of behavioral development.* New York: Academic Press.

Wohlwill, J. F. (1980). Cognitive development in childhood. In O. G. Brim & J. Kagan (Eds.), *Constancy and change in human development* (pp. 359–444). Cambridge, MA: Harvard Univ. Press.

Yarrow, L. J., Klein, R. P., Lomonaco, S., & Morgan, G. A. (1975). Cognitive and motivational development in early childhood. In B. X. Friedlander, G. M. Sterritt, & G. E. Kirk (Eds.), *Exceptional infant* (Vol. 3, pp. 491–502). New York: Brunner/Mazel.

Yarrow, L. J., McQuiston, S., MacTurk, R. H., McCarthy, M. E., Klein, R. P., & Vietze, P. M. (1983). Assessment of mastery motivation during the first year of life: Contemporaneous and cross-age relationships. *Developmental Psychology,* **19,** 159–171.

Yarrow, L. J., & Messler, D. J. (1983). Motivation and cognition in infancy. In M. Lewis (Ed.), *Origins of intelligence* (pp. 451–477). New York: Plenum.

Zigler, E. (1971). The retarded child as a whole person. In H. E. Adams & W. K. Boardman (Eds.), *Advances in experimental clinical psychology* (Vol. 1, pp. 47–120). Oxford: Pergamon.

METAPHORIC COMPETENCE IN COGNITIVE AND LANGUAGE DEVELOPMENT

Marc Marschark and Lynn Nall

DEPARTMENT OF PSYCHOLOGY
UNIVERSITY OF NORTH CAROLINA AT GREENSBORO
GREENSBORO, NORTH CAROLINA

I. Introduction

During the 1960s and early 1970s, the study of language development was guided largely by assumptions of what children could not do, from an adult-centered viewpoint, and by a desire to chart the developmental waning of grammatical incompetence. However, young children consistently were

ADVANCES IN CHILD DEVELOPMENT
AND BEHAVIOR, VOL. 19

shown to be more flexible than would be expected from the then-popular linguistic theories (Chomsky, 1965; McNeill, 1970). Wetstone and Friedlander (1973), for example, demonstrated that children as young as 2 years old could understand nongrammatical language, and Slobin (1966) demonstrated that passive sentences were no harder than active sentences for 6-year-old children to understand, if all other factors were equated. Researchers therefore were faced with having to explain children's responding correctly and apparently effortlessly to language that was incorrect or complex to the adult.

Armed with a new concern for children's competencies rather than incompetencies, researchers in the 1980s have become more interested in the content of what children say and the extent to which it might reflect their understanding of language and the world. Investigations of young (3–7 years old) children's figurative language abilities have been an important part of this "new look" especially because these abilities previously were assumed to require complex linguistic and cognitive knowledge not acquired until age 10 or 11 (e.g., Asch & Nerlove, 1960; Billow, 1975; Piaget, 1926/1974). A difficulty sometimes encountered is seeing exactly how such research and even figurative skills themselves fit in the larger context of development. The following discussion, therefore, evaluates the extent of children's figurative abilities in terms of their roles as learning devices as well as indicators of cognitive and linguistic competence.

If one takes preschoolers' language production at face value, they appear either to exhibit considerable metaphoric expertise or not to know that trucks cannot die, that horses cannot be "doggies," or that hair cannot be spaghetti. Alternatively, given the differences in the ways that adults and children "carve up" the world (Bronowski & Bellugi, 1970; Denney & Ziobrowski, 1972), what is nonliteral for the adult may not be so to the child. Young children may use language constructions such as "My truck died" not out of error or figurative expertise, but because it describes a state of affairs quite accurately in terms of their knowledge of the world, that is, the truck has ceased its normal functioning (see Lakoff & Johnson, 1980; Pollio & Pickens, 1980; for discussions of related alternatives).[1] Similarly, a child's calling an umbrella a "rain roof" may indicate that from that child's perspective, *roofs* is a category containing umbrellas, awnings, trees, and other functional roofs, just as the child's *fish* category may include whales and porpoises and her *bird* category may not include ostriches or penguins. The extent to which children (intentionally or unintentionally) violate conceptual "boundaries" in apparently figurative statements thus

[1]Similar arguments against considering adults as analogs in understanding young children have been made by Fagan, Rovee, and Kaplan (1976) with regard to infant perception and Offenbach (1983) with regard to children's concept learning.

may reflect the breadth and flexibility of their category knowledge (see Section VIII for further discussion). Figurative productions then become interesting phenomena not so much because they occur, but because of the ways in which they reflect children's understanding of the world and affect their interactions with others and with the environment.

Drawing a distinction between learning to comprehend language literally and nonliterally requires consideration of differences in adults' and children's conceptual abilities and knowledge as well as a definition of nonliteral language appropriate from both perspectives. In this article, we will consider these differences and the related argument of whether metaphor use can be seen in "the genius of early child language" (Winner, McCarthy, & Gardner, 1980a) or is dependent on a metalinguistic awareness that is not really observed until later stages of development (Asch & Nerlove, 1960; Inhelder & Piaget, 1958; Piaget, 1926/1974). Following discussions of the bases and necessity of children's creative language constructions, the relevant literature on figurative comprehension and production will be reviewed. Evaluation of recent research findings in the area will be shown to reveal that who (i.e., what aged child) has figurative abilities depends on how these skills are evaluated (Gardner, Winner, Bechhofer, & Wolf, 1978; Reynolds & Ortony, 1980). We therefore will delineate what nonliteral skills are apparent in the language of children of different ages and the role of nonliteral language in language and cognitive development at large.

II. Distinguishing Figurative Language in Children

According to most generally accepted definitions, true metaphor involves intentional but implicit comparisons between entities in two distinct domains. The domains of the subject (or *topic*) and predicate (or *vehicle*) have aspects of both similarity (their *ground*) and dissimilarity (their *tension*), and their juxtaposition serves to define or highlight some aspect of the topic by transferring to it qualities of the vehicle (Tourangeau & Sternberg, 1981). The aspect of this definition most difficult to apply unequivocally in evaluating children's utterances is intention. Pollio and Pickens (1980) have noted the traditional argument that children use metaphor inadvertently because they are unaware of the linguistic constraints inherent in their words, lack sufficient vocabulary for literal description, "play" with language in ways otherwise unacceptable, or make jokes using language that appears figurative but is not intended to be so (e.g., "My truck died"). However, some current researchers, like Pollio and Pickens, have taken a more functional view of figurative language, addressing themselves to "the purpose or function of the usage for the speaker'' (Pollio & Pickens, 1980, p. 312). Although determining intention on the part of a young child may be difficult, that assessment nonetheless is necessary in order to distinguish errors and apparently figurative but actually literal productions from those that are truly figurative.

The problem of ascertaining intention in children's nonliteral language is the same as that encountered in ascertaining object substitution in symbolic play, because in both cases purposeful symbolic extension requires a priori knowledge of both conventional and nonconventional (i.e., standard and novel) usage (Lakoff & Johnson, 1980; McCune–Nicolich, 1981). Borrowing from the symbolic play literature, therefore, we assume attribution of intention in metaphoric comparisons to be appropriate when based on verbal commentary (e.g., explicit comment, accompanying laughter, or requests for approval), alternate use of both conventional and nonconventional functions of the same term within the same context, or demonstrated generality of a novel comparison across contexts (McCune–Nicolich, 1981). Other empirical methods of determining intentionality may be possible, but we believe that the most common method—the multiple-choice test—may have serious flaws. Researchers must be wary of generalizing results obtained from comprehension tasks to spontaneous production, because selection of a metaphorical sentence from a small set of alternatives may involve different competencies from generating such a construction in a novel context. This issue is considered at length in Sections V and VII. A single example here will suffice to demonstrate the importance of distinguishing the functions of children's nonliteral productions aside from their comprehension abilities.

Mendelsohn, Robinson, Gardner, and Winner (1984) recently devised a task purported to determine whether preschoolers' nonliteral renamings (e.g., calling a streak of skywriting a ''scar'') actually reflected ''intentional category violations (and hence are metaphors) or simply one of several 'literal' ways in which preschoolers classify'' (p. 187). A bit of ''straw man'' logic was involved there, as this distinction was considered only in terms of whether the child actually thought, for example, a yellow baseball bat *was* corn, or chose to call it so in order to emphasize the perceptual similarity. The possibility of the child's simply pretending the bat was corn (without the intention of communicating a similarity/dissimilarity relation) was not considered. In their experiment, 4-year-old children were given a multiple-choice test in which a target element (e.g., a cherry lollipop) could be matched to one of three others: a taxonomically or associatively related element (e.g., a chocolate bar), a visually similar element (e.g., a stop sign), or an unrelated element (e.g., the sky at night). Mendelsohn *et al.* found that across three different stimulus modalities, taxonomic and associative matches were more likely than "metaphorical," perceptual matches and were more easily explained by the children. They concluded that because preschoolers in this multiple-choice experiment said that lollipops were best put with chocolate bars rather than stop signs, "we can now assert with considerable confidence that preschoolers' renamings [in other, naturalistic contexts] are genuine perceptual metaphors" (p. 192). We find awkward, however, the argument that because children display literal classification skills in one task (that explicitly biases them in that direction), they are being nonliteral in a different task when they produce different utterances for different reasons. Drawing the conclusion that Mendelsohn et al. seem to want requires insight into the aspects of object similarity and dissimilarity relevant in children's (implicit or explicit) comparison statements.

The importance laid to similarlity and dissimilarity in metaphor comprehension varies with several theoretical perspectives (see Marschark, Katz, & Paivio, 1983; Tourangeau & Sternberg, 1982, for discussion), but relevant discussions virtually always are in terms of adult perceptions thereof. Even relatively simple nominative ("an A is a B") metaphors may have attributes of similarity and/or dissimilarity significant for adults but not children (of any particular age) or the other way around, but this possibility need not mean that one group or the other is language deficient. Unfortunately, the dimensions of figurative language that affect its comprehension by children have not been mapped as well as for adults (Katz, Paivio, & Marschark, 1985; Marschark et al., 1983), and so determining exactly what is nonliteral from the perspective of the young child is difficult.[2]

One likely source of variation in adult–child perceptions of literalness is the extent to which metaphoric topics and vehicles share perceptual, functional, action, or conceptual properties (Calhoun, 1984; Silberstein, Gardner, Phelps, & Winner, 1982; cf. Clark, 1973; Nelson, 1973, for discussions of the importance of those characteristics in literal language). Silberstein et al. (1982) presented subjects 25 incomplete sentences, each followed by five possible endings that would yield metaphorical statements; a sixth ending combined two grounds, and a seventh yielded a literal statement. The resulting metaphorical statements were based on grounds of shape, color, sound, movement, or abstract ("conceptual") similarity. For example, "The popped red balloon is . . . " was followed by the choices "a limp washcloth" (shape), "a bottle of ketchup" (color), "a washed away sandcastle" (conceptual: impermanence), "an empty auditorium after a concert" (sound), and "an apple peel" (combination of color and shape). "A traffic

---

[2]Most likely, many children's utterances deemed correct and literally true by adults are actually figurative or erroneous from the child's perspective (i.e., a wrong, but contextually acceptable message has been inferred). This possibility is even harder to examine empirically, however, and apparently has not been considered seriously in any previous research.

jam is . . . '' was followed by "many cars in one place" (literal) and "a creeping caterpillar" (movement) among other choices. Silberstein *et al.* found relative ground preferences to change with age. The youngest subjects (6 years old) preferred perceptual endings based on color or shape, somewhat older subjects (12–14 years old) preferred endings based on sound and movement, and the oldest subjects (18–22 years old) preferred nonperceptual, conceptual grounds.

The findings of Silberstein *et al.* (1982) and similar results obtained by Calhoun (1984) can be considered in the context of children's acquiring their first words, as discussed by Clark (1973), Macnamara (1972), and Nelson (1973). Taken together, these studies provide evidence that the same processes are likely involved in young children's "solving the problem" of referential (word–object) pairings and their later discovery of nonliteral relationships between linguistic units and speakers' intended meanings. Both children's first words and their first use of figurative statements depend on the same perceptual characteristics of objects. Those characteristics most easily distinguished from the identity of the object itself and associated with a verbal label become the earliest tools for psycholinguistic generalization and creativity. In fact, several researchers have suggested that metaphor provides one of the basic ways of learning about the world. Its mapping of different, previously unrelated domains onto each other is seen to extend children's knowledge to that which is unfamiliar, thus making it a tool as well as a skill (Arnheim, 1974; Petrie, 1979; Piaget, 1926/1974).

III. Theoretical Views of Children's Figurative Language

The role of children's nonliteral language as a learning device has not been considered from the two orientations that have generated most of the recent research on figurative language abilities of adults and children, an omission that we believe seriously limits their theoretical utility. One of these orientations, the traditional, formal view, derives from literary considerations of metaphors. In this view, nonliteral deviations from "standard" language are based on knowledge of both the meaning of the literal statement and the implications of the nonliteral use (e.g., Piaget, 1926/1974; see also, Ziff, 1964, for a linguistic consideration). From this perspective, most apparently figurative constructions of younger children must be considered errors because the producers lack the linguistic and metalinguistic competencies assumed necessary for reconciling metaphoric tension and ground.

An alternative, currently popular view espoused by Winner (1979; Winner *et al.*, 1980), Billow (1975), and Verbrugge (1979) seems a radical response to the formal orientation. According to their criteria, almost any verbal or nonverbal response that crosses behavioral or conceptual boundaries to an observer can be considered a metaphor. Children's "eating" a yellow baseball bat as though it were corn (Mendelsohn *et al.*, 1984), seeing clouds as lions (Verbrugge, 1979), or noticing a perceptual similarity between a wrinkled face and a wrinkled apple (Dent & Dupree, 1983) thus are all given special status as indicative of metaphoric competence, despite the lack of independent evidence concerning the communicative intentions or competencies of the children involved. The problem with this view is that any apparently nonliteral statement is accepted as a valid figure if it communicates some meaning to the listener, even if that meaning differs in denotation or connotation from the meaning intended by the speaker. In a modified version of this theoretical view, Pollio and Pickens (1980) inquired into the purposes of children's metaphoric statements, but they failed to consider differences in the purpose of the speaker and the purpose inferred by the listener.

The present view of children's nonliteral language obviously differs from both the traditional, formal view and its current, liberal alternative. Our view of figurative language is essentially the traditional one: true figurative use of a linguistic unit depends on the presence of a ground (or semantic features or selection rules) that make the utterance acceptable to the speaker while still being aware of the violation or believed violation of someone else's semantic categorizations (Lakoff & Johnson, 1980). The status that we give to the apparently figurative constructions produced by incompetent young speakers, however, is that they often may be neither error nor metaphor. Rather, much if not most such language may be intended literally. Consider again a 3 year old's use of "My truck died." According to the traditional definition above, this utterance simply would be considered a production error. The assumption is that even though the sentence would likely be considered metaphorical if uttered by an adult, 3 year olds lack the necessary "operational intelligence" to understand the analogy and likely have "incorrect" notions of animacy that lead them to believe that trucks can die. According to the more liberal view of figurative production, in contrast, "My truck died" is clearly metaphorical, regardless of whether the child knows that trucks cannot literally die. Finally, from the present perspective, the utterance at issue is nonliteral for adult listeners, by virtue of having crossed the "adult" conceptual boundary of animacy, but need not be for the child. If the 3 year old's meaning of "died" involves the cessation of functions characteristic of living things (movement, making noise, having all parts intact, etc.), the statement cannot be a semantic error, but it also lacks any intentional conceptual violations and thus also

cannot be a metaphor. The statement simply is literal, because it functionally conveys a literally believed state of affairs.

Examples similar to the above appear occasionally in the literature on
children's figurative language, and others are available anecdotally from
almost any parent. However, we assume that many situations occur in which
children's literally unacceptable sentences are misperceived by adult observers. Such statements might be taken to have a literal or figurative intent
different from that actually intended by the child or be taken as an error
of misnaming or overgeneralization. Gardner, Kirchner, Winner, and Perkins (1975), for example, studied children's figurative language production.
They presented 3 to 19 year olds a series of vignettes for which the subjects
had to provide appropriate endings. The vignettes ended with incomplete
similes, and subjects were encouraged to produce unusual completions. In
addition to a variety of obviously figuative constructions (e.g., "quiet as a
magic marker"), Gardner *et al.* found a number of similar productions that
they ruled out as nonsensical. Although they may have been so to the adult
researchers, those productions may not have been meaningless to their producers. Gardner *et al.,* for example, classified "a boy as tall as a light
switch" as an anomalous production. In our view, this statement seems
likely to represent a literal description from the viewpoint of a child not
yet tall enough to turn on bedroom lights.

Our suggestion is that children of various ages may have different (or
additional) definitions of words from adults, and that those differences can
make for mistaken communications and classifications thereof in linguistic
interactions (Asch & Nerlove, 1960; Nelson, 1974). Admittedly, this functional restriction of metaphor and related constructions creates a problem
for investigators of children's figurative language. The boy who calls his
sister a cow after describing her ponderous, bovine qualities now can be
credited with having used a metaphor. But can such competence be inferred
if the same epithet were hurled without overt prior description? Declaring
for the affirmative is tempting, and would be consistent with the positions
of Verbrugge (1979) and Billow (1975). But the determining factor in the
decision must be whether the statement is intended or seen as a category
violation by the child, because experimenter-defined criteria may differ substantially (Lange & Jackson, 1974; see Section VIII for further discussion).

IV. Why Children Use Metaphor

Ortony (1975) suggested that although metaphor can be used as an artistic
device, it also has a natural and often necessary function in more mundane
language interaction (see also Beck, 1978, for the anthropological view, and
Petrie, 1979, for the educational view). He described three bases for the

necessity of figurative language, all of which appear to have particular implications for the development of figurative competence. Most important in this context is Ortony's *inexpressibility* thesis. He suggested that some things, by their nature, are not easily described. This feature results from the continuous nature of experience precluding the possibility of having distinct word readings for every conceivable detail that one might want to convey (Ortony, 1975, p. 49). Nonliteral language allows children (as well as adults) to communicate unnameable or not easily named characteristics implicitly, by predicating one domain (of the vehicle) on another (of the topic).

For the child, inexpressibility likely arises frequently, because of the imbalance between relatively good sensorimotor acuity, with accompanying exploration and curiosity, as compared to relatively poor linguistic and metalinguistic skills. When discovery develops faster than the ability to describe or inquire about new findings, the words or constructions necessary for "literal" communication frequently will be unavailable, either because they are not in the repertoire at all or because their applicability in a particular context is not apparent. Nelson (1974) and others (e.g., Leopold, 1948; Werner & Kaplan, 1964; see also Marschark & West, 1984, 1985) have noted that in such situations, children are prone to linguistic invention.

Although situations of inexpressibility for a child thus can lead to apparently figurative productions, careful consideration must be given to the status of those utterances from the child's perspective. Utterances deriving from inexpressible situations and appearing figurative may be literally true, erroneous, or figurative for the child. For example, consider a child encountering a platypus for the first time. The statement "It's a Donald Duck," likely considered a perceptually based overgeneralization (*platypus = duck*) by an adult observer, could indicate a literal intention of the child, who may always call ducks "Donald Ducks" and believes the platypus to be a duck. Alternatively, the child may be familiar with platypuses from books and television, but may not recognize this particular animal as a platypus. Given the child's knowledge base then, "It's a Donald Duck" (= "It's a duck") is truely an error. Finally, the child may realize that the platypus is unfamiliar and, noticing the similarity of fur to Donald Duck's clothing or a fur coat, use the metaphorical statement "It's a Donald Duck" (= "It looks like Donald Duck") or even "It's a Donald Duck with a fur coat."

How is this figurative use to be discerned by an observer? Here, we must defer to the criteria described in Section II. If the child made one of the above statements in simile form ("It's like Donald Duck with a fur coat") or accompanied the utterance with laughter or other evidence of nonliteral recognition, we would credit the child with a figurative utterance. The child's descriptions of similarities and differences between Donald Duck and the platypus or descriptions of other animals in terms of cartoon characters also would be taken to indicate that the child knows a platypus is similar to, but not the same as a duck. Beyond these possibilities, the status of the utterance may be uncertain, although the age of the child, context of the utterance, and the similarity of a platypus to other things within the child's ken may provide additional cues.

Inexpressibility, whether for a child or an adult, connotes a lack of linguistic choice. When a "correct" literal form of expression is unavailable, an alternative form must be used. These forms are undoubtedly creative (Marschark & West, 1985) and nonliteral, but are not necessarily figurative for the child. This interpretation of Ortony's inexpressibility thesis leads to three important predictions. First, the more novel and difficult to-be-communicated information is for the child, the greater should be the incidence of creative linguistic constructions, including figurative expressions. Although no direct evidence has been offered with regard to this prediction, indirect support can be inferred from findings related to a second prediction. This prediction is that as children get older and their language repertoire increases, the frequency of inexpressible situations, and hence apparently nonliteral language, should decrease, at least until they are able to use more intentional, "artistic" figurative language. A related but largely unexplored possibility is that some forms of nonliteral language may decrease in frequency with age while others increase regularly. Findings consistent with at least the general, age-related prediction have been reported by Pollio and Pollio (1974, 1979) for a written task involving children 8–11 years old and by Marschark and West (1984) for a sign language production task with deaf children 8–15 years old. Further consideration of these and other age-related findings are discussed later, in Section VII.

A third prediction arising from the inexpressibility thesis concerns the nonliteral language of deaf and other language-impaired children. Simply stated, to the extent that deaf children (or any others) are language deficient relative to hearing peers (as noted by Furth, 1973; Liben, 1978), they should have a greater incidence of "inexpressible events" and hence should produce more nonliteral language. In contrast, if nonliteral language use is the culmination of linguistic and metalinguistic skill, such disordered populations should produce less figurative language than nondisordered populations. The nonliteral comprehension abilities of deaf children have been examined in several studies with mixed results (see Iran-Nejad, Ortony & Rittenhouse, 1981; Marschark & West, 1985, for reviews). Conley (1976) compared deaf and hearing children's abilities to interpret English idioms. She found that despite her matching subjects on reading ability, deaf children still scored significantly lower than their hearing peers. Iran-Nejad *et al.* (1981), however, demonstrated that when verbal and nonverbal contexts are supplied, deaf children can learn to distinguish metaphorical from nonmetaphorical story endings. They concluded that deaf children do not suffer from any particular metaphor-related deficit, but lack the linguistic experience necessary for dealing with (English) figurative language (see Marschark & West, 1985, for similar conclusions).

Studies of deaf children's nonliteral language production (rather than comprehension) are practically nonexistent. Marschark and West (1985), had deaf and hearing children 12–15 years old tell stories on two fantasy-based themes similar to those used by Pollio and Pollio (1974). For example, they were asked to describe what would happen if they awakened one morning and found that all of the animals and people in the world had exchanged roles. Story productions were videotaped (and translated in the case of the signed productions of deaf subjects) and later examined for nonliteral constructions. Both groups produced stories containing several classes of figurative language. Consistent with the inexpressibility prediction, and contrary to previous claims of language rigidity in deaf children, the deaf students showed considerable nonliteral language use within sign language. They produced traditional types of figurative constructions (e.g., metaphor, simile) at a rate slightly higher than their hearing age mates and reliably surpassed them in four other nonliteral categories appropriate for oral and sign production but not written prose.

Among the scoring categories used by Marschark and West (1984, 1985) in examining nonliteral constructions in signed and oral productions was one that included novel modification of signs or words. These modifications provided additional meaning or more vivid communication than would have been possible with literal production or regular American Sign Language inflections (Klima & Bellugi, 1979). For example, one deaf child restricted her signing space to denote an infant speaker; one hearing child, similarly, changed to a creaky voice to denote an aged speaker. These and similar modifications often were accompanied by literal statements expressing the same information, and the linguistic adjustments thus appeared primarily to serve the function of making the message more vivid. But were such modifications simply embellishments of the literal message, or were they necessary to communicate some additional information?

Ortony (1975) suggested in his *vividness* thesis that figurative language is necessary, in part, because it allows one to bridge the gap between the continuity of experience and the discreteness of symbolic descriptions, thereby increasing the probability that a listener will understand a speaker's message as it is intended (p. 50; see also Henle, 1972; Johnson & Malgady, 1980). The importance of nonliteral language for relatively young children may be strongly linked to its vividness, in that figurative constructions can facilitate the communication of ideas to and from them at the concrete level at which they are most adept. Consistent with this assumption, Gardner (1974), Honeck, Sowry, and Voegtle (1978), Iran–Nejad *et al.* (1981), and others have obtained results indicating that the comprehension of nonliteral statements is facilitated by presentation of a pictorial context that concretizes the metaphoric ground. More specifically, Paivio (1979) pointed out that a metaphoric vehicle acts as a conceptual peg for comprehension of an entire metaphor since "it promotes retrieval of images and verbal information that intersects with information aroused by the topic" (p. 168). Given the importance of concreteness to such conceptual pegs in paired-associate learning, Paivio argued that the image-evoking value (or vividness) of metaphoric vehicles should be particularly important for metaphor interpretation. On this basis, vehicle imagery would be expected to be especially important to younger children's figurative comprehension. Direct experimental support for this prediction at the adult level is lacking, and normative studies by Marschark *et al.* (1983) and Katz *et al.* (1985) have yielded only inconsistent relationships between ratings of vehicle imagery and comprehensibility.

However, Nall (1983) recently obtained some support for Paivio's prediction in a study involving third, fifth, and seventh graders (mean ages 9:3, 11:2, and 13:0 years, respectively). She tested metaphor comprehension in a multiple-choice task involving materials drawn from the Marschark *et al.* (1983) study. The metaphors were presented in riddle form (e.g., "Why is an ant a bulldozer?") and were followed by three possible response choices: a correct ground for the metaphor ("both are strong"), a literally true sentence relevant to the topic ("an ant is an insect"), and a false sentence relevant to both topic and vehicle ("an ant is made of steel"). Children pointed to the responses that "solved" the riddles, and the total number of correct responses for each item were then analyzed in terms of the norms of Marschark *et al.* (1983). Rated imageability of (whole) metaphors was the only predictor of comprehension reliable at all three age levels in Nall's task, but imageability of the predicate was a better predictor for the third graders. Predicate imagery was not a reliable predictor of correct performance for the fifth and seventh graders, who, like the university-aged subjects in the Marschark *et al.* study, would not be tied to concrete levels of language comprehension (Asch & Nerlove, 1960; Billow, 1975).[3]

Ortony's (1975) *compactness* thesis, like the vividness thesis, was based on a reconstructive view of metaphor. One characteristic of figurative language is that it holistically communicates large, conceptually rich chunks of information in a very efficient manner. This efficiency eliminates the

[3]A possible alternative explanation for the observed lack of imagery effects was offered by Mary Walsh (personal communication, November 15, 1983). She suggested that the imagery processes tapped in these tasks might underlie only one facet of figurative comprehension: the perception of similarity. Vehicle concreteness then could help identify which aspects of the vehicle domain are relevant without guiding "higher," or more abstract (presumably semantic) aspects of the comprehension process.

need for the speaker to provide all details of a message explicitly, thereby reducing the time required for communication relative to exact, literal transmission. At the same time, the memory load and parsing demands on the listener are reduced, facilitating comprehension. The compactness of nonliteral language therefore should be especially important to the young child. As a comprehender, the rich instantiation of a nonliteral comparison allows the child to leap "the epistemological chasm between old knowledge and radically new knowledge" (Petrie, 1979, p. 440). The diverse set of associations activated in memory upon hearing such an utterance also increases the probability of some overlap in the intended and derived messages by providing multiple pathways to memory (Marschark & Hunt, 1985), while simultaneously constraining the scope of that activation (Ortony, 1979). As language producers, the freedom to violate (as well as the lack of knowledge about the existence of) semantic and syntactic selection restrictions provides children the means to express themselves in a way nearer to the continuous, holistic nature of their perceptual experience (Shepp, Burns, & McDonough, 1980). Interpreted by developmental psycholinguists as metaphors, statements such as "Your hair is spaghetti" communicate more information than is "literally" expressible given the vocabulary and presumed processing capacity limitations of young children. Although no research has specifically addressed this issue, the effects of compactness seem evident in the variety of findings indicating that metaphor and simile comprehension increase when those constructions occur at the end of verbal contexts and concisely summarize them (e.g., Gardner *et al.*, 1975; Vosniadou & Ortony, 1983b; Vosniadou, Ortony, Reynolds, & Wilson, 1984).

In summary, nonliteral language appears to satisfy several needs of young language users, both as comprehenders and as producers. Use of such language by children, and perhaps more pervasively by others to children, frequently provides a communication medium more appropriate to children's level of general cognitive competence than does literal language. The fact that most nonliteral language serves to concretize and particularize the world thus should not be seen as coincidental to the young child's frequent concretization and particularization in literal language. "In a word, the line of development of language, as of perception, is from whole to the part, from syncretism to analysis, and not vice versa" (Piaget, 1926/1974, p. 146).

V. Children's Verbal and Nonverbal Metaphoric Comprehension

Implicit in the preceding discussion was the verbal nature of metaphor. This position is not universally accepted, but examination of findings that fall on opposite sides of the question "Do young children have metaphoric competence?'' have varied in the extent to which such competence was limited to the verbal domain. At one extreme was Piaget's 1926 procedure of asking children if they understood proverbs and then asking them for explanations. (Piaget's finding that young children professed to understanding the proverbs but provided unsatisfactory interpretations spawned the idea of verbal syncretism.) Honeck *et al.* (1978), however, found that 7- to 9-year-old children could perform at above-chance levels in a proverb task when they pointed to pictures representing nonliteral interpretations of the proverbs, rather than providing verbal descriptions.

A similar case of apparently contradictory results following from verbal versus nonverbal figurative contexts is that of Asch and Nerlove's (1960) classic study and Gardner's (1974) redesigned replication. Asch and Nerlove asked 3- to 12-year-old children to explain double-function words, referring to both physical properties of objects and psychological properties of people (e.g., *sweet, cold, hard*). They found a developmental sequence of explanation abilities in which object reference was understood first, followed by psychological reference of the word as a homonym (rather than as an extension of the concrete word), and finally, awareness of double-function qualities. Gardner (1974) made Asch and Nerlove's task largely nonverbal by examining how children mapped polar adjectives onto novel, perceptual domains. Pairs such as *light/dark, happy/sad,* and *warm/cold* were presented to subjects 3–19 years old who were asked to map the words onto orthogonally paired stimuli from several sensory domains (e.g., colors, faces, objects). Although even preschoolers were relatively good in the matching task (57–76% correct, chance = 50%), they and other young subjects were relatively poor in explaining their matches. These and similar findings obtained by Douglas and Peel (1979) and Lesser and Drouin (1975) suggest that either the associative pairings in nonverbal "metaphor" tasks "are made on an immediate or intuitive basis rather than as a deduction from the logical properties of the task or of the language" (Gardner, 1974, p. 90) or that the stimulus relationships important to the child are not always describable to the adult.

In either case, studies like those of Gardner (1974) and Honeck *et al.* (1978) have suggested to researchers that the basics of nonliteral thought are developed by $3\frac{1}{2}$ years of age, at least as measured by nonverbal comprehension tasks. Similar findings obtained with various other paradigms have demonstrated clearly that young children can in fact map objects and attributes across domains, as is required for nonliteral comprehension (e.g., Gentner, 1977). Yet those abilities seem of a rather elementary level, below what is required for similar comprehension in the absence of visual aids. For example, Gentner (1977) had preschool children map human facial and body features onto pictures of trees and mountains. The fact that they were able to make those "cross-domain" transfers despite manipulations of picture orientation and detail was taken as evidence for metaphoric competence. Her forced-choice task, however, emphasized the spatial relationships that were being tested. Actually, only elements in a single domain, body parts, were involved, and they are explicitly taught to children according to their location. No evidence was offered indicating that children of the same age can spontaneously produce such mappings, and even if they could, their metaphoric underpinnings still would be in some doubt. As Vosniadou and Ortony (1983a) have noted,

> If in calling a green carpet "grass" the child is merely noticing an (interesting) similarity and texture, this hardly seems sufficient to justify calling the production metaphorical. Nor is it enough to know that the child knows the word for carpet. Rather, what seems to be needed is that the child also knows that carpets and grass belong to different conventional categories. (pp. 154–155)

Still involving nonverbal responding but demonstrating somewhat more complex nonliteral skills are a series of experiments reported by Vosniadou and Ortony (1983b) and Vosniadou *et al.* (1984). They presented to 4- to 8-year old children short stories ending with literal or metaphorical sentences and had the children act them out using specially constructed toy layouts. Results consistently showed that even the youngest children could act out metaphoric story endings, when the endings were highly predictable from the stories. For less probable endings such performance was only approached in the older subjects, who also were able to provide verbal explanations of the metaphors. These studies then, like the nonverbal two-choice studies noted above, reveal that young children have some prerequisites necessary for nonliteral competence. However, an important point is that the demonstrated scope of those skills is still rather restricted, being apparent only when the alternatives are limited. The same caveat also applies to several studies that have shown nonliteral comprehension in young children given entirely verbal tasks. Vosniadou and Ortony (1983a) presented children 3–6 years old perceptual comparison sentence frames with the last word omitted (e.g., "A river is like a . . . "). The child's task was to select one of two words to complete each sentence, when the pairs provided metaphorical and literal, literal and anomalous, or metaphorical and anomalous alternatives. Their results indicated that children as young as 4 could distinguish anomalous sentences from ones that were literally or figuratively possible, but the bases of those judgments remain uncertain (see also Calhoun, 1984; Nall, 1983).

Although children younger than 5 years old clearly exhibit the rudiments of nonliteral comprehension in verbal and nonverbal tasks, the limitation of such performance to restricted-alternative situations seems to evidence an ability rather different from that sought by Piaget (1926/1974), Asch and Nerlove (1960), and others. The difference is essentially the same as that encountered frequently in the developmental literature with regard to the question of what constitutes evidence for "true" cognitive abilities in young children confronted with Piagetian and similar tasks (e.g., Brainerd, 1983). Ortony and colleagues (Iran-Nejad *et al.,* 1981; Reynolds & Ortony, 1980; Vosniadou & Ortony, 1983a,b; Vosniadou *et al.,* 1984), have argued that children's difficulties in metaphor comprehension often are attributable to factors that are unrelated to its nonliteral quality per se. "Such factors are limited knowledge of the world, limited knowledge of the language, difficulty in creating an appropriate context for interpreting metaphorical language" (Vosniadou & Ortony, 1983b). Indeed, when those factors are controlled, metaphor comprehension is seen to increase, presumably because that control eliminates sources of confounding. Nevertheless, all these factors seem to us an essential part of what complex language skills such as metaphor comprehension are all about. The fact that children evidence understanding of nonliteral statements in limited, artificial situations does not necessarily mean that such understanding will generalize to other settings. As with the classic Genevan tasks, doubt exists whether such limited demonstrations should be considered indicative of *competence.* Vosniadou and Ortony (1983b) themselves pointed out that true metaphor comprehension, like comprehension of language in general, "is a complex interaction between various difficulty sources some of which have to do with the predictability of the linguistic input within its already established context, and others with the complexity of the linguistic input itself" (pp. 12–13). Removing these sources of difficulty thus substantially changes the nature of the nonliteral problem.

VI. Children's Verbal and Nonverbal Metaphoric Production

Paivio (1979) pointed out that metaphor comprehension and production involve awareness of similarity and relations between domains as well as the integration of analogous elements into new wholes. Nall (1983) further suggested that there is a developmental progression in the achievement of these abilities, as children first come to identify similarities between objects, then understand relationships between similarities, and, finally, can produce new concepts from diverse elements. However, successful performance in multiple-choice tasks such as hers and the enactment paradigm of Vosniadou and Ortony (1983b; Vosniadou *et al.,* 1984) may tap only the first and second stages of nonliteral language competence. The synthesis of new meaning seems untouched by such tasks. Nonliteral language production might provide an indicator of such competence, but disagreement over what constitutes nonliteral output has prevented any consensus on who has such abilities. This disagreement is compounded by what appear to be qualitative differences in children's creative productions involving physical–physical mappings (e.g., using a stick as a horse), physical–verbal labelings (e.g., calling a stick a snake), and verbal–verbal or verbal–conceptual analogies (e.g., saying that children's minds are sponges). In our view, only the last should be considered true metaphorical production. We do not deny the desire of many investigators to consider observed relationships between unlike elements as metaphorical relationships (e.g., Beck, 1978). The labeling of a Picasso painting as a metaphor, for example, seems quite justifiable from the adult perspective. For the young child, however, noticing that a particular cloud looks like a lion (Verbrugge, 1979) seems a far cry from saying that clouds (in general) are dancers, and understanding the role of nonliteral statements in the child's language and thought requires a distinction between the two.

McCune-Nicolich (1981) has suggested that "children use both play and language to 'try out' various representational equivalences and so learn about the range of acceptable transformations" (p. 791), but several researchers have observed the creativity in children's symbolic play and equated it with metaphoric competence. Verbrugge (1979) was perhaps the most liberal in accepting evidence for this inference, describing instances of "metaphoric perception," "metaphoric action," and "both at once (when searching for an appropriate stick and riding around on it as if it were a horse)" (p. 78). Both Billow (1981) and Winner (1979; Winner *et al.*, 1980a) also labeled the symbolic play of preschoolers as metaphor but required verbal accompaniment. Billow (1981) was the more generous of the two investigators, as "each word or phrase uttered by the child which ordinarily would not be used to describe the particular object, feeling, or event was considered a metaphor" (p. 6), unless they were repetitions or frozen metaphors (i.e., nonliteral expressions such as "I lost my footing" that were once novel but have gained a near-literal status through repeated use).

Winner (1979) was more conservative than Billow (1975) in her analysis of one child's figurative language. Winner suggested that "the pretend object substitutions of symbolic play are not unlike the transformations reflected in metaphoric renaming" (p. 473). In scoring utterances as metaphors, Winner required that the child had used an object's literal name in close enough temporal proximity to show that the child knew the "real" label. Vosniadou and Ortony's (1983a) warning that renamings are not always metaphors should be kept in mind here, insofar as the relative frequencies with which Winner's subject made figurative comparisons and simply noted perceptual similarities are unclear. Whether or not a child actually understands the figurative intent of a nonliteral production ultimately depends on whether both the tension and the ground are perceived (Lakoff & Johnson, 1980; Ogden & Richards, 1960). For example, if we assume that a child knows that a green carpet is not literally grass, then we also logically must assume that the child knows that there exists some difference, or tension, between them. If there is no conscious awareness of a difference between two domains, their relationship is one of literal identity to the child even if that relationship appears to be an overgeneralization to the adult. Metaphor production therefore requires that the producer be aware that the objects of comparison belong to different categories. Otherwise, there is no categorical boundary to be violated intentionally.

An alternative method to observing children at play for assessing children's nonliteral production abilities relies on prompted vocalizations of children in the absence of particular, to-be-described referents (e.g., in story telling, compositions, descriptions of absent people or objects). This method does not remove figurative language from context (a concern raised by Vosniadou & Ortony, 1983b), but places its elicitors entirely in a child's linguistic and cognitive intentions. Allowing children the freedom to generate novel constructions only as needed, for example in telling about what it would be like to be picked up by a flying saucer, also avoids the pitfall of attempting to determine their metaphoric competence on the basis of nonliteral explanation tasks (e.g., Asch & Nerlove, 1960; Piaget, 1926/1974) that are difficult even for adults (Marschark & Hunt, 1985). Nonliteral production in the relatively naturalistic, experimenter-prompted situation therefore is likely to be a more accurate indicator of figurative skills than are forced-choice discrimination tasks, observations of perceptually based renamings, or proverb interpretation tasks.

Using the prompted production method, M. R. Pollio and colleagues (Pollio & Pickens, 1980; Pollio & Pollio, 1974, 1979) have provided several findings concerning children's nonliteral, verbal production skills. Pollio and Pollio (1974) used three different tasks designed to tap figurative production abilities. In their *multiple sentences* task, the 8-, 9-, and 10-year-old subjects were asked to create sentences describing as many different meanings as possible for five different words (e.g., "How many different meanings are there for the word *run*?"). In their *comparisons* task, children were presented three word pairs and asked to describe as many similarities as possible for each (e.g., "How are *box* and *can* related?"). Finally, in their *compositions* task, children wrote stories on fictional topics such as "What would you do if all trees disappeared?" or "How would you feel if you were in a pet store and one of the goldfish started to talk to you?'' The results of both the multiple sentences and comparisons tasks indicated increases over grade in the frequencies of novel and frozen figurative language. On the composition task, in contrast, Pollio and Pollio found that the frequency of novel figures of speech decreased from 8 to 9 to 10 years (means were 1.30, 0.80, 0.70 figures per 100 words of text, respectively). Pollio and Pollio (1974) suggested that this discrepancy resulted from children's increasing fear of sanctions against (written) figurative language in successive grades. The interpretation favored here is that the frequency of inexpressible events decreases with age as lexical and syntactic abilities increase (see Section IV). Unfortunately, neither alternative can be ruled out on the basis of any data currently available, but in either case, the production of novel figurative language observed in the composition task clearly indicates some kind of context-free nonliteral competence by 8 years of age.

In summary, Pollio and Pollio's (1974) results as well as those of Marschark and West (1984, 1985) indicate that children's nonliteral language abilities can be assessed in more naturalistic ways than those provided by two-choice visual discrimination tasks. Those results also seem to suggest a more valid measure of nonliteral production ability than the observation of perceptual renaming, and the differences in the findings from the different tasks lend support to the present caution against generalizing from simpler to more complex tasks in assessing metaphoric competence. In the relevant research however, age frequently has been confounded with experimental paradigm for determining nonliteral linguistic skill. Generally, those researchers who wanted to demonstrate figurative abilities in younger children have had to adopt more lenient criteria or to develop simpler methodologies. The question thus remains whether the more generous indicators tap the same abilities as the less generous, and thus at what age and with what evidence nonliteral intention can be inferred.

VII. Age and Figurative Competence

The two preceding sections have indicated that the more complex the nonliteral language task, the later will be the apparent age of nonliteral competence. Such findings leave several questions unanswered. Perhaps the most central of these questions concerns the relationship of task-specific nonliteral performance and more general cognitive abilities of the child that underlie that performance. Therefore, in determining the age at which a child might be expected to exhibit metaphoric competence, various levels or components of nonliteral use must be considered. The relationships between these levels and the ages of their emergence in children's language

are considered here to highlight several threads of development (see Gardner *et al.,* 1978, for different threads). One question to be kept in mind
throughout this discussion is whether the observed changes with age in nonliteral language abilities are indicative of a relatively continuous growth in
one ability or the successive emergence of several distinct abilities. For example, is the oft-noted temporary decline in figurative abilities around 7 to
9 years of age (e.g., Pollio & Pollio, 1974; Winner *et al.,* 1980a) best accounted for as the result of development in a single domain or the result
of several, perhaps more pervasive changes?

A number of diverse age-related changes in "nonliteral behavior" have
been described by several investigators of children's metaphor use. In terms
of our theoretical perspective on the development of metaphoric competence, these changes seem to be quite orderly. Early on, concurrent with
the emergence of language, intentional symbolic behavior marks the existence of a vivid and active internal world for the young child. Although
investigators have not as yet mapped such creative abilities onto various
linguistic measures (e.g., mean length of utterance), such investigations
likely would be informative. At 18 months, for example, children have at
their disposal vocabularies of about 50 words. Still before any significant
use of two-word phrases, these often idiosyncratic labels are primarily
nouns, referring to objects in the environment (Nelson, 1973). Gardner *et
al.* (1978) have noted the child's nonverbal, symbolic play at this age (e.g.,
cradling a spoon like a doll) and refer to it as "metaphoric object substitution" (p. 16). To deny that this action is metaphor, as we do, is not to
maintain that the child is making a mistake (e.g., thinks a spoon is a baby;
cf. the limited alternatives offered by Mendelsohn *et al.,* 1984). Rather, the
denial suggests that some object is temporarily used to denote another, not
to highlight properties or relations but just as a tool of imagination. Later,
such pretend actions will not require placeholders such as spoons, but can
be done on an entirely verbal–symbolic level. This change presumably reflects a decrease in cognitive and linguistic inexpressibility limitations, as
the child can say things such as "You be the baby." Such behavior is still
play, however, not metaphor. Initial similarities and differences between the
"topic" (the listener) and "vehicle" (the suggested role) are irrelevant. In
contrast to statements such as "Stop being such a baby!" a form of behavior is being requested here, not being figuratively described.

We find interesting the fact that 18-month-old children have not been
described as using any of their 50 or so words for (apparently) intentional
misnaming. At times they may rename things (intentionally or not) in the
course of firming up conceptual boundaries, but parents and researchers
would tend to view these utterances as errors of overgeneralization (Clark,
1973) rather than perceptual renamings. Mismatches between names and

things do not come to be appreciated by parents until their children are about 2 years old and are putting words together into two-word phrases. At this point, children have the common/proper noun distinction, "knowing" that people and people-surrogates (such as dolls) have specific and constant names, while common objects can easily be renamed (Gardner *et al.*, 1978; Katz, Baker, & Macnamara, 1974). But renaming familiar objects in play is quite different from applying familiar names to unfamiliar objects. Verbal attempts to classify novel stimuli correctly are no more indicative of metaphor than would be nonverbal attempts to see if objects do what similar things can do (e.g., whether grandmother's china can fly like a Frisbee). These attempts at verbal classification may represent the idiosyncratic first steps in bridging gaps between the familiar and unfamiliar, but lack the purpose, intentionality, and balancing of ground and tension characteristic of true figurative language use.

During the third year, a shift occurs from symbolic play with objects to renaming them on the basis of how they look (Winner, 1979) or how they move (Calhoun, 1984). This shift marks the beginning of a movement out of strictly nonverbal creative functioning into a period of sensorimotor-based conceptual and linguistic categorization. Previously, the child dealt with objects holistically (Macnamara, 1972; Shepp *et al.*, 1980), and did not distinguish specific features in any way that could allow metonymic or synecdochical renaming. The separation of attributes (e.g., size) from their possessors (e.g., cows, hippoptamuses, and elephants) provides the first opportunity for intentional figurative references to people and objects that possess those qualities. Renaming now is taken very seriously by the child-metaphor investigator, and perhaps too seriously. For example, Gardner *et al.* (1978) called preschoolers' naming of their artwork (e.g., "It's a snake") metaphoric in the same way as they did other perceptual renaming. Naming one's artwork and figurative renaming seem fundamentally different to us, however. The 4-year-old boy who draws "Mom" seems to think the portrait an accurate depiction. The statement "It's Mom" thus is intended only to identify the relationship of the markings to their referent and is no more metaphorical than is verbally identifying a photograph of his mother. But in the Gardner and Winner class of renamings, the boy's labeling is assumed to be false and recognized as such. He is portrayed as making the intentional error of calling a set of inanimate markings on a page his mother, with the implicit understanding that the listener will not take him literally. Artwork itself may be metaphorical (Beck, 1978), but naming a painting or any other object for what it is believed literally to represent is not.

Renaming of objects in the third year also has to be distinguished from unintentional overgeneralization (Clark, 1973). As with the 2-year-old child, separating intentional renaming from unintentional errors is difficult, and both might serve similar assimilative functions. Nevertheless, overgeneralization (as well as undergeneralization) reveals the child's conceptual boundaries still to be unstable, while renaming requires distinct categories that are intentionally violated. Relevant here are several findings from Vosniadou and Ortony's (1983a) study. They found that 3-year-old children reliably chose literal and metaphorical sentence endings over anomalous ones, so that a river was said to be like a lake or a snake, but not a cat. In categorizations however, the 3 year olds were not reliably above chance in completing sentences of the form "A river is the same kind of thing as a . . . " (lake, snake). The latter task is more difficult than the verbal–nonverbal renaming task, and seems to require a qualitatively different skill: one of reflecting on meaning rather than just labeling a perceptual component. Vosniadou and Ortony's results suggest to us that although 3-year-old children know what things are and what they are not, similarity relationships even within a category are not particularly salient at a verbal–conceptual level. If the child does not have a particular conceptual dichotomy available at a given time, that boundary cannot be violated intentionally in service of nonliteral creativity.

By 4 years of age, children respond appropriately in both comparison and categorization tasks such as those of Vosniadou and Ortony (1983a). Calhoun (1984) used a metaphoric/anomalous discrimination task like that used by Vosniadou and Ortony (1983a) in her investigation of how various ground types affect children's metaphor comprehension. She asked preschoolers to choose the "most true or real" member of sentence pairs such as "A puppy's tail is like a windshield wiper" and "A puppy's tail is like a trashcan," that differed in whether their grounds were based on static-perceptual, action, or functional similarities. She found that metaphorical alternatives were most likely to be selected over their anomalous counterparts when based on action rather than static-perceptual or functional grounds (see Silberstein *et al.*, 1982, for discussion). Further, in subsequent explanations of items to which they correctly responded, children provided acceptable interpretations for proportionately more action-based items than any others.

Children can deal with cross-category similarity between objects at age 4, but similes based on conceptual grounds still present problems, and will for some time (Vosniadou & Ortony, 1983b). Gardner *et al.* (1978) suggested that in similes like *That pencil looks like a rocket ship,* "the child is explicitly confronting the tension entailed" (p. 17) in mentioning elements from two distinct domains in the same sentence. This confrontation may be inherent in adults' use of simile, insofar as they recognize that, for example, pencils and rocket ships differ in more ways than they are similar (i.e., the tension). However, we hesitate to classify children's "looks like" utterances as similes, because there is no evidence at all that tension really is being "confronted." In fact, children's behavior suggests just the contrary: that they are experimenting only with similarity, for example by putting pencils and rocket ships in the same perceptual category. Only later, with the ability to cross-classify on several dimensions simultaneously at about age 6 or 7 (McCauley, Weil, & Sperber, 1976; Steinberg & Anderson, 1975) do children reconcile tension and ground in nonliteral competence. Noticing physically present similarity is one thing; the active self-regulation of metalinguistic hedging is yet another.

The frequency of comparisons using "like" increases substantially from 5 to 6 years of age. This change could indicate increasing sensitivity to listeners, either their need for information (Winner, 1979) or the likelihood of listeners to reprimand unqualified renamings as errors (Pollio & Pollio, 1974). Alternatively, the added explanation inherent in similes may be serving as both a linguistic hedge and a means of self-monitoring in new categorizations and generalizations. Rather than obtaining feedback from an external listener, the child, through overt (and eventually covert) vocalization, can judge the applicability of the vehicle domain in a given context (Luria, 1961). In either case, children now find similes easier to act out than metaphors for the first time. They now explain metaphorical story endings (e.g., "Johnny was a dog burying his bones"), but tend to do so literally, in terms of "make-believe" (e.g., "He pretended he was a dog") rather than figurative relations (Vosniadou *et al.*, 1984). The most popular interpretation of this latter situation is that the development of comprehension skill simply outpaces the metalinguistic skills necessary for making mental events public. To us, literal interpretations of metaphors reveal that the nonliteral competence displayed in both multiple-choice and enactment paradigms is still somewhat syncretic. The child's appropriate responding in such tasks (especially given the limited-alternative constraints described earlier) is no guarantee of awareness of the nonliteralness of the situation. Correct performance simply may be based on a temporary (or more long-term superstitious) literal link between two concepts, the persistence of which is a function of other cognitive and linguistic experience. Although metaphoric competence thus seems imminent, mental juxtaposition of elements with the emergence of abstract relationships (Ogden & Richards, 1960) seems unlikely at this age.

Prior to the emergence of figurative explanation proficiency around age 11 (Billow, 1975; Gardner, 1974; Gardner *et al.*, 1978), a period from approximately 6 to 10 years old can be observed in which children evidence verbally based, nonliteral comprehension skills. During these years, they correctly pair double-function words with "metaphorically related" referents and usually respond to queries about the bases of their judgments.

Although these responses still tend to be relatively concrete and idiosyncratic (Gardner, 1974; Winner, Rosenstiel, & Gardner, 1976), some competence is evidenced by consistency in supplying alternative uses for the
double-function terms (Pollio & Pollio, 1974). The ability to paraphrase
nonliteral statements correctly also increases during these years (Cometa &
Eson, 1978; Douglas & Peel, 1979; Pollio & Pickens, 1980; Vosniadou *et
al.*, 1984). However, given the simplicity of the relevant research methodologies, the increased ability to paraphrase may reflect the ability to make
use of verbal context, but still without complete nonliteral appreciation.
For example, lack of explanatory competence is still apparent, because the
ability to act out metaphoric story endings is significantly better than the
ability to paraphrase them even with contextual support (Vosniadou & Ortony, 1983b; see also Cometa & Eson, 1978).

Metaphor comprehension, as measured by verbal multiple-choice tasks,
increases during this period from age 6 to age 10 (Pollio & Pickens, 1980)
and reaches near-ceiling performance when alternative choices are improb-
able (Nall, 1983; Vosniadou & Ortony, 1983a; Winner *et al.*, 1980a). Researchers who have focused on the perceptual bases of nonliteral
(supposedly metaphoric) competence at this age have shown that children
exhibit a consistent preference for static properties, especially shape, in
multiple-choice comprehension (Winner *et al.*, 1980a; Dent & Dupree,
1983). As noted earlier however, Silberstein *et al.* (1982) demonstrated a
reliable decrease in the preference for perceptual metaphoric grounds during this period, accompanied by a reliable increase in the preference for
conceptual/abstract grounds, when such alternatives were available to subjects. Billow (1975) similarly demonstrated the beginnings of abstract, nonliteral analysis, in that children at age 7 were able to give appropriate
explanations for more than twice as many similarity metaphors as children
at age 5, even without pictorial support. By age 9, Billow's (1975) subjects
also were able to explain almost half of the more difficult proportional
metaphors he presented, even though proficiency therein was not expected
until formal operations (his 13-year-old subjects reached only about 75%
correct on the proportional items).

During the ages 7–10, in contrast to figurative comprehension skills, the
production of written figurative language declines (Pollio & Pickens, 1980;
Pollio & Pollio, 1974). This decrease heralds the beginning of what some
investigators see as a "literal" stage in language use (e.g., Gardner *et al.*,
1978). Although the extent of this "literal period" remains unclear, it seems
more a function of an increased language repertoire and regularizing of
linguistic skills (Marschark & West, 1984) or a concession to perceived academic and task demands (Pollio & Pollio, 1974) than a more pervasive
inflexibility in cognitive functioning. As noted above, some forms of non-

literal production may decrease during this period, while other types of constructions may increase. For example, Marschark and West (1984) found that in a sample of 20 deaf children aged 8-15, novel modifications of existing signs increased reliably with age (as assessed in a story-telling task) while the invention of new signs decreased. Further investigation of the alleged decline in the production of figurative constructions between the ages of 7 and 10 years is clearly in order.

Explanatory competence is the last nonliteral language skill to develop (Billow, 1975). All other methodological and ideological issues aside, the ability to give appropriate explanations for novel, and perhaps even familiar, figurative expressions does not emerge until the time that other abstractive abilities emerge, at around 10-12 years. Gardner (1974), as well as Asch and Nerlove (1960), found that younger children apparently could not explain the relationships between psychological and physical reference of words, even though Gardner (1974) showed that they could pair attributes with objects and vice versa. Piaget (1926/1974) similarly found school-aged children unable to explain proverbs they asserted they understood, even though they produced figurative language spontaneously under other conditions (Piaget, 1951). Billow (1975) found that 11-year-old children were able to explain only about 10% of proverbs he presented, and 13 year olds' performance was still below 50%.[4]

These and similar results from other studies provide evidence of some syncretism in nonliteral language competence even during the later school years. The important aspect of syncretism in this context is the listener's tendency to assume holistic comprehension rather than ensure it through conceptual analysis. Most people have had the experience of seeing and understanding a word or phrase in context, but being unable to explain its meaning independent of that particular use. Interpreting a proverb, for example, requires more conscious analysis than does acknowledging its applicability in a particular instance or even using it appropriately, either of which might occur correctly on the basis of having heard it previously rather than understanding it. Proverb explanation requires not only the ability to see similarities and relations across conceptual boundaries, but also the ability to describe an internal production, the *Gestalten* of ground and tension in the nonliteral comparison (see Piaget, 1926/1974; Winner, Engle, &

---

[4]We do not know how far one can generalize from metaphor to proverb research findings, although findings from Marschark and Hunt's (1985) study suggest that it is not too far. Poetic metaphors, for example, have been shown to be harder to interpret, comprehend, and image (among other reliable differences in the same direction; Katz *et al.,* 1985) than the more commonly used experimenter-constructed metaphors. Such findings suggest that lack of stimulus controls in proverb research might contribute to some underestimates of children's proverb-related nonliteral competence.

Gardner, 1980b). As such, the ability to explain nonliteral constructions appropriately both requires and reflects complex abilities not available to or at least not evident in the younger child.

VIII. Metaphor and Developing
Cognitive Organization

By definition, the comprehension of metaphors involves the transfer of vehicle properties to an unfamiliar topic or to a familiar topic in an unfamiliar way. This process requires a kind of "head-fitting" by children, whereby they attempt to understand the content of such utterances by assimilating them into their existing conceptual frameworks. We noted in Section III that these frameworks may differ substantially from those of adults. Similarities or relations that appear obvious to adults may not appear so to children, and vice versa (see discussion by Nelson, 1974, p. 269). Understanding what is and is not figurative for a particular child therefore requires consideration of that child's cognitive abilities and knowledge of the world.

Consistent with this view, Paivio (1979) suggested that the perception of metaphorical relations is affected by both mediation and categorization. Although the categorization process involved in understanding nonliteral language remains unclear, it must involve activation of some subset of attributes common to both topic and vehicle domains. Rosch's (1973) emphasis for nominal category judgments (similar to nominal metaphors) is on the similarity of to-be-classified elements and the prototype of the potential category (see also Rips, Shoben, & Smith, 1973). Oden (1977) similarly suggested a continuous criterion for class membership in which all sets are essentially fuzzy, with some elements being neither clearly a member nor not a member of any particular one. In the case of nonliteral comparisons, the goal is to identify characteristics common to the prototypes of both topic and vehicle domains. The more information one has about these domains, presumably the greater the amount of information that is linked to the prototypes, and thus the more extensive the potential grounds that are available. Therefore, the likelihood of a particular statement receiving more than a single, literal interpretation should increase with the age, knowledge, and cognitive–linguistic flexibility of the comprehender.

Findings of Rosch (1973), McCauley *et al.* (1976), and others suggest that the categorical structure of long-term memory does change with age in ways relevant to nonliteral language comprehension. Rosch (1973) observed that children make more errors than adults in judging whether peripheral exemplars are members of a category. Thus, a fly is less likely than a lion to be judged an animal, just as would overzealous boyfriends and less-than-attractive blind dates. To complicate the researcher's situation further, Denney and Ziobrowski (1972) and Inhelder and Piaget (1958) demonstrated that young children's categorizations often are based on more functional, thematic, or complementary relationships (e.g., pipe—tobacco) rather than on the taxonomic or similarity relationships evident in older children. Because of this, when a child indicates that A is more like B than C, one cannot take for granted that the relationship is the same as that obvious to the adult observer nor even that reported by another child of some other age.

Given the subjective nature of class membership, we find tantalizing the possibility of an essential link between children's unintentional overgeneralizations and their early use of apparently nonliteral language. Both appear to depend on the fuzziness of categorization and the mapping of that internal structure onto the external world. In fact, a body of literature on children's category clustering (in recall output) exists that seems to support this link. Although a variety of studies have shown that clustering increases with age, the age at which clustering strategies are first used regularly is a matter of empirical debate. Some studies have purportedly identified clustering as early as age 2 (e.g., Horowitz, 1969; Moely, Olson, Hawles, & Flavell, 1969), but others have suggested that it does not emerge until at least about age 10 (e.g., Arlin & Brody, 1976; Lange, 1973; Lange & Jackson, 1974). These discrepancies parallel the similar controversy in the metaphoric competence literature and may have a similar resolution. Lange (1973) has argued that properties of the stimuli used in the clustering studies may account for the discrepant findings observed. When "same-category" items are not strong natural associates, preadolescents do not evidence clustering in recall. When items are highly associated, such relationships do appear functional, independent of any conscious attempt at organization by the subjects (Corsale, 1978; Haynes & Kulhavy, 1976). Lange (1978) suggested that when the child is familiar with the stimuli, clustering may not reflect higher order strategies, but the child may simply be "struck" by an organization that is automatically incorporated in encoding.

Nonliteral language comprehension may represent one instance in which weakly associated items require conscious "clustering" in order to determine any similarities between the elements. When topic and vehicle domains do not exude similarity, such combination or comparison becomes far more difficult and unlikely, especially for preadolescents. However, when topics and vehicles are brought down to the associative level of the younger child, as in using metaphors like "A river is a snake" rather than ones like "The wind is a rocking chair," displays of spontaneous "clustering" and nonliteral competence become more likely. This facilitation suggests that manipulations of topic–vehicle semantic relatedness should have marked effects on metaphor comprehension (Johnson & Malgady, 1979), especially for younger children. In fact, Nall (1983) found that semantic relatedness was the best predictor of 8-year-old children's performance in her comprehension task (accounting for 30% of the variance), although not a reliable predictor for 10 or 12 year olds. More explicit evaluation of this relationship is clearly in order, but the research described in this section generally indicates that understanding children's nonliteral competence requires consideration of their other cognitive capabilities. In all likelihood, there will be a fair return on our investment, as this research helps to elucidate other aspects of child development.

IX. Summary and Conclusions

Consideration of the age-related changes in children's language and cognitive development suggests qualitative changes in their creative language use. Many, if not most, researchers in the area have argued that some metaphoric competence emerges far earlier than would be expected on the basis of explanation or interpretation tasks alone. These same researchers, however, appear largely to have neglected consideration of the cognitive prerequisites for such abilities and differences between what is nonliteral for the adult and nonliteral for the child. If figurative language is defined as involving intentional violation of conceptual boundaries in order to highlight some correspondence, one must be sure that children credited with that competence have (1) the metacognitive and metalinguistic abilities to understand at least some of the implications of such language (Lakoff & Johnson, 1980; Nelson, 1974; Nelson & Nelson, 1978), (2) a conceptual organization that entails the purportedly violated conceptual boundaries (Lange, 1978), and (3) some notion of metaphoric tension as well as ground.

Having stacked the definitional cards, we doubt that many investigators would assert that 2-year-old children at nonverbal symbolic play are doing anything that is literally metaphorical in our terms. But neither will we deny that one can observe creative components in the verbal and nonverbal play of the young child that are precursors of later nonliteral language skills (see McCune-Nicolich, 1981, for discussion). We simply do not see these creative abilities as specific to language in any way that justifies calling them *metaphoric competence*. Rather, the child's abilities to deal flexibly with the world, to "play" with possible alternative organizations of it, and to see similarity in diversity represent the bases of subsequent cognitive as well as language development. Far from being an exceptional aspect of development, apparently nonliteral language should be considered a fundamental tool in the young child's construction of both internal and external worlds (McCune-Nicolich, 1981; Vygotsky, 1978). If one is willing to accept that children's conceptual organization might not match that of adults, then what is appropriately called nonliteral language in the young child must be reexamined. We find it strange that researchers acknowledge differences, for example, in children's notions of animacy, and yet assume that errors of animacy attribution are figurative constructions indicative of an ability to supercede a level of analysis the child does not have. If a child makes a statement that is literally true in terms of that child's world view, that statement cannot be considered nonliteral for that child, even if its interpretation is nonliteral for the adult.

One thing made clear from all of the preceding is that much more information is needed on the interface of children's language creativity and their knowledge of the world. The challenge of considering the child more holistically, in interaction with verbal and nonverbal environments, is not easily met, especially when dealing with nonliteral, often inferred, relationships. Nonetheless, the bases of young children's language productions are markedly different from those of college students and require separate consideration rather than generalization from studies involving the older subjects. Language development, like other aspects of development, has to be evaluated in terms of the organization and experiences of one with relatively limited knowledge of linguistic and logical rules or conventions. Determination of the psycholinguistic variables underlying children's nonliteral comprehension, the nature of the apparent literal period in language development, and similar questions are not likely to be resolved without taking into account the larger contexts of cognitive and language development.

ACKNOWLEDGMENTS

Preparation of this article was supported by grants to the first author from the National Institute of Neurological and Communication Disorders and Stroke (Grant 1-RO1-NS20064-01), and the Research Council of The University of North Carolina at Greensboro. We thank the members of the UNC-Greensboro Language Research Group for their comments and constructive criticisms of the ideas expressed herein, and Hayne Reese and Gilbert Gottlieb for their helpful comments on earlier drafts of this article.

REFERENCES

Arlin, M., & Brody, R. (1976). Effects of spatial representation and blocking on organization and verbal recall at three grade levels. *Developmental Psychology, 12,* 113–118.
Arnheim, R. (1974). *Visual thinking.* Berkeley: Univ. of California Press.

Asch, S., & Nerlove, H. (1960). The development of double function terms in children: An exploration study. In B. Kaplan & S. Wapner (Eds.), *Perspectives in psychological theory.* New York: International Universities Press.

Beck, B. E. F. (1978). The metaphor as a mediator between semantic and analogic modes of thought. *Current Anthropology, 19,* 83-97.

Billow, R. (1975). A cognitive-developmental study of metaphor comprehension. *Developmental Psychology, 11,* 415-423.

Billow, R. (1981). Observing spontaneous metaphor in children. *Journal of Experimental Child Psychology, 31,* 430-445.

Brainerd, C. J. (1983). Varieties of strategy training in Piagetian concept learning. In M. Pressley & J. R. Levin (Eds.), *Cognitive Strategy Research: Educational Applications.* New York: Springer Verlag.

Bronowski, J., & Bellugi, U. (1970). Language, name, and concept. *Science, 168,* 669-673.

Calhoun, A. W. (1984). *The effects of perceptual, functional, and action based grounds on children's comprehension of metaphors.* Unpublished master's thesis, University of North Carolina-Greensboro.

Chomsky, N. (1965). *Aspects of the theory of syntax.* Cambridge, MA: MIT Press.

Clark, E. (1973). What's in a word: On the child's acquisition on semantics in his first language. In T. E. Moore (Ed.), *Cognitive development and the acquisition of language.* New York: Academic Press.

Cometa, M. S., & Eson, M. E. (1978). Logical operations and metaphor interpretation. *Child Development, 49,* 649-659.

Conley, J. E. (1976). The role of idiomatic expressions in the reading of deaf children. *American Annals of the Deaf, 121,* 381-385.

Corsale, K. (1978). *Factors affecting children's use of organization and recall.* Unpublished doctoral thesis. University of North Carolina at Chapel Hill.

Corsale, K., & Ornstein, P. A. (1980). Developmental changes in the use of semantic information in recall. *Journal of Experimental Child Psychology, 30,* 231-245.

Denney, N., & Ziobrowski, M. (1972). Developmental changes in clustering criteria. *Journal of Experimental Child Psychology, 13,* 275-282.

Dent, C. H., & Dupree, K. A. (1983). *Figurative description of objects by children and adults: Effects of perceptual information and background knowledge.* Unpublished manuscript.

Douglas, J. D., & Peel, B. (1979). The development of metaphor and proverb translation in children grades one through seven. *Journal of Educational Research, 73,* 116-119.

Fagan, J. W., Rovee, C. K., & Kaplan, M. G. (1976). Psychophysical scaling of stimulus similarity in 3-month-old infants and adults. *Journal of Experimental Child Psychology, 22,* 272-281.

Furth, H. (1973). *Deafness and learning.* Belmont, CA: Wadsworth.

Gardner, H. (1974). Metaphors and modalities: How children project polar adjectives onto diverse domains. *Child Development, 45,* 84-91.

Gardner, H., Kirchner, M., Winner, E., & Perkins, D. (1975). Children's metaphoric productions and preferences. *Journal of Child Language, 2,* 125-141.

Gardner, H., Winner, E., Bechhofer, R., & Wolf, D. (1978). The development of figurative language. In K. E. Nelson (Ed.), *Children's language* (Vol. 1). New York: Gardner.

Gentner, D. (1977). If a tree had a knee where would it be? Children's performance on simple spatial metaphors. *Papers and Reports on Child Language Development, 13.*

Haynes, C. R., & Kulhavy, R. M. (1976). Conservation level and category clustering. *Developmental Psychology, 12,* 179-184.

Henle, P. (1972). Metaphor. In P. Henle (Ed.), *Language, thought, and culture.* Ann Arbor, MI: Univ. of Michigan Press.

Honeck, R. P., Sowry, B. M., & Voegtle, K. (1978). Proverbial understanding in a pictorial context. *Child Development, 49,* 327-331.

Horowitz, A. B. (1969). Effect of stimulus presentation modes on children's recall and clustering. *Psychonomic Science,* **14,** 297-298.

Inhelder, B., & Piaget, J. (1958). *The growth of logical thinking from chilhood to adolescence.* New York: Basic Books.

Iran-Nejad, A., Ortony, A., & Rittenhouse, R. K. (1981). The comprehension of metaphorical uses of English by deaf children. *Journal of Speech and Hearing Research,* **24,** 551-556.

Johnson, M. G., & Malgady, R. G. (1979). Some cognitive aspects of figurative language: Association and metaphor. *Journal of Psycholinguistic Research,* **8,** 253-265.

Johnson, M. G., & Malgady, R. G. (1980). Toward a perceptual theory of metaphoric comprehension. In R. P. Honeck & R. R. Hoffman (Eds.), *Cognitive and figurative language.* Hillsdale, NJ: Erlbaum.

Katz, A. (1982). Metaphoric relationships: The role of feature saliency. *Journal of Psycholinguistic Research,* **11,** 283-296.

Katz, A., Paivio, A., & Marschark, M. (1985). Poetic comparisons: Psychological dimensions of metaphoric processing. *Journal of Psycholinguistic Research,* **19,** 365-383.

Katz, N., Baker, E., & Macnamara, J. (1974). What's in a name? A study of how children learn common and proper names. *Child Development,* **45,** 469-473.

Klima, E. S., & Bellugi, U. (1979). *The signs of language.* Cambridge, MA: Harvard Univ. Press.

Lakoff, G., & Johnson, M. (1980). *Metaphors we live by.* Chicago: Univ. of Chicago Press.

Lange, G. (1973). The development of conceptual and rote recall skills among school age children. *Journal of Experimental Child Psychology,* **15,** 394-406.

Lange, G. (1978). Organization-related processes in children's recall. In P. A. Ornstein (Ed.), *Memory development in children.* Hillsdale, NJ: Erlbaum.

Lange, G., & Jackson, P. (1974). Personal organization in children's free recall. *Child Development,* **45,** 1060-1067.

Leopold, W. F. (1948). Semantic learning in infant language. *Word,* **4,** 179.

Lesser, H., & Drouin, C. (1975). Training in the use of double-function terms. *Journal of Psycholinguistic Research,* **4,** 285-302.

Liben, L. S. (1978). Experiential deficiencies: Developmental perspectives. In L. S. Liben (Ed.), *Deaf children: Developmental perspectives.* New York: Academic Press.

Luria, A. R. (1961). *The role of speech in the regulation of normal and abnormal behaviour.* Oxford: Pergamon.

Macnamara, J. (1972). The cognitive basis of language learning in infants. *Psychological Review,* **79,** 1-13.

Marschark, M., & Hunt, R. R. (1985). On memory for metaphor. *Memory and Cognition,* in press.

Marschark, M., Katz, A., & Paivio, A. (1983). Dimensions of metaphor. *Journal of Psycholinguistic Research,* **12,** 17-40.

Marschark, M., & West, S. A. (1984). *A developmental study of creative language abilities in deaf children.* Paper presented at meetings of the Southeastern Conference on Human Development, Athens, GA.

Marschark, M., & West, S. A. (1985). Creative language abilities of deaf children. *Journal of Speech and Hearing Research,* **28,** 73-78.

McCauley, C., Weil, C. M., & Sperber, R. D. (1976). The development of memory structure as reflected by semantic priming effects. *Journal of Experimental Child Psychology,* **22,** 511-518.

McCune-Nicolich, L. (1981). Toward symbolic functioning: Structure of early pretend games and potential parallels with language. *Child Development,* **52,** 785-797.

McNeill, D. (1970). *The acquisition of language.* New York: Harper.

Mendelsohn, E., Robinson, S., Gardner, H., & Winner, E. (1984). Are preschoolers' renamings intentional category violations? *Developmental Psychology,* **20,** 187-192.

Moely, B., Olsen, F. A., Hawles, T. G., & Flavell, J. H. (1969). Production deficiency in young children's clustered recall. *Developmental Psychology,* **1**, 26–34.

Nall, L. (1983). *Dimensions of metaphor comprehension in third, fifth, and seventh graders.* Unpublished master's thesis, Wake Forest University, Winston-Salem, NC.

Nelson, K. (1973). Structure and strategy in learning to talk. *Monographs of the Society for Research in Child Development,* **38** (1–2, Serial No. 149).

Nelson, K. (1974). Concept, word, and sentence: Interrelations in acquisition and development. *Psychological Review,* **81**, 267–285.

Nelson, K. E., & Nelson, K. (1978). Cognitive pendulums and their linguistic realization. In K. E. Nelson (Ed.), *Children's language* (Vol. 1). New York: Gardner.

Oden, G. C. (1977). Fuzziness in semantic memory: Choosing exemplars of subjective categories. *Memory and Cognition,* **5**, 198–204.

Offenbach, S. I. (1983). The concept of dimension in research on children's learning. *Monographs of the Society for Research in Child Development,* **48**(6).

Ogden, C. K., & Richards, I. A. (1960). *The meaning of meaning.* London: Routledge & Kegan Paul.

Ortony, A. (1975). Why metaphors are necessary and not just nice. *Educational Theory,* **25**, 45–53.

Ortony, A. (1979). Beyond literal similarity. *Psychological Review,* **86**, 161–180.

Paivio, A. (1979). Psychological processes in the comprehension of metaphor. In A. Ortony (Ed.), *Metaphor and thought.* London and New York: Cambridge Univ. Press.

Petrie, H. G. (1979). Metaphor and learning. In A. Ortony (Ed.), *Metaphor and thought.* London and New York: Cambridge Univ. Press.

Piaget, J. (1951). *Play, dreams, and imitation in childhood.* New York: Norton.

Piaget, J. (1974). *The language and thought of the child.* New York: Meridian Books (original work published 1926).

Pollio, M. R., & Pickens, J. P. (1980). The developmental structure of figurative competence. In R. P. Honeck & R. R. Hoffman (Eds.), *Cognition and figurative language.* Hillsdale, NJ: Erlbaum.

Pollio, M. R., & Pollio, H. (1974). The development of figurative language in children. *Journal of Psycholinguistic Research,* **3**, 185–201.

Pollio, M. R., & Pollio, H. (1979). The comprehension of figurative language in children. *Journal of Child Language,* **6**, 111–120.

Reynolds, R. E., & Ortony, A. (1980). Some issues in the measurement of children's comprehension of metaphorical language. *Child Development,* **51**, 1110–1119.

Rips, L. J., Shobin, E. J., & Smith, E. E. (1973). Semantic distance and the verification of semantic relations. *Journal of Verbal Learning and Verbal Behavior,* **12** 1–20.

Rosch, E. H. (1973). On the internal structure of perceptual and semantic categories. In T. E. Moore (Ed.), *Cognitive development and the acquisition of language.* New York: Academic Press.

Shepp, B. E., Burns, B., & McDonough, D. (1980). The relation of stimulus structure to perceptual and cognitive development: Further tests of the separability hypothesis. In F. Wilkening, J. Becker, & T. Trabasso (Eds.), *The integration of information by children.* Hillsdale, NJ: Erlbaum.

Silberstein, L., Gardner, H., Phelps, E., & Winner, E. (1982). Autumn leaves and old photographs. The development of metaphor preferences. *Journal of Experimental Child Psychology,* **34**, 135–150.

Slobin, D. I. (1966). Grammatical transformations in childhood and adulthood. *Journal of Verbal Learning and Verbal Behavior,* **5**, 219–227.

Steinberg, E. R., & Anderson, R. C. (1975). Hierarchical semantic organization in six-year-olds. *Journal of Experimental Child Psychology,* **19**, 544–553.

Tourangeau, R., & Sternberg, R. J. (1981). Aptness in metaphor. *Cognitive Psychology,* **13,** 27–55.

Tourangeau, R., & Sternberg, R. (1982). Understanding and appreciating metaphors. *Cognition,* **11,** 203–244.

Tversky, A. (1977). Features of similarity. *Psychological Review,* **84,** 327–352.

Verbrugge, R. R. (1979). The primacy of metaphor in development. *New Directions for Child Development,* **6,** 77–84.

Vosniadou, S., & Ortony, A. (1983a). The emergence of the literal-metaphorical-anomalous distinction in young children. *Child Development,* **54,** 154–161.

Vosniadou, S., & Ortony, A. (1983b). *Testing the metaphoric competence of the young child: Paraphrase versus inactment.* Paper presented at the Biennial Meeting of FRDC, Detroit, Michigan.

Vosniadou, S., Ortony, A., Reynolds, R. E., & Wilson, P. T. (1984). Sources of difficulty in the young child's understanding of metaphorical language. *Child Development,* **55,** 1588–1606.

Vygotsky, L. S. (1978). *Mind in society.* Cambridge, MA: Harvard Univ. Press.

Werner, H., & Kaplan, B. (1964). *Symbol formation.* New York: Wiley.

Wetstone, H. S., & Friedlander, B. Z. (1973). The effect of word order on young children's responses to simple questions and commands. *Child Development,* **44,** 734–740.

Winner, E. (1979). New names for old things: The emergence of metaphoric language. *Journal of Child Language,* **6,** 469–491.

Winner, E., McCarthy, M., & Gardner, H. (1980a). The ontogenesis of metaphor. In R. P. Honeck & R. R. Hoffman (Eds.), *Cognitive and figurative language.* Hillsdale, NJ: Erlbaum.

Winner, E., Engel, M., & Gardner, H. (1980b). Misunderstanding metaphor: What's the problem? *Journal of Experimental Child Psychology,* **30,** 22–32.

Winner, E., Rosenstiel, A. K., & Gardner, H. (1976). The development of metaphoric understanding. *Developmental Psychology,* **12,** 289–297.

Ziff, P. (1964). On understanding 'Understanding utterances.' In J. A. Katz & J. J. Fodor (Eds.), *The structure of language.* New York: Prentice–Hall.

THE CONCEPT OF DIMENSIONS IN
DEVELOPMENTAL RESEARCH

Stuart I. Offenbach and Francine C. Blumberg[1]

DEPARTMENT OF PSYCHOLOGICAL SCIENCES
PURDUE UNIVERSITY
WEST LAFAYETTE, INDIANA

I. Introduction

In the 1960s and 1970s, many studies of children's concept development were, generally speaking, limited to the context of discrimination learning or concept identification tasks. In addition, the focus was on the age range represented by the older preschool child (4–5 years of age) through the elementary school years (11 or 12 years of age). These interests were sharply defined by White in his theoretical statement describing a hierarchical struc-

[1]Present address: National Assessment of Educational Progress/Educational Testing Service, Princeton, New Jersey 08541.

83

ture of children's learning (White, 1965). White formalized what others had incorporated into the developmental framework (e.g., Kendler & Kendler, 1962), namely that an important transition takes place between the ages of 5 and 7 years. White proposed that younger children's learning is described by a stimulus–response conditioning model and that learning by older children is controlled by more complex cognitive functions. This two-stage theory was an advance over extant approaches in that learning by the older child had to be reevaluated in terms of internalized cognitive structures that more easily could include covert language, preprocessing, and classification of the stimulus world, and more thoughtful (often slower) responding. However, White's position also implied that what is learned must be qualified by cognitive capabilities that can limit or influence how the child interprets the stimuli in the learning environment. One example of the direction research took after 1965 was the careful analysis of the role played by internal mediators in learning (particularly in discrimination shift problems; see reviews and comments by Esposito, 1975; Gollin & Rosser, 1974; Wolff, 1967).

In the 1970s, new procedures and approaches were developed to describe some of these cognitive controls of learning. Gholson's (Gholson, Levine, & Phillips, 1972) modifications and extensions of Levine's hypothesis testing theory are one example of this trend; Hale's use of his component selection task is another (Hale & Morgan, 1973). Another important direction of the research and theory-building efforts since 1965 has been the attempt to describe learning by even younger children in terms of cognitive structures (e.g., Cohen & Strauss, 1979; Denney & Acito, 1974; Kemler, 1983). Together, these efforts have redirected some of the issues and research relevant to the study of learning in children. One example of note is that investigators of discrimination learning turned to a consideration of potential influences on children's perception of the stimuli (e.g., preference, salience, or dominance). Unfortunately, these investigators ignored (at least initially) an important issue: When and how do children categorize or class particular stimuli as members of a set or as exemplars of a concept? Furthermore, investigators spoke of stimulus dimensions as though they knew not only what they meant but also how the child was thinking about the stimuli. That turned out to be a misleading assumption. The vast research on the effects of stimulus preferences and dimensional salience and/or dominance led only to the not very surprising conclusion that learning could be influenced by some sort of preprocessing of the stimuli.

Yet these issues, how children conceptualize and interpret the stimuli within a dimensional or conceptual framework (if they do), continue to be the focus for potentially important contributions to our understanding of developmental changes in learning. In particular, the issue of how children interpret the stimulus and task has been approached more directly. Research designed to reveal how perceived stimuli interact to influence learning has been replaced by research on the more fundamental question of how children define stimulus dimensions and become able to categorize perceived stimuli (e.g., Kemler, 1983; Offenbach, 1983; Rosch, 1978; Shepp, 1983). This newer research is based on at least one assumption that differs from past research: that children always organize and categorize (or classify) stimulus inputs in some manner. Thus, an important research question, one that stimulated much of Piaget's research, is to specify not only when and how children organize and categorize stimuli, but also why and under what circumstances children *do not* do so. The study of why children fail to learn, fail to classify, fail to organize information, is one important organizing principle behind recent research (e.g., Levine, 1971; Offenbach, 1980). However, the question that has received the greatest amount of theoretical and experimental attention has been and continues to be how and when children organize, classify, and learn.

In Section II of this article, we shall examine some of the results of the latter activities, and describe some of the additional work that we believe is necessary. We shall analyze some aspects of these new approaches and suggest some deficiencies in them. We also shall present some data to support our contentions. Finally, in Section III, we shall try to integrate these approaches and suggest some solutions and directions for future research. We begin by reviewing some different theoretical approaches to the definition and formation of concepts.

II. Theories of Concepts

In most discrimination learning tasks, sorting tasks, and classification tasks (and, of course, the variations of all of these), stimuli are described by experimenters in terms of dimensions, attributes, or concepts (e.g., Gholson *et al.,* 1972; Hale & Morgan, 1973; Kemler & Smith, 1979; Kendler & Kendler, 1970). These descriptions and labels are based on an underlying assumption that the stimuli are exemplars of some common class or classes of objects or things. Sometimes these classes are concrete or quite easily verbalizable. Color, shape, and size are examples that seem to fit these criteria. Other sets of stimuli have been more difficult to describe, at least in words. Brightness and saturation differences of a single hue, random shapes, and collections of common objects (of the type often used in learning set experiments) are examples of these stimulus classes. One common denominator that underlies both types of collections is that the members of a set may be described by how similar or dissimilar they are to one another.[2] In each case, the stimulus items can be typed, grouped, or rank ordered on the basis of similarity as determined by a human sorter. These collections and the items in them are then given the status of a "concept" or a "class," and the items in the class are then considered "exemplars" of it. The observer can either assign new items to the class using some rule of similarity or infer whether additional members of the collection exist.

For example, given the exemplars *robin, eagle,* and *penguin,* the class of *bird* might come to mind. The actual similarity or other criterion that individuals use to decide that these items (or any other set of items) constitute a class is subject to much debate (see Murphy & Medin, 1985, for a discussion of possible criteria). But it does seem clear that the knowledge that such a class exists and is operating in a specific situation is sufficient to enable children or adults to impute membership in the class to new exemplars and/or to learn how to sort exemplars of the class into categories. The possible ways in which such judgments can be made are numerous, but three come easily to mind. First, concrete or abstract similarity among the class members might be used to make decisions of class membership. Second, the individual could construct some "theory" describing the items that belong in a category or class (Murphy & Medin, 1985). Third, the child might be biologically predisposed to detect some differences and not others. As an example, research by Bornstein (1981) on early color perception might be interpreted as supporting the existence of "built-in" color detectors. Each of these different views is well represented in the recent research on concept attainment and development. Because the similarity point of view is reasonably formalized, we shall examine its strengths and weaknesses in some detail. In addition, we shall consider two other approaches to the development of conceptual behavior: a prototype approach (Bornstein, 1981; Posner & Keele, 1968; Younger, 1984; Younger & Cohen, 1983a,b) and the concept theory approach of Murphy and Medin.

---

[2] A number of difficulties are associated with definitions of the term *similarity.* Many of these difficulties have been discussed in detail by Gregson (1975). We agree with Gregson's criterion for similarity: a quantifiable measure independent of the psychological theory (or process) is necessary to define similarity. Thus, the definitional problem is easier for attributes such as color, number, and shape of legs of animal figures, form, than for attributes that are primarily conceptual or based on verbal associations (e.g., similarity of nonsense trigrams, word associations) because in the latter cases, the similarity measure is not independent of the psychological response.

A. SIMILARITY THEORIES

The view that similarity relations are important in categorization has had, over the long term, the strongest influence on the study of children's learning. One reason is that similarity has been clearly represented in terms of an easily understood distance model (e.g., Coombs, 1964; Shepard, 1962). The distance model represents stimuli as points in a multidimensional space (such as those in Fig. 1) and similarity as the distance between the points. Thus, the stimuli represented by points A and B in Fig. 1 are more similar (closer together) than are the stimuli represented by points A and C. Asked to state which of these two pairs of stimuli are most alike or similar, children and adults class A and B together (Offenbach, 1983).

One other point should be made about the distance model, or models, since several different representations of distance are available. The most common distance model, depicted in Fig. 1, represents distances in a Euclidean space (the Euclidean "metric" or space is one case of the more general mathematical Minkowski model; a second case, the "city-block"

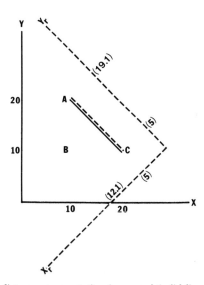

Fig. 1. *Euclidean distance representation in normal (solid lines) and in a rotated space (dashed lines). The numbers in parentheses are the X, Y values in the rotated space. The distance between points A and C can be "traversed" via the solid line or the dashed line. The distance between A and C can be computed by establishing the right triangle (ABC) in the unrotated space.*

metric is described below). That is, the distance D between points A and C is equal to

$$D_{ac} = \sqrt{D_{ab}^2 + D_{bc}^2} \qquad (1)$$

which is familiar as the formula used to compute the hypotenuse of a right triangle.

Another distance model that has been used in descriptions of concept acquisition is the city-block metric in which distance can be computed only along the principal axes of the space. The formula for the distance between points A and C in Fig. 1 according to the city-block model would be

$$D_{ac} = D_{ab} + D_{bc} \qquad (2)$$

That is, to get from point A to C, one must go by way of point B. Later, we shall see that both of these metrics have been used to describe concept learning and categorization, and the developmental changes in each.[3]

Garner (1974, 1978) has incorporated these metrics in a theory of how individuals (mostly adults) organize and categorize dimensional stimuli. Garner ascribes an important role to similarity in his formulation of holistic or integral stimulus attributes and analyzable or separable stimulus attributes. His views have been particularly influential in developmental research (Garner, 1983), having been adapted by Shepp and others (Kemler, 1983; Kemler & Smith, 1979; Shepp, 1983) into what is essentially a perceptual learning framework.

1. The Developmental Separability Hypothesis

Perceptual learning has had its most important impact on developmental psychology through the work of Gibson (e.g., Gibson, 1969; Gibson & Spelke, 1983). Focusing on the active nature of perception, Gibson argued that perception consists of extracting information (called affordances) from stimuli in the environment. These affordances reflect "the possibilities for action that are offered by the objects, events, and places that surround us" (Gibson & Spelke, 1983, p. 52). Perceptual learning was seen by Gibson to be a progression toward finer discriminations and the differentiation of cues in a stimulus complex that enables the developing child to acquire specific goals and a broad range of responses to achieve those (perceptual) goals. This process might be viewed as learning to select out and respond to information in the environment that had not been processed previously. De-

---

[3]Note that the computations of the distance AC in both the Euclidean and the city-block space require computation from a right triangle. However, if the spatial coordinates of A and C are known, the required triangle can be generated to compute the distance.

velopmentally, the trend in perception was from an undifferentiated or global type of processing to a more differentiated selective type of processing.

More recent versions of perceptual learning also incorporate the view that children's perception of the stimulus becomes increasingly more differentiated. Perception is seen to develop from a mode based on the physical or psychophysical similarity of a set of stimuli to organization based on actual dimensions, physical, psychophysical, or conceptual, that can be used to describe arrays of stimuli. The most prominent of these is Garner's proposal that describes different kinds of dimensional interactions. These types of dimensions were derived from a taxonomy of stimulus attributes postulated by Garner and associates (Garner, 1974, 1978; Garner & Felfoldy, 1970), in which attempts were made to identify and define the psychological stimulus in terms of the perceived structure or impact that different combinations of stimulus dimensions have on the individual. Two such classes of dimensional interactions were identified: integral and separable.

If a stimulus can be adequately specified only by reference to its values, or levels, on several dimensions, these dimensions are said to be *integral.* Saturation and brightness are integral dimensions, according to Foard and Kemler Nelson (1984). According to the *separability hypothesis,* stimuli that differ on these two dimensions need to be identified by reference to both (e.g., a bright, highly saturated color). The stimuli are sensed as holistic or integrated units and are difficult (perhaps impossible) to analyze subjectively into components based on the two dimensions (i.e., brightness is not perceived independent of saturation). Further, stimuli constructed from integral dimensions are, according to Garner, embedded in space described by the Euclidean metric. The property of distance (similarity) relations in the Euclidean space noted above is relevant to integral dimensions; the distances (similarity) between stimuli A and C in Fig. 1 remain constant even if the axes of space or the configuration of the three points are rotated. Separable dimensions, in contrast, can be more readily analyzed into isolated stimulus components on the basis of dimensional characteristics. Stimuli that vary on separable dimensions can be identified by referring to values of just one of the dimensions. For example, size and brightness are considered to give rise to analyzable and separable perceptions (Foard & Kemler Nelson, 1984) and one could identify a stimulus by ignoring one dimension and describing it as "the large one" or the "bright one" (by contrast, speaking of the "bright one" of stimuli that differ on brightness and saturation presumably would be confusing). In addition, in the stimulus space representing separable attributes, distance relationships are sensitive to changes in the orientation of the space, a characteristic of the city-block metric rather than the Euclidean metric. In the city-block metric, changes of the axes via rotation alter the distances (and similarity) between the points (Fig. 2), even though similarity is still represented as distance in the city-block metric. As a result, the psychological relationship between stimuli in city-block space may be quite different from the relationship in Euclidean space (Fig. 1).

In the developmental version of the separability hypothesis, Shepp (1978) proposed that some combinations of stimulus dimensions that are perceived as separable by the older child and adult are perceived as integral by the younger child. Shepp and colleagues focused not only on the structure of the stimulus and how the child interprets the structural cues, but also on how that interpretation changes with age and experience. However, Shepp has not discussed precisely how or why these changes take place. Nor have the potential underlying cognitive mechanisms that would mediate these perceptual developments been specified. These proposals regarding developmental changes also separate Shepp's approach from that of Garner. Although both investigators interpreted the psychological stimulus in terms of analyzable versus nonanlyzable dimensions, they seem to disagree with regard to the perceived status of these dimensions over time. That is, Garner

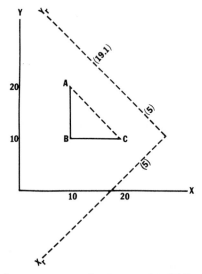

Fig. 2. City-block distance representation in normal (solid lines) and in a rotated space (dashed lines). The numbers in parentheses are the X,Y values in the rotated space. In order to compute the distance AC, a right triangle must be generated [for eq. (2) to be true]. The distance between points A and C can be "traversed" only by moving parallel to the X and Y axes: in the normal space only via the solid line and in the rotated space only via the dashed line.

saw dimensions as more stable or "pure" characteristics of the stimulus; Shepp viewed stimulus dimensions as undergoing change as a result of the child's more sophisticated perceptual processes.

2. Support for the Separability Hypothesis

Much of the evidence supporting Shepp's hypothesis is drawn from experiments in which various forms of classification tasks were used. For example, Shepp and Swartz (1976) examined dimensional classification among younger (aged 6 years) and older (9 years) children using both a speeded classification task and a free-sort task. In the speeded classification task, the children had to use a rule provided by the experimenter to sort a deck of cards into two piles as rapidly as possible. In free-sort tasks, the same stimulus combinations might be employed, but the child decided how to categorize cards and divide the pile. Each card contained stimuli that differed on one or two of three binary-valued dimensions (hue: two shades of red identified as Munsell 5–Red and 10–Red; brightness: Munsell value of 4/ or 6/; and shape: square or circle). Hue and brightness were considered to be integral dimensions and the combination of hue and shape represented separable dimensions. Three different sorts were made. In one, the child had to separate the cards into piles of, say, 5–Red and 10–Red cards (a unidimensional sort). Other sorts had the two dimensions correlated (e.g., 5–Red circles vs 10–Red squares). The children had to place the cards with a 5–Red circle in one pile and those with a 10–Red square into another pile. The third type of sort, called an orthogonal dimensions task, involved stimuli in which the values of the second dimension were paired equally often with those of the first dimension (these stimuli were similar to those used in most discrimination learning tasks). The child still had to sort on the basis of one dimension (e.g., 5–Red squares and 5–Red circles go in one pile; 10–Red squares and 10–Red circles go in a second pile).

Shepp and Swartz (1976) predicted that stimuli that varied on integral dimensional combinations would not be analyzed (dimensionally), so that the sorting times with these stimuli should not differ regardless of which task was presented. Differences in sorting were predicted when separable dimensions were used, particularly for the orthogonal dimensions task (because the child would have to look at both stimulus dimensional values). The results supported these expectations, but only for the older children, whose data were similar to those reported for adults. The younger children sorted the decks of cards as if they all contained only integral dimensions. Thus, the three decks were sorted in the same way.

The results of studies in which unrestricted classifications can be made also have supported the separability hypothesis (Kemler, 1982, 1983; Kemler & Smith, 1979; Smith & Kemler, 1977). The classification task used incorporates stimuli that differ on two dimensions. A representation of this type of stimulus arrangement is depicted in Fig. 3. Note that A and B share a value on one of the two dimensions (dimension X) but that C differs from A and B on both dimensions. The subject is asked which two stimuli go together. If the dimensional combination is perceived as integral, similarity relations govern the response and stimuli A and C would be grouped together (A and C differ by one unit while A and B differ by three units). If, however, the dimensional combination is analyzable and the dimensions are separable, the classification is made on a dimensional basis. Because stimuli A and B share a dimensional value, they would "go together." The same match would be made with the triad on the right side of Fig. 3, where C and B are more similar than are A and B (again because A and B share a value). Kemler (1983) summarized the results of several studies in which these types of sorts have been compared. She noted that children aged 6 years or less (3 year olds were the youngest children tested) consistently respond in this task by classifying stimuli on the basis of presumed similarity, and older children (10 years and above) group stimuli on the basis of dimensions.

3. Unresolved Issues Regarding the Separability Hypothesis

A number of difficulties confront the separability hypothesis. Perhaps the most important of these is the absence of criteria for deciding, a priori, whether a dimensional combination will be perceived as integral and non-analyzable or separable and analyzable. The lack of such a criterion leads to confusion because the same dimension is integral in one combination and separable when paired with a different dimension. Foard and Kemler Nelson (1984) used as an integral pair of dimensions saturation and brightness. However, when brightness is combined with size, stimuli that vary on this pair of dimensions are perceived as separable.

L. B. Smith (1980) and Kemler Nelson (J. D. Smith & Kemler Nelson, 1984) each proposed a modification of the developmental separability hy-

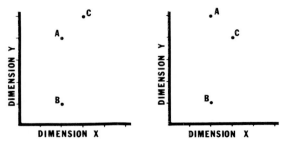

Fig. 3.   Representations of two stimulus triads used in testing for integral vs separable dimensions (from Kemler, 1982, Fig. 1).

pothesis that seemed to be an attempt to overcome, at least in part, this difficulty. They hypothesize that the integral–separable distinction represents a continuum of analyzability ranging from nonanalyzable (integral) to analyzable (separable). The manner in which a stimulus is interpreted is a function of a "processing mode" that "encompass(es) a combination of stimulus variables, processor variables, and task variables" (Foard & Kemler Nelson, 1984, p. 95). Unfortunately, the nature of this "processing mode" has not been clearly defined or explicated, and the relative contributions of the task, the individual, and the setting in which analytic or holistic processing occurs are unknown. As a result, the continuum proposal adds little to predictability or explanation of perceptual phenomena and development. In fact, it may lead to an experimental dead end in which a taxonomy of (mostly) integral and (mostly) separable dimensions is formulated in the place of predicting when dimensions shall be analyzable or explaining why and how dimensions can be analyzed.

Another criticism of the Shepp–Kemler Nelson position should be noted. Gibson (1983) observed that the tasks and settings in which the separability hypothesis has been evaluated are quite limited, and perhaps bear little relationship to "real-world perception and organization" (a criticism that could be directed at many different researchers, not just proponents of the separability hypothesis). She noted further that perception is an exploratory process demanding organization and structuring of everyday experience carried out by an active individual ("perceiver"). Finally, Gibson complained that the experimental tasks used in much of perceptual research represent something more like a "snapshot" of a static environment than the complex ongoing flow of "events that are continuously monitored" (p. 308). But Gibson's implication, that the principles and theories derived from such tasks are not valid because the task is static and limited in perceptual information and variability, is itself largely untested (see Blumberg & Offenbach, 1984, for one attempt to test this general assumption). Generalization may or may not occur. The fact that the developmental separability hypothesis applies only to a limited set of conditions does not by itself invalidate the hypothesis. This issue of generality actually poses difficulties for the separability hypothesis in a far more complex manner than even Gibson suggested.

This generalization question cuts two ways. First, it refers to the issue that Gibson raised regarding the application of experimental findings to more complex environmental events. Second, the principles derived from this theory also should be applicable to unidimensional stimuli. That is, perception is more than a fusion of two or more dimensions. We often perceive and interpret information about unidimensional objects or situations in the real world as well as in the laboratory. Unfortunately, generalizing the developmental separability hypothesis to the unidimensional case does not seem to be any easier than generalizing it to the multidimensional natural environment case. Additionally, even for multidimensional situations, human adults and children may attend to only one attribute and treat stimulus (or other environmental) differences as unidimensional. Thus, limiting Kemler Nelson's processing mode to multidimensional stimuli cannot be correct, as children (and adults) may ignore some dimensions of stimulus or event differences and process, interpret, and decide using only a single attribute of the situation. We believe conclusions drawn from tasks currently used to test the separability hypothesis must be shown to generalize not only to the more complex natural environment (as Gibson suggested), but also to the more restricted case of unidimensional judgments.

B. PROTOTYPES AND CONCEPTS

Questions of integrality and separability deal with the kind of percept a multidimensional stimulus gives rise to (i.e., holistic or analyzable). Prototype theories, in contrast, more often have dealt with how a perceiver declares a specific stimulus item to be a member of one or another category. Thus, Bornstein, Cohen, and other prototype theorists focused much of their research on how and when concepts first are formulated; and proponents of the separability hypothesis, including Shepp, Kemler Nelson, and Garner, have been concerned more with dimensions of stimuli.

1. Basic Categories

The prototype approach is derived in part from the idea of natural categories formulated by Rosch (1973). She proposed that a category is definable in terms of "features" that are common to most, many, or even all members of the category. An important point Rosch made was that in the real world, features are not equally probable and they do not convey equal amounts of information to the perceiver. Some combinations of features are more likely to be observed than are other combinations. For example, the combination of wings and flying ability has a higher probability of occurrence than does the combination of wings and absence of flying ability. But both do occur, and organisms that possess either pair of attributes may be categorized as birds (e.g., robins and penguins). A high correlation should prevail among sets of features such as these in order to identify category members. Natural categories are those defined by such sets of correlated features.

Objects and events can be grouped together in any one of several sets or levels arranged in a hierarchy. The "basic category" is the set or level at which the cluster of correlated features maximizes the information available. In addition, the within-category similarity of the exemplars is maximized relative to similarity between different categories (Mervis & Rosch, 1981). The process of forming such basic categories is considered a "basic process" in the sense defined by Flavell and Wellman (1977) for basic processes in memory phenomena—it is automatic and a part of the individual's original behavioral repertoire. The critical variable seems to be that the exemplar of a basic level category has some minimum number of highly correlated important or criterial features. The one object that is the "best" representative of the category, which perhaps has the greatest number of criterial features, is considered a prototype of the category.

A review of the research examining the development of natural concepts and categories reveals two major emphases. A significant amount of research has been conducted on the origins of prototypes and basic level categorization (e.g., Bornstein, 1981; Cohen & Strauss, 1979). Second, investigators have been concerned with the nature and structure of basic concepts (e.g., Rosch, 1978; Smith, 1984).

2. Origins of Basic Categories and Concepts

Basic concepts apparently may arise from experiences and interactions with the environment as well as biological biases. Evidence for learning these concepts has been reported by Younger and Cohen (1983b). They described a series of experiments in which the correlation among features was varied. Infants under 1 year of age could form categories based on perceptually salient features of animals and of faces (Fig. 4). These categories were

Fig. 4. Examples of the types of stimuli used by Younger and Cohen (1983b). In this case, five dimensions (type of body, shape of tail, shape of feet, ear structure, and number of legs) of animal features are varied to create novel stimulus variations.

acquired more easily and at earlier ages when features were highly correlated. Whether the development of less salient and less important categories
would be observed in such young children is a question yet to be answered.
Nor can we conclude that these early categories or concepts serve the same
functions that they do for older children. For example, an interesting test
might be to use stimuli such as those of Younger and Cohen's in discrimination shift tasks or classification tasks. We recognize that successfully
adapting these concepts and methods for use with infants is a significant
challenge to the experimenter's ingenuity, but it is a challenge that presumably can be met. The results of such an experiment might show that these
concepts are analyzed in the same manner by infants and preschool-aged
children (see Section III).

   Our speculation that at least some of these primitive concepts may be
biologically determined was suggested by the results of Bornstein's experiments with color. In those experiments, Bornstein (1981) demonstrated that
by 4 months of age, infants differentially dishabituated to color stimuli that
varied qualitatively. That is, dishabituation was observed when a stimulus
crossed a color boundary (say from green to blue), but not when an alter-
ation in the training stimulus did not cross the qualitative boundary (from
one shade of green to another shade of green). These different reactions
occurred even though the quantitative changes in the physical stimuli were
identical. In the absence of specific training in categorizing color stimuli,
Bornstein's results suggest that at least some concepts may have a biological
or innate component. Of course, in the case of color, these differentiations
may result from specific receptors (cones in the case of color vision) more
or less "tuned" to one level of stimulus energy. What we are suggesting is
that other early differentiations may also have a biological or structural
base. However, as with the learned concepts, the role these concepts might
play in later cognitive development is unknown.

3. Conclusions and Implications

   One of the most significant questions confronting prototype theories is
how to define a feature (Murphy & Medin, 1985). The question is not triv-
ial, although it may appear so. Rather, it relates to the basic process of
identifying items that are members of a class as well as items that are similar. This question may also provide a significant link to the separability
hypothesis, on the proposition that only features from separable, analyzable dimensional combinations could be abstracted and compared. With
holistically perceived compounds, no such features should be identifiable.
Again, the issue is one of noting a priori which elements of a stimulus or
an array could be perceived as "features" to be analyzed and compared.

   The data reported by Bornstein (1981) and by Cohen and colleagues

(Cohen & Strauss, 1979; Younger & Cohen, 1983a,b) enable the investigator to identify at a gross level some stimulus features that can be used to identify and to formulate classification "rules." These data also must be interpreted as showing that, at some level, an analysis of the dimensions that differentiate a set of stimulus items is accomplished by young infants (at least 5 or 6 months of age). This conclusion is inconsistent with the premise of the developmental form of the separability hypothesis that all dimensional combinations are initially integral (and thus are not analyzed into components). However, the extensive research on infant concepts (e.g., Linn, Reznick, Kagan, & Hans, 1982; Nelson, 1973; Rose, Gottfried, Melloy-Carminar, & Bridger, 1982; as well as the research discussed above by Bornstein and Cohen) seems to us to strengthen the conclusion that some form of classification and analysis does take place in early infancy. A logical question to ask is whether such analysis also fits the definition of "dimensional analysis."

These observations support the hypothesis that the young infant has available structures or predispositions that can facilitate the development of concepts and/or categories (possibly in both form and content). As a result, the operations leading to the forming of categories, the organizing— or attempts to organize—environmental inputs into a meaningful framework and the processing of stimulus features, do not have to be learned. They are as much a part of the biological structure of the organism as eating, walking, and sensing the external environment. We also speculate from the experimental evidence that some early categories serve as a superstructure upon which later learned differentiations may be built. Finer judgments of color, use of color information, etc. may be based on the perceived structure of color differences that may have been available from birth. Finally, we also draw the following inference: the features of these early categories are concrete and are, perhaps, easy for experimenters and observers to specify. As a result, these concrete categories may at some later developmental period be integrated into more complex and abstract verbal concepts that mediate performance in a wide variety of tasks (and may be more difficult to specify). Later in this article, we shall examine some research findings that would support this view. First, however, we examine one remaining proposal regarding the nature of concepts and categories.

C. CATEGORIZATION BY THEORY

1. A New View of a Concept

Among the recent additions to the literature on concept attainment and definition are the proposals of Medin (Medin, 1983; Murphy & Medin, 1985). By focusing on how individuals decide which items are classed as members of a category (categorical inclusion), Medin seems to rely more on cognitive operations than on stimulus–response relationships. Murphy and Medin also were more concerned with the nature of abstract concepts and of domains of information (or events) that are based on the individual perceiver's "theory" of the various "domains," as being the important interpretative component of categorical judgments. Murphy and Medin's "theories" are loosely defined, and refer to one of many "mental 'explanations'" rather than formal, organized theories in the scientific sense. Murphy and Medin explicitly stated that "one's theory about a domain helps to structure the concepts about that domain" (Murphy & Medin, 1985, p. 4). Further judgments of categorization, combinations of concepts, and individual definitions of attribute relations apparently are based on these "theories." Thus, the "conceptual glue" (Murphy and Medin's term) that is the basis of categorization and concept formation are these idiosyncratic rationales for grouping objects rather than the attributes of the objects themselves (as was the case in the two ideas discussed in Sections II,A and II,B).

In fact, Murphy and Medin rejected both similarity and feature analysis as the basis for categorization. Regardless of whether one agrees with their basic approach, Murphy and Medin have made some significant comments about the difficulty involved in trying to explain concept development and categorization. For example, similarity has not been adequately defined. On what basis are two stimuli to be judged similar? Many of us have used the term *similarity* in a loose and poorly defined manner, seeing similarity as a framework for explaining what a concept is or why objects are grouped together. "Similarity" judgments are at the heart of many psychological processes (e.g., psychophysical judgments, generalization, and learning), but the processes involved in deciding what constitutes similarity have not been satisfactorily defined. One popular approach is that similarity can be represented by the matching of important features of the stimuli. However, this approach simply defers definitional problems. Thus, we would ask (as did Murphy and Medin) the following questions: What is a feature? How many features must match before two things are considered similar? How do we decide which are the most important features in matching? Murphy and Medin's conclusion that similarity cannot "stand unadorned as a principle of category structure" is correct. However, we would point out that this conclusion does not warrant throwing out the concept of similarity. Rather, the problem is to define similarity in a way that gives it explanatory power. A definition of similarity may be elusive, but that does not justify moving on to constructs that are equally elusive.

The second valid point Murphy and Medin made was that the current model of concepts based on correlated features (i.e., Rosch's theory) is "insufficient." Although Murphy and Medin did not reject the idea that correlations are part of categorization, they did state that the presence of correlations among category members is a consequence rather than a cause. The correlational model is based in part on similarity. However, it is elaborated in a number of ways. Specifically, similarity is relatively unstructured, but the correlational model specifies detectable links among a set of stimuli. As a result, the correlated features model is subject to many of the same criticisms as the similarity model. One additional difficulty with the correlated features model, according to Murphy and Medin, is determining how the important relevant correlations (for categorizing) are discriminated from what may be a large set of correlations among features, many of which are irrelevant to concept formation and/or categorization.

2. Developmental Implications

Medin has not yet dealt specifically with developmental change, or the potential for developmental change. Rather, he seems to have accepted some of the tenets of the developmental separability hypothesis (Medin, 1983, p. 227). But according to that hypothesis, the shift in processing stimuli from integral to separable dimensions results from the child's supposed ability to deploy attention more effectively and to use attention selectively. That Murphy and Medin did not consider the potential implications of the "mental glue" postulates on development is understandable. Medin and colleagues have focused primarily on mature categorization processes. At some point, however, the manner in which a child or an adult decides whether the "theory" that binds a particular concept or category together is correct or incorrect (or useful or not useful) must be considered. How the child learns to formulate hypotheses to test is an important consideration because theory construction at any level, including the theories of concepts that Medin proposed, must follow a path of hypothesis creation (via deduction or induction) and testing. The developmental separability hypothesis, which Medin seems to have adopted (at least in part), is not itself consistent with some aspects of the idea that hypotheses must be tested to build theories or that categories are held together by theories. The position we describe here is that stimulus dimensions have an important role in concept development and in the formation of categories (whether well defined or ill defined).

Finally, when Medin (1983) discussed the developmental separability hypothesis and the role of attention, he also appeared to shift the focus from "categories" alone to a mixed "category"–"dimension" conglomerate. Medin (1983) commented that predicting how learning would occur or which hypotheses would be tested when the stimuli are exemplars drawn from some "ill-defined" categories is difficult in the hypothesis testing framework. Yet it should be remembered that most hypotheses tested in discrimination learning are based on simple associations of one value of a *dimension* with reward. Hypotheses relevant to ill-defined categories would have to describe a complex association between some *category feature* and reward in order to be useful.

Medin's position is really not very different from those discussed in Section II,A and II,B in that one important issue remains. Proponents of these different positions often treat dimensions, concepts, and categories as interchangeable constructs, each representing the same (or similar) psychological processes. We believe that the use of multiple semantic labels, each with its own load of surplus meaning, has been a source of much potential and actual confusion. We hope to resolve some of these issues in the discussion that follows.

III. Concepts and Dimensions

The theoretical positions we described in Section II tend to blend together as proponents of each try to identify significant problems, explain research findings, and carry out new experiments. However, we believe some important issues must be resolved before these theories can enable us to enlarge our understanding of children's cognitive development. These issues concern the relationship between dimensions and concepts or categories. The kinds of dimensions that underlie concepts and categories and how the mechanisms or processes underlying the perception (or construction) of these dimensions change with age need to be explicated. These are two of the issues we consider in the following discussion. Another important issue is the relationship between dimensions and concepts, and we describe a system in which attributes (or concepts or categories) may be decomposed into a set of basic dimensions.

The terms *dimension, concept,* and *category* have been used often without a formal definition by investigators studying concept development or learning (although some recent exceptions include Garner, 1978; Offenbach, 1983; Shepp and colleagues, in Tighe & Shepp, 1983). In our view, this lack of consistency has been partly responsible for the conflicting results and theoretical interpretations of learning experiments.

Concepts and categories have been defined by Clark (1983) as "a set of properties that are associated with each other in memory and thus form a unit" (p. 789). This definition refers to what we have called "attributes" in the present discussion. We would define concepts and categories as cognitive "sets of properties" that can be used to organize stimuli or events as superordinate classes. We view dimensions as a possible framework upon which these complex concepts and categories are structured. Further, concepts and categories may be decomposed into one or more constituent dimensions (of which there are at least two types). These "structural" dimensions are defined by responses to the physical similarity of the items or stimuli making up the dimension. The point we are making is that both higher order concepts and basic dimensions coexist, and probably neither is a prerequisite for the other. As an example, variations in the hue component of the more general color attribute represent two different dimensions—red–green and blue–yellow—derived from physical differences in the wavelength of the stimuli. These and other structural dimensions organize early color perception. However, with increasing age and experience, variations in stimuli such as hue may function as a dimension, independent of whether such variations are consistent with the underlying structural dimensions (e.g., red–green and blue–yellow). In that case, the stimulus differences represent a component, or a subclass, of the overall attribute of "color."

These differences represent an intermediate class of dimension that combines aspects of concepts and categories with aspects of the basic perceptual dimensions. That is, attributes, concepts, or categories sometimes exhibit properties both of structural dimensions and of higher level cognitive "sets of properties." As a result, intermediate level sets may function as attributes and concepts to organize cognitive information or as structural dimensions that mediate stimulus and response relationships. We use the term *conceptual dimensions* to refer to these cognitive sets when they function as dimensions or mediators, although in practice the distinction between the intermediate conceptual dimensions and the two types of structural or perceptual dimensions may become blurred or may even disappear. However, understanding the nature and acquisition of both the basic and intermediate "levels" of dimensions that are the structure on which attributes, concepts, or categories are based is an important component of perceptual and cognitive theorizing. Dimensions serve to mediate stimulus relationships and generalizations, as well as the development of more abstract structures that link stimuli or ideas together as high-level collections (e.g., attributes, concepts, categories).

A. PERCEPTUAL DIMENSIONS

Perceptual dimensions may be assessed by examining the child's (or the adult's) psychological response to real physical differences among a set of stimuli (see footnote 2). In order to be decomposed into perceptual dimensions, a domain or a set of stimuli must be capable of being rank ordered on one or more physical measures. Most likely, all attributes are initially analyzed on the basis of (or are decomposed into) one of two types of perceptual dimensions. One type consists of sets of elements that can be rank ordered on the basis of learned cues or associations. The other type depends on biological factors. Dimensions of both types may play an important role in mediating children's development as perception and learning, based upon the dimensional combinations Shepp, Kemler, and others have called integral, yield to those combinations that have been labeled or classified as separable.

The dimensions which we believe to be based on biological factors (such as hue and perhaps shape) may also reflect stimulus-processing biases built into the organism. For these attribute domains, differences among stimuli are detected by "prewired" biological structures. For example, for the domain of color, the organism may have specific hue or wavelength detectors. The edge and movement detectors of the visual system may mediate some aspects of shape perception. The perception of differences that result from the operation of these detectors serves as the basis of dimensions that may organize perception without the necessity for any prior learning.[4] The other type of perceptual dimension results when associations are formed between an object or set of objects (stimuli as they are detected) and the perceived salient features of the object or set of objects. The dimensions used by Strauss (Cohen & Strauss, 1979; Strauss, 1979; Strauss & Curtis, 1981) and by Cohen and colleagues (e.g., Husaim & Cohen, 1981; Younger, 1984; Younger & Cohen, 1983a,b) in their studies of infant perception and learning may be prototypes of these dimensions.

As we indicated, color is a good example of the first class of perceptual attributes. Physically and psychologically, color can be decomposed into a hue (wavelength) structure, a brightness (intensity) structure, and a saturation structure (related to the amount of radiant energy contributed by the dominant wavelength to achromatic white light). These dimensions or substructures already have been extracted from individuals' perceptual behavior in a variety of psychophysical studies of color (e.g., Helm, 1964; Indow & Ohsumi, 1972; Offenbach, 1983, experiment 1). Shape is another attribute that has been studied in this manner, yielding a variety of constituent dimensions (see Brown & Owen, 1967; Künnapas, Mälhammer, & Svenson, 1964; Offenbach, 1983, experiment 2).

Examples of dimensions that may be derived from simple associations are those based on animal form studied by Younger and Cohen (1983a,b). The psychological responses to stimuli that varied on physical measures such

[4]Another speculation is that these dimensions may develop even without prior exposure or experience.

as number and shape of legs and feet apparently were differentiated as a result of experience (in a habituation task). The result was that these arrays of stimulus differences then could be treated as perceptual dimensions. The salience of the physical features (or cues) that are the basis of these dimensions may be determined biologically, but the psychological response to the dimensional aspects or variations in the stimuli appear to be learned. That is, the perception of these features might be mediated by specialized receptors or some preprocessor present at birth. However, the mere presence of such specialized receptors does not in itself guarantee that the psychological dimensions will develop. Rather, some critical experiences that result in learned associations might be necessary—either to activate the receptors or to make the dimensions useful. Both (or either) of these two classes of dimensions thus form the framework for the more general attributes. Finally, the distinction between dimension and attribute is made quite easily in cases such as these (e.g., hue in the case of color, number of legs in the case of animal). Such is not the case for conceptual dimensions.

B. CONCEPTUAL DIMENSIONS

The conceptual dimensions into which attributes and/or categories may be decomposed are based on sets of properties within which differences are mediated by some abstract associational structure. Unlike perceptual dimensions, conceptual dimensions do not have an independently defined similarity metric. Therefore, stimuli drawn from a conceptual dimension are rank ordered on the basis of the perception or interpretation of *psychological* differences instead of physical differences. As a result, the similarity metric is not independent of the abstract associations or the links in memory that bring the stimuli into the same domain (see Section III,A). Concepts tied directly to language represent one example of conceptual dimensions. For other concepts or categories, such as colors and shapes, the organization or framework of the concept may shift from being based on perceptual dimensions to being based on abstract associations, that is, conceptual dimensions. These conceptual dimensions may in fact function as concepts or dimensions, depending upon the setting. Thus, what we refer to as conceptual dimensions may be the same as what others simply have called *concepts* or *dimensions* (e.g., this usage more closely matches the use of the term *dimension* in many reports of studies of learning, concept attainment, etc.).

Conceptual dimensions represent a higher level of organization than the two types of perceptual dimensions described in Section III,A. One difference between the two may lie in how encoding or analyzing a complex stimulus display takes place. Offenbach has argued elsewhere (1983) that young children under 4 or 5 years of age, who are limited to responding to the concrete aspects of a stimulus display, also analyze stimuli only in terms of perceptual dimensions. As a result, complex stimuli are organized in a rather stereotyped manner, with no elaborate system of learned associations to make interpretation more efficient. The inability to organize complex stimuli in terms of conceptual dimensions may be similar to the mediational deficiency hypothesis proposed by Reese (1962). Our proposal includes some significant differences from a deficiency model. We show below that young children are capable of producing and using mediators, provided that the stimulus variations match the structural dimensions of the stimulus domain. Some of the advantages of cognitively organized conceptual dimensions are that more broadly based generalizations may be made and the conceptual organization may be useful in a greater variety of situations. At this time, we would add another potential difference. Analyzing stimulus displays into component perceptual dimensions may represent a primary process, automatically called into play. Decomposing a complex display into conceptual dimensions may require that the automatic process be inhibited while a more reflective process is carried out. This suggestion is drawn from ideas developed by White (1965). The analogy is that perceptual "analysis" is at the same level as conditioning, and decomposition of a domain into conceptual dimensions is at the same level as a cognitive learning process.

Because both perceptual and conceptual dimensions enable the child to mediate stimulus differences and response relationships, confusion is possible, particularly for older children who have both levels of organization available. Younger children, in contrast, may be limited in their potential for mediation. For example, if young children, whose dimensional organization is limited to perceptual variations, attempt to organize a set of stimulus differences that actually vary conceptually, they may produce mediators that fail to facilitate performance. The observer might mistake that failure for the absence of a capacity rather than the child's (or the experimenter's) inappropriate management of the learning environment.

Finally, we note that more complex conceptual and cognitive frameworks are not automatically acquired. The associational structure necessary for a conceptual dimension may require special training or experience. Some aspects of color may be in that category. Artists and scientists studying the physical or psychological structure of color perception may acquire a conceptual understanding of color saturation (Munsell chroma) that most other adults do not acquire. The result would be that in some experiments (such as those described in Section III,C,2 with reference to the developmental separability hypothesis), these trained adults would analyze chroma differences as "normal" adults analyze form differences.

C. TWO APPLICATIONS OF PERCEPTUAL
AND CONCEPTUAL DIMENSIONS

Our analysis has the potential to explain some of the disparate results that have been obtained in the developmental literature. We shall discuss two issues and show how a more precise consideration of what constitutes dimensions and concepts can be applied to them. The first of these is the discrimination shift paradigm, and the second is the new position proposed by Shepp and colleagues. For discrimination learning, we show that young children's performance is more like that of their older counterparts so long as the learning task stimuli vary along perceptual dimensions. The analysis of integral and separable dimensions is focused on the use of perceptual and conceptual dimensions as a mechanism underlying the developmental pattern that has been observed.

1. Discrimination Learning

In the discrimination shift literature, experimenters, including the present authors, often refer to stimuli as varying on the "dimensions" of form or color. This usage is incorrect, or at least imprecise, because color and form stimuli are linked by abstract associations. Color and form stimuli would be organized as (conceptual) dimensions only by older children. Younger children can mediate differences in color and form if and only if the stimulus variations conform to the basic perceptual structure of these domains. In many published reports of discrimination shift experiments, color and form attributes (or other attributes) were implicitly assumed to have the same properties as those we have described for perceptual dimensions. We believe that assumption is not justified as far as young children are concerned. Young children may do poorly on the shift task precisely because they cannot "properly" organize or analyze the stimulus differences.

Having made these assertions, we examine some discrimination shift results that provide some support for our proposals. Within-dimension (reversal and intradimensional) shifts often are easier to learn than shifts to different dimensions (nonreversal and extradimensional shifts), particularly by older children and adults. The reversal is easier because the older children learn to respond to (or attend to, mediate, or test dimensional hypotheses about) the relevant "dimension" in original learning. Because that "dimension" remains relevant in the reversal and intradimensional shifts, the same dimensional response continues to be rewarded, and learning the shift task is facilitated relative to a shift to a formerly irrelevant "dimension" or to a new "dimension." Young children's failure to learn the reversal shift more rapidly than the nonreversal shift has been interpreted by many to reflect an inability to mediate (e.g., Kendler's early mediation theory: Kendler & Kendler, 1962; Kendler & Kendler, 1970) or a limited attentional capacity (e.g., Zeaman and House's 1963 attentional model). However, another possibility is suggested by our analysis of perceptual and conceptual dimensions.

Early in development, stimulus relationships are mediated only by perceptual dimensions (which would determine the ease with which a shift would be acquired). As a result, reversal and intradimensional shifts are facilitated for young children only when an appropriate perceptual dimension is involved. Otherwise the shift may be interpreted by the young children as the more difficult nonreversal or extradimensional shift. Older children, however, interpret variations in stimuli on a cognitive level. For them, the stimulus differences vary as conceptual dimensions. Therefore, the shift from one to another color would be interpreted as the easier reversal or intradimensional shift. Because all shifts from one dimension to another dimension appear to be difficult, children who acquire a reversal or intradimensional shift more slowly than a nonreversal or extradimensional shift may do so because they perceive the stimuli to be from different perceptual dimensions rather than from a single conceptual dimension. That is, children who have difficulty with the reversal may see the stimuli as representing two or more perceptual dimensions rather than the one conceptual dimension that the adult experimenter used to organize the attribute.

Offenbach (1983, experiment 4) conducted a discrimination shift experiment that demonstrates these principles. The stimuli used varied on perceptual dimensions, namely, the two hue dimensions of red–green and blue–yellow. These stimuli were constructed by pairing colored squares like those symbolized in Fig. 5. In each presentation, a red square and a blue (or yellow) square constituted one stimulus while green and yellow (blue)

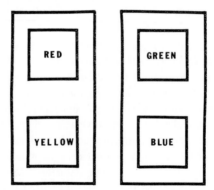

Fig. 5.   Color combinations consistent with underlying perceptual dimensions used in experiment 4 by Offenbach (1983).

squares made up the other stimulus. (The top and bottom location of the color squares was random and irrelevant.) Young children (age 5), who in other studies have been found to learn a reversal shift only with difficulty, quickly learned this reversal from red to green, making fewer errors and taking fewer trials to attain the criterion than children who were shifted from red to blue. These results are similar to the results for older children in studies in which the manipulated "dimensions" have been color and form. Offenbach also conducted a replication study in which the stimuli were combined in a nondimensional manner (one stimulus setting is symbolized in Fig. 6). That study also yielded results consistent with our hypothesis that young children do analyze dimensions: all shifts were equally difficult to learn. The older children in both of Offenbach's experiments shifted from one color to another with equal facility. These data were interpreted as reflecting "dimensional" responding with "conceptual" dimensions. That is, the older children apparently treated the stimulus differences as being the same—variations on a "dimension" of color. Thus, all shifts were within the same dimension and all were learned rapidly and with few errors.

2. Integral and Separable Dimensions

The impreciseness noted in Section III,C,1 seems also to characterize some of the research on integral and separable dimensions, although Burns, Shepp, McDonough, and Wiener-Erlich (1978) carefully analyzed some of the properties of integral and separable dimensions. Different types of dimensions (perceptual and conceptual) have been combined in different studies, and have led to conclusions that a particular dimensional combination is integral in one case and separable in another case. Burns *et al.* (1978) noted that even for adults, size of circle and angle of line are some-

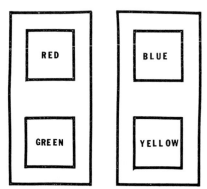

Fig. 6.   *Color combinations not consistent with the underlying perceptual dimensions used in the replication of experiment 4 by Offenbach (1983).*

times perceived as integral and other times as separable. Further, these inconsistencies have been a major factor in leading Shepp and colleagues to propose the developmental separability hypothesis. We do not quarrel with the developmental pattern, but we do wish to propose an alternative explanation for the developmental trend.

Our view is that holistic or analytic processing of the environment is primarily activated by the perceiver, and represents a more general case of strategy usage not unlike the strategies used in hypothesis formation and testing during learning tasks and in encoding and processing of information to be stored or retrieved from memory. A more fruitful approach than compiling lists of types of dimensions might be to discover when children invoke "this" strategy rather than "that" strategy or when a dimension is perceived in one manner rather than another.

Separable dimensional combinations may result whenever one or more perceptual dimensions are combined with one or more conceptual dimensions (or attributes). Dimensional combinations may be perceived in a more holistic manner and be less subject to decomposition when the constituent dimensions are perceptually defined (perceptual dimensions). Further, the availability or the development of an associational structure in memory for what may have been a perceptual dimension makes that dimension subject to more detailed or deeper analysis. This transformation may be what happens with stimuli that differ in hue. When such stimuli are linked by a set of associations as "colors," dimensional combinations with color may become separable. However, if in an experimental setting, color stimuli continue to vary only on perceptual dimensions, they would continue to generate integral combinations. Burns *et al.* (1978) reported two experiments with hue and chroma (experiments 5 and 6) that highlight the latter effect. The stimuli, four levels of intensity of the same hue (the Munsell notations were 2.5R, 5R, 7.5R, and 10R) were combined with four chroma levels. In that the hues were from the same perceptual dimension, we would expect them to produce integral combinations. This is the result Burns *et al.* obtained. Perhaps the use of hues from different perceptual dimensions (e.g., Munsell R, Y, and G) would have produced combinations that were separable.

Another example of the effects of mixing dimensional classes can be seen in Foard and Kemler Nelson's (1984) research on the developmental separability hypothesis. They combined brightness and size, expecting (correctly) that the resulting stimulus combinations would be separable. Although brightness qualifies as what we have termed a perceptual dimension, size does not. Size is an attribute that can be decomposed (using psychophysical procedures) into height, width, and area dimensions. Note also that each of these dimensions conforms to the criterion of similarity required for perceptual dimensions. Values on each can be rank ordered on the basis of physical differences. The stimuli used by Foard and Kemler Nelson varied on some of these dimensions because different sized squares were used. We would expect such stimulus compounds to be analyzable. However, if the size variations were made along only one of the perceptual dimensions, the resulting compounds might be perceived as integral. The test of these proposals awaits further experimentation.

IV. Summary

In the present article, the terms *attribute, concept,* and *category* were deliberately used to demonstrate how such terms share a common meaning, at least at one level. This is precisely the level at which interpretive misunderstandings seem to abound. The misunderstandings are not limited to any group of theorists, but apply equally to many of us. Actually, the problem is not very different from that which exists for similarity. In an extensive analysis of the similarity construct, Gregson (1975) remarked that one reason for its popularity was that the lack of a precise definition could be "dangerously versatile." Versatility at the expense of precise definition does not improve either predictability or our understanding of complex developmental processes. That understanding is our goal, and if the suggestions we have made lead to more clearly defined research designs and more consistent results, our goals shall have been achieved.

ACKNOWLEDGEMENTS

We would like to thank Charles Nelson, Robert V. Kail, and Hayne W. Reese, each of whom read and commented on an earlier version of this article. Their assistance helped clarify our ideas, and made the presentation of those ideas much clearer. S. I. Offenbach would like also to acknowledge and thank William J. Meyer for his support and encouragement over the years, without which this and other works would never have been completed.

REFERENCES

Blumberg, F. C., & Offenbach, S. I. (1984). *Effects of directed response training on incidental learning.* Paper presented at the meeting of the American Psychological Association, Toronto, August.

Bornstein, M. H. (1981). Two kinds of perceptual organization near the beginning of life. In W. A. Collins (Ed.), *Minnesota symposia on child psychology* (Vol. 14, pp. 39–91). Hillsdale, NJ: Erlbaum.

Brown, D. R., & Owen, D. H. (1967). The metrics of visual form: Methodological dyspepsia. *Psychological Bulletin,* **68,** 243–259.

Burns, B., Shepp, B. E., McDonough, D., & Wiener-Erlich, W. K. (1978). The relation between stimulus analyzability and perceived dimensional structure. In G. H. Bower (Ed.) *The psychology of learning and motivation* (Vol. 12, pp. 77–115). New York: Academic Press.

Clark, E. V. (1983). Meanings and concepts. In P. H. Mussen (Series Ed.), *Handbook of child psychology* (Vol. 3, pp. 787–840). New York: Wiley.

Cohen, L. B., & Strauss, M. S. (1979). Concept acquisition in the human infant. *Child Development, 50,* 419–424.

Coombs, C. H. (1964). *A theory of data.* New York: Wiley.

Denney, N. W., & Acito, M. A. (1974). Classification training in two- and three-year-old children. *Journal of Experimental Child Psychology, 17,* 37–48.

Esposito, N. J. (1975). Review of discrimination shift learning in young children. *Psychological Bulletin, 82,* 432–455.

Flavell, J. H., & Wellman, H. M. (1977). Metamemory. In R. V. Kail & J. W. Hagen (Eds.), *Perspectives on the development of memory and cognition* (pp. 3–33). Hillsdale, NJ: Earlbaum.

Foard, C. F., & Kemler Nelson, D. G. (1984). Holistic and analytic modes of processing: The multiple determinants of perceptual analysis. *Journal of Experimental Psychology: General, 113,* 94–111.

Garner, W. R. (1974). *The processing of information and structure.* Hillsdale, NJ: Erlbaum.

Garner, W. R. (1978). Aspects of a stimulus: Features, dimensions, and configurations. In E. Rosch & B. B. Lloyd (Eds.), *Cognition and categorization* (pp. 99–139). Hillsdale, NJ: Erlbaum.

Garner, W. R. (1983). Asymmetric interactions of stimulus dimensions in perceptual information processing. In T. J. Tighe & B. E. Shepp (Eds.), *Perception, cognition, and development: Interactional analyses* (pp. 2–38). Hillsdale, NJ: Erlbaum.

Garner, W. R., & Felfoldy, G. L. (1970). Integrality of stimulus dimensions in various types of information processing. *Cognitive Psychology, 1,* 225–241.

Gholson, B., Levine, M., & Phillips, S. (1972). Hypotheses, strategies, and stereotypes in discrimination learning. *Journal of Experimental Child Psychology, 13,* 423–446.

Gibson, E. J. (1969). *Principles of perceptual learning and development.* New York: Appleton.

Gibson, E. J. (1983). Commentary on the development of perception and cognition. In T. J. Tighe & B. E. Shepp, (Eds.), *Perception, cognition, and development: Interactional analyses* (pp. 307–322). Hillsdale, NJ: Erlbaum.

Gibson, E. J., & Spelke, E. S. (1983). The development of perception. In P. H. Mussen (Series Ed.), *Handbook of child psychology* (Vol. 3, pp. 1–76). New York: Wiley.

Gollin, E. S., & Rosser, M. (1974). On mediation. *Journal of Experimental Child Psychology, 17,* 539–544.

Gregson, R. A. M. (1975). *Psychometrics of similarity.* New York: Academic Press.

Hale, G. A., & Morgan, J. S. (1973). Developmental trends in children's component selection. *Journal of Experimental Child Psychology, 15,* 302–314.

Helm, C. E. (1964). Multidimensional ratio scaling analysis of perceived color relations. *Journal of the Optical Society of America, 54,* 256–262.

Husaim, J. S., & Cohen, L. B. (1981). Infant learning of ill-defined categories. *Merrill–Palmer Quarterly, 27,* 443–456.

Indow, T., & Ohsumi, K. (1972). Multidimensional mapping of sixty Munsell colors by nonmetric procedures. In J. J. Vos, L. F. C. Friele, & P. L. Walraven (Eds.), *Color metrics* (pp. 124–133). Soesterberg: AIC Holland.

Kemler, D. G. (1982). Classification in young and retarded children: The primacy of overall similarity relations. *Child Development, 53,* 768–799.

Kemler, D. G. (1983). Holistic and analytic modes in perceptual and cognitive development. In T. J. Tighe & B. E. Shepp, (Eds.), *Perception, cognition, and development: Interactional analyses* (pp. 77-102). Hillsdale, NJ: Erlbaum.

Kemler, D. G., & Smith, L. B. (1979). Accessing similarity and dimensional relations: Effects of integrality and separability on the discovery of complex concepts. *Journal of Experimental Psychology: General,* **108,** 133-150.

Kendler, H. H., & Kendler, T. S. (1962). Vertical and horizontal processes in problem solving. *Psychological Review,* **69,** 1-16.

Kendler, T. S., & Kendler, H. H. (1970). An ontogeny of optional shift behavior. *Child Development,* **41,** 1-27.

Künnapas, T., Mälhammer, G., & Svenson, O. (1964). Multidimensional ratio scaling and multidimensional similarity of simple geometric forms. *Scandinavian Journal of Psychology,* **5,** 249-256.

Levine, M. (1971). Hypothesis theory and nonlearning despite ideal S- R-reinforcement contingencies. *Psychological Review,* **78,** 130-140.

Linn, S., Reznick, J. S., Kagan, J., & Hans, S. (1982). Salience of visual patterns in the human infant. *Developmental Psychology,* **18,** 651-657.

Medin, D. L. (1983). Structural principles in categorization. In T. J. Tighe & B. E. Shepp (Eds.), *Perception, cognition, and development: International analyses* (pp. 203-230). Hillsdale, NJ: Erlbaum.

Mervis, C. B., & Rosch, E. (1981). Categorization of natural objects. *Annual Review of Psychology,* **32,** 89-115.

Murphy, G. L., & Medin, D. L. (1985). The role of theories in conceptual coherence. *Psychological Review,* **92,** 289-316.

Nelson, K. (1973). Some evidence for the cognitive primacy of categorization. *Merrill-Palmer Quarterly,* **19,** 21-39.

Offenbach, S. I. (1980). Children's learning as a function of hypothesis set size. *Child Development,* **51,** 1050-1056.

Offenbach, S. I. (1983). The concept of dimension in research on children's learning. *Monographs of the Society for Research in Child Development,* **48**(6, Serial No. 204).

Posner, M. I., & Keele, S. W. (1968). On the genesis of abstract ideas. *Journal of Experimental Child Psychology,* **77,** 353-363.

Reese, H. W. (1962). Verbal mediation as a function of age level. *Psychological Bulletin,* **59,** 502-509.

Rosch, E. (1973). Natural categories. *Cognitive Psychology,* **4,** 328-350.

Rosch, E. (1978). Principles of categorization. In E. Rosch & B. B. Lloyd (Eds.), *Cognition and categorization* (pp. 27-48). Hillsdale, NJ: Erlbaum.

Rose, S. A., Gottfried, A. W., Melloy-Carminar, P., & Bridger, W. H. (1982). Familiarity and novelty preferences in infant recognition memory: Implications for information processing. *Developmental Psychology,* **18,** 704-713.

Shepard, R. N. (1962). The analysis of proximities: Multidimensional scaling with an unknown distance function. II. *Psychometrika,* **27,** 219-246.

Shepp, B. E. (1978). From perceived similarity to dimensional structure: A new hypothesis about perceptual development. In E. Rosch & B. B. Lloyd (Eds.), *Cognition and categorization* (pp. 135-167). Hillsdale, NJ: Erlbaum.

Shepp, B. E. (1983). The analyzability of multidimensional objects: Some constraints on perceived structure, the development of perceived structure, and attention. In T. J. Tighe & B. E. Shepp (Eds.), *Perception, cognition, and development: Interactional analyses* (pp. 39-75). Hillsdale, NJ: Erlbaum.

Shepp, B. E., & Swartz, K. B. (1976). Selective attention and the processing of integral and non-integral dimensions: A developmental study. *Journal of Experimental Child Psychology,* **22,** 73–85.

Smith, J. D., & Kemler Nelson, D. G. (1984). Overall similarity in adults' classifications: The child in all of us. *Journal of Experimental Psychology: General,* **113,** 137–159.

Smith, L. B. (1980). Development and the continuum of separability. *Perception and Psychophysics,* **28,** 1132–1145.

Smith, L. B. (1984). Young children's understanding of attributes and dimensions: A comparison of conceptual and linguistic measures. *Child Development,* **55,** 363–380.

Smith, L. B., & Kemler, D. G. (1977). Developmental trends in free classification: Evidence for a new conceptualization of perceptual development. *Journal of Experimental Child Psychology,* **24,** 279–298.

Strauss, M. S. (1979). Abstraction of prototypical information by adults and 10-month-old infants. *Journal of Experimental Psychology: Human Learning and Memory,* **5,** 618–632.

Strauss, M. S., & Curtis, L. E. (1981). Infant perception of numerosity. *Child Development,* **52,** 1146–1152.

Tighe, T. J., & Shepp, B. E. (Eds.). (1983). *Perception, cognition, and development: Interactional analyses.* Hillsdale, NJ: Erlbaum.

White, S. H. (1965). Evidence for a hierarchical arrangement of learning processes. In L. P. Lipsitt & C. C. Spiker (Eds.), *Advances in child development and behavior* (Vol. 2, pp. 187–220). New York: Academic Press.

Wolff, J. L. (1967). Concept-shift and discrimination-reversal learning in humans. *Psychological Bulletin,* **68,** 369–408.

Younger, B. A. (1984). Category segregation by 10-month-old infants. *Infant Behavior and Development,* **7,** 392 (Abstract).

Younger, B. A., & Cohen, L. B. (1983a). *Developmental change in infants' perception of correlated attributes.* Paper presented at the Biennial meeting of the Society for Research in Child Development, Detroit, April.

Younger, B. A., & Cohen, L. B. (1983b). *Infants' acquisition of correlated vs. uncorrelated categories.* Paper presented at the Biennial meeting of the Society for Research in Child Development, Detroit, April.

Zeaman, D., & House, B. J. (1963). The role of attention in retardate discrimination learning. In N. R. Ellis (Ed.), *Handbook of mental deficiency* (pp. 159–223). New York: McGraw-Hill.

EFFECTS OF THE KNOWLEDGE BASE ON CHILDREN'S MEMORY STRATEGIES

Peter A. Ornstein

DEPARTMENT OF PSYCHOLOGY
UNIVERSITY OF NORTH CAROLINA AT CHAPEL HILL
CHAPEL HILL, NORTH CAROLINA

Mary J. Naus

DEPARTMENT OF PSYCHOLOGY
UNIVERSITY OF HOUSTON—UNIVERSITY PARK
HOUSTON, TEXAS

I. Introduction

Two themes characterize current approaches to the development of memory in children. The first concerns the operation of children's mnemonic strategies (see, e.g., Hagen, Jongeward, & Kail, 1975; Ornstein & Corsale, 1979a; Naus & Ornstein, 1983). Many researchers have suggested that the growth of children's memory strategies during the elementary school years is related directly to improvements in their ability to commit material to

ADVANCES IN CHILD DEVELOPMENT
AND BEHAVIOR, VOL. 19

memory. A second emphasis in the literature focuses on the role of the permanent memory system or "knowledge base" in influencing the acquisition, retention, and retrieval of information (e.g., Chi, 1978, 1985; Naus & Ornstein, 1983). During the same time that young children are acquiring the use of more efficient memory strategies, they are also learning more about the world around them and about their native language, and this increased knowledge has also been shown to correspond to age-related changes in memory performance.

These themes of the development of strategies and the development of the knowledge base have been treated as independent components of memory development. However, as Naus and Ornstein (1983) have suggested, they are interactive and must be studied concurrently in order to understand the developing memory system. Here it is argued that neither factor alone is adequate to explain age-related changes in memory; rather, it is only by means of an extensive analysis of the interrelationships between strategies and underlying knowledge that some of the inconsistencies and unanswered questions concerning each literature can be resolved.

Given that to date the strategy and knowledge base literatures have primarily been considered separately, Sections II and III of this article deal with selected reviews in these areas. Reviews of these literatures are available elsewhere (e.g., Chi, 1985; Ornstein & Corsale, 1979a), and therefore the treatment here is selective, designed to highlight the major empirical findings and to articulate yet unanswered questions. These overviews provide the background for Section IV in which research that approaches the linkage between the knowledge base and memory strategies is presented. Specifically, different ways by which the changing knowledge base can influence the utilization of memory strategies are defined and illustrated.

To facilitate a consideration of these issues, a classification system is used that differentiates between the effects of the knowledge system upon current performance, on the one hand, and more long-term developmental consequences, on the other. Current performance effects are considered to reflect the structure of the knowledge base and the relative ease of gaining access to stored information. In contrast, long-term effects reflect the influences of changes in the system and practice in remembering on the refinement in memory strategies. It is hoped that a treatment of the literature in terms of this classification system will encourage a truly developmental and more comprehensive analysis of children's memory.

II. Memory Strategies

A substantial research literature attests to the importance of subject-controlled processes in the memory performance of both adults and children (e.g., Puff, 1979; Tulving & Donaldson, 1972). A somewhat smaller, but still good-sized literature demonstrates convincingly that during the elementary school years, children become increasingly proficient at a number of important mnemonic strategies for storing and retrieving information. Although little is yet known about the emergence, development, and generalization of these strategies (Ornstein & Naus, 1978; Ornstein, Baker-Ward, & Naus, 1985a), their implementation seems to be strongly related to recall success. Thus, for example, substantial developmental changes appear in the rehearsal and organizational techniques children employ when they are asked to memorize verbal materials; in turn, these changes are responsible for much of the recall improvement typically observed. Age differences in strategy use are summarized briefly in Section II,A, whereas current problems and unsettled issues are indicated in Section II,B.

A. DEVELOPMENTAL TRENDS IN STRATEGY USE

. The use of paradigms to "externalize" memory strategies so that they can be examined systematically—e.g., overt rehearsal procedures (Rundus & Atkinson, 1970) and sort/recall tasks (Liberty & Ornstein, 1973; Mandler, 1967)—has resulted in a composite picture of the transition of children from relatively "passive" to relatively "active" memorizers. Consider, for example, the operation of rehearsal strategies, as illustrated in an experiment by Ornstein, Naus, and Liberty (1975, experiment I). Children between 9 and 14 years of age were presented a list of 18 unrelated words to recall in an overt-rehearsal free-recall task. The research participants were asked to rehearse aloud as each list item was presented, and then to recall the words in any order.

As shown in Fig. 1A, recall performance improved with age, with major developmental differences in the recall of items from the initial serial po-

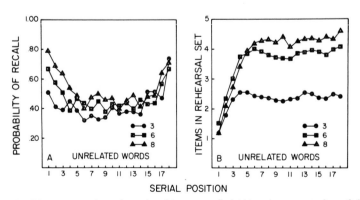

Fig. 1. Mean proportion of unrelated items recalled (A) and mean number of different items in each rehearsal set (B), as a function of serial position for 9, 12, and 14 year olds (third, sixth, and eighth graders). (From Ornstein et al., 1975.)

sitions of the list. Paralleling these changes in recall were corresponding differences in children's rehearsal techniques. An examination of the rehearsal "sets," the rehearsal associated with the presentation of each new item, revealed that the 9 year olds tended to repeat each stimulus item alone as it was presented, or in combination with one other item. In contrast, the older children showed a greater tendency to rehearse each newly presented word along with several previously presented items. Data such as these for two typical research participants can be seen in Table I; clearly, the older child has intermixed several different items in rehearsal in an active fashion, whereas the younger child has not done so and is rehearsing passively. Average data for all of the subjects in this experiment are displayed in Fig. 1B, indicating substantial age changes in the number of different or unique items that are rehearsed together.

A great deal of evidence is now available (Ornstein & Naus, 1978; Naus & Ornstein, 1983) to indicate that these changes in degree of rehearsal activity are related directly to developmental improvements in recall, especially with relatively unstructured materials. Research on children's organizational strategies (e.g., Lange, 1978; Moely, 1977; Ornstein & Corsale, 1979b) is quite compatible with the rehearsal literature, suggesting that young children's organizing is less systematic than that of older children, when recall is explicitly requested. Central to these demonstrations of the operation of memory strategies are training experiments indicating that the memory performance of children can be facilitated by the provision of instructions concerning strategy deployment (e.g., Belmont & Butterfield, 1977; Butterfield, Siladi, & Belmont, 1980; Borkowski & Cavanaugh, 1979). The likelihood of success in strategy training is increased when children (1) are motivated and provided a rationale for the benefits of strategy deployment (Cavanaugh & Borkowski, 1979; Paris & Cross, 1983; Paris, Newman, & McVey, 1982), (2) are given feedback concerning the success of their recall efforts as a function of strategy use (Pressley, Borkowski, & O'Sullivan,

TABLE I
Typical Rehearsal Protocols[a]

Word presented	Rehearsal sets	
	14 year old	9 year old
1. Yard	Yard, yard, yard	Yard, yard, yard, yard, yard
2. Cat	Cat, yard, yard, cat	Cat, cat, cat, cat, yard
3. Man	Man, cat, yard, man, yard, cat	Man, man, man, man, man
4. Desk	Desk, man, yard, cat, man, desk, cat, yard	Desk, desk, desk, desk

[a] From Ornstein *et al.* (1975, experiment I).

1985; Pressley, Levin, & Ghatala, 1984), and (3) are given information processing supports such as visual access to the to-be-remembered items (Ornstein, Medlin, Stone, & Naus, 1985b).

The importance of strategies is further seen in the fact that major age changes in memory performance are observed most clearly in tasks that call for the use of such mnemonic techniques. In situations in which strategies cannot be systematically applied, as for example in recognition tasks (Perlmutter & Lange, 1978), only minimal age changes are found in memory performance. Further, when incidental learning situations are examined, age differences in memory performance are often minimal (Brown, 1975; Naus & Halasz, 1979; Ornstein & Corsale, 1979a).

These findings demonstrate that young children often have information available to them that could be used, but typically is not, for the formation of task-appropriate strategies. Although the available knowledge of young children is clearly incomplete relative to that of older children and adults, nonetheless their performance often is characterized by this discrepancy between available knowledge and the strategic use of that knowledge. Indeed, children's mnemonic activities vary—to a much greater extent than is true with adults—as a function of the task setting. Their failure to utilize available knowledge may result from an incomplete understanding of the usefulness of that knowledge (see, e.g., Cavanaugh & Perlmutter, 1982; Flavell & Wellman, 1977). Motivational and other factors may also contribute to the varied performance observed with children who show more "sophisticated" levels of functioning in informal play contexts as opposed to formalized laboratory situations (e.g., Baker-Ward, Ornstein, & Holden, 1984; Istomina, 1975). Further, as will be seen in Section III, children's use of mnemonic techniques may vary as a function of their knowledge of the stimulus materials. For discussions of these issues, see papers by Naus and Ornstein (1983), Ornstein *et al.* (1985a), Ornstein and Corsale (1979a,b), and Paris (1978a).

B. DEFINITIONAL ISSUES AND UNANSWERED QUESTIONS

In spite of the fact that there has been extensive work over the past 15 years that has documented and analyzed the direct relationship between age-related changes in memory strategies and performance, a number of important questions about the development of strategy use and its role in memory development remain unanswered (see Naus & Ornstein, 1983; Ornstein *et al.,* 1985a; Ornstein & Naus, 1979). First, current investigations of strategy development contribute little to an understanding of the mechanisms that might underlie developmental changes in memory techniques. What factors in the world of the child influence the emergence of memory techniques and govern the acquisition of skill and efficiency in their deployment? Second, although it has been demonstrated that strategy use in young children appears to be task specific, very little is known about the conditions that influence the generalization of these techniques over the elementary school years. Third, as research has accumulated, it has become quite apparent that the precise definition of strategy is unclear, particularly in terms of how these memory processes relate to the more automatic, nonattentional aspects of memory processing (see Hasher & Zacks, 1979; Naus & Halasz, 1979; Schneider & Shiffrin, 1977; Shiffrin & Schneider, 1977). In this article (following Ornstein et al., 1985a; see also Ornstein & Naus, 1978; Naus & Ornstein, 1983), strategies are viewed as subject-controlled activities that are employed in the service of a memory goal. Further, there are subcomponents of strategies that can be automated to varying degrees, and with increases in practice an entire study/remember sequence may become routinized to some extent.

It seems likely that the eventual resolution of these issues requires a consideration of strategies in the broader context of the child's changing general knowledge of the world. The influence of the child's knowledge on memory performance is discussed next in Section III, and the relationship between knowledge and strategies is treated in Section IV.

III. The Knowledge Base

Much research has stressed the effects of an individual's prior knowledge on the processing and acquisition of information. For example, central to information-processing accounts of cognition (e.g., Anderson, 1976; Collins & Loftus, 1975; Norman & Bobrow, 1976) and cognitive development (Kail & Bisanz, 1982; Klahr & Siegler, 1979; Siegler, 1983) are issues of the representation of information in a knowledge base and the processes that serve to operate on that information. Admittedly, there are differences among various information-processing treatments of knowledge representation, and serious questions have been raised about the usefulness of the information-processing approach (e.g., Brown, 1979, 1982; Bransford, Nitsch, & Franks, 1977). Nonetheless, there is general agreement that what is known already is of major importance for what can be known (see, e.g., Brown, 1975; Brown, Bransford, Ferrara, & Campione, 1983; Chi, 1978; Norman, Rumelhart, & the LNR Research Group, 1975). Perhaps the most compelling illustrations of this principle can be seen in the classic (Bartlett, 1932; Binet & Henri, 1894) and recent (Bransford & Franks, 1972; Cofer, 1973; Jenkins, 1974; Paris, 1975, 1978b) demonstrations of constructive activities in the memory performance of both children and adults. Additional indications of the effects of prior knowledge are seen in studies of experts and novices in particular subject matter domains (e.g., Chase & Simon, 1973).

Given that the contents and structure of information available in a knowledge system change markedly with age, it is of particular importance to examine developmentally the linkage between knowledge and memory performance. Indeed, it seems reasonable to assume that age-related differences in what is known about language and specific bodies of knowledge contribute to corresponding changes in remembering new information. Thus, not only does an older child have available more task-appropriate strategies, but, in addition, there is a more articulated permanent memory system through which incoming information can be interpreted, stored, and retrieved. Recently, there have been a number of demonstrations of the influence of the growing knowledge base on age-related changes in memory performance. This literature is summarized briefly in the next section, followed by a discussion of problems and future directions.

A. KNOWLEDGE AND MEMORY DEVELOPMENT

Major credit for calling attention to the role of prior knowledge in children's memory must be given to Chi (1977, 1978). In an initial experiment, Chi (1977) determined that both strategy and knowledge base differences contributed to age changes in memory span. She found that under conditions in which photographic stimuli were equally familiar for children (e.g., pictures of their classmates) and adults (e.g., pictures of colleagues), and in which adults were prevented from utilizing strategies, age differences in memory span were almost completely eliminated. The operation of the knowledge base was probed more deeply in a follow-up study in which Chi (1978) asked subjects of different ages to remember the position of chess pieces in modified memory span tasks. In this experiment, Chi varied the degree of knowledge about the game of chess by comparing expert chess players with novices who had a working knowledge of the game. A critical manipulation was the knowledge variable, in that the novice players were adults and the experts were children who averaged 10 years of age. Performance was tested in two different ways, first by providing one trial to determine how many chess pieces could be replaced correctly in their positions, and second, by giving feedback and continuing the task for as many trials as were necessary to reconstruct the layout on the chessboard.

Chi (1978) found that with both measures of performance, the child experts demonstrated better memory for chess positions than the adult novices, thus providing strong support for the view that knowledge is of considerable importance in determining memory performance. As a control, to demonstrate that these effects were actually mediated by knowledge of chess and not by intelligence or some other variable, Chi presented her subjects with comparable memory tasks involving sets of digits. As expected, the results of these tasks were the reverse of those with the chess materials. Figure 2 presents an illustration of these findings for both the chess and digit tasks.

Dramatic reversals of age-related improvements in cognitive performance are always very striking, and Chi's (1978) data generated considerable interest. Another striking set of findings was reported by Piaget and Inhelder (1973). In fact, Piaget and Inhelder made one of the strongest statements in support of the close linkage between knowledge and memory, by suggesting that memory performance depends on the child's operative level, defined in the context of the Piagetian framework. They argued that a child's ability to remember is influenced by changes in cognitive structures, even to the extent that long-term retention of some materials may actually improve as a function of developmental changes in the understanding of certain fundamental concepts. Piaget and Inhelder presented a number of

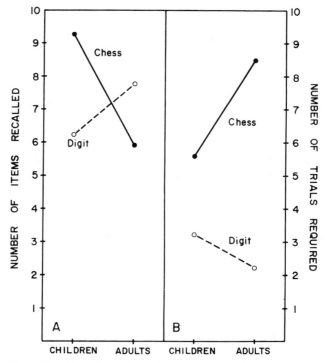

Fig. 2.   Immediate (A) and repeated (B) recall of chess stimuli and digits for adults and children. (From Chi, 1978.)

different confirmations of this thesis, the most popular of which was the assertion that 5-year-old children's recall of arrays of sticks of increasing size improved over a 6-month period, presumably because of developments in the children's concepts (schemata) of seriation. The novelty of the Piagetian argument—actual improvement, and not deterioration of memory during a long interval—resulted in a great deal of interest.

In addition to the Chi (1978) and Piaget and Inhelder (1973) studies of nonverbal memory, several other investigations of children's memory have been designed to study the linkage between the knowledge base and remembering. By manipulating the characteristics of the stimulus materials presented to children, Richman and colleagues (Chechile & Richman, 1982; Richman, Nida, & Pittman, 1976), Lindberg (1980), and Bjorklund and Thompson (1983), among others, were able to alter recall patterns substantially. Arguing that the recall of older children may be facilitated because they have a more elaborated set of associations to verbal stimuli than younger children, Richman *et al.* (1976) and Chechile and Richman (1982) varied the meaningfulness of the stimulus words. Familiar three-letter words that varied as a function of the number of associations they elicited, that is, items that differed in meaningfulness (Noble, 1953), were used as stimuli. The results indicated typical age differences in recall when a common stimulus list was employed, with the meaningfulness values of the words varying positively with age. In contrast, with words selected such that meaningfulness was equated across age (using different stimulus lists), age differences in recall were minimized.

In Lindberg's (1980) study, 9-year-old children and adults were compared on the recall of words drawn from "standard" taxonomic categories (Battig & Montague, 1969) and words taken from children's everyday experiences. The latter set of words included items in the "categories" of current children's television programs, the names of school teachers, the titles of books in standardized reading curricula, etc. As expected, the children recalled child-centered words much better than the taxonomic materials used in most previous memory investigations. Performance of the adults, in contrast, was better with the taxonomic categories than with the children's materials.

Bjorklund and Thompson (1983) presented 5, 8, and 11 year olds a cued-recall task involving both typical and atypical category exemplars, as determined by both child and adult norms. As might be expected, overall recall of the lists derived from the children's normative data was superior to that of lists based on adult norms. Moreover, recall of typical category exemplars was superior to that of atypical instances, and this finding held with the lists derived from both sets of norms. Bjorklund and Thompson (1983) suggested that the typicality effect (Rosch, 1973, 1975) with the child-derived materials reflected differences in the degree to which the exemplars resemble their category prototypes. In contrast, they felt that performance with the adult-derived lists reflected lack of awareness of the categories to which the atypical items belonged. The implications of these findings are consistent with those of Richman (Chechile & Richman, 1982; Richman *et al.*, 1976) and Lindberg (1980) studies, namely, that the degree of knowledge children possess in reference to the to-be-remembered items affects their memory performance.

More recent work by Chi and colleagues (Chi, 1981, 1985; Chi & Koeske, 1983) has focused on case studies of particular domains of knowledge. Chi and Koeske (1983), for example, generated detailed representations of a single 5 year old's knowledge of the dinosaur domain, and related these structures to recall performance. Although this child was an expert in dinosaurs, it was possible to examine subsets of better known and lesser known dinosaurs. Production protocols were used to map semantic networks, including the relevant concept nodes and their connecting links, for the two subsets. The two mappings were evaluated in terms of the number of links, strengths of these links, and the cohesiveness of the networks, and clear differences were found between the better known and lesser known subsets. Moreover, the better known (and structured) set of dinosaurs was found to be more easily remembered and retained over the course of a year. This work suggests a clear relationship between the details of the information in the knowledge base and memory performance.

B. PROBLEMS AND PROSPECTS

The research described above provides an outline of the influence of prior knowledge on children's memory performance. Nonetheless, interpretation of this influence is limited in at least two fundamental ways, by the absence of an in-depth analysis of "knowledge" and a corresponding consideration of the mechanisms by which the knowledge base mediates memory performance. To move beyond the demonstration level, it is necessary to define knowledge more specifically, and to chart its development in a systematic fashion. Concurrently, serious consideration of the mediational question is required.

In contrast to studies of semantic development (e.g., Anglin, 1977; Nelson, 1978; see also, Bjorklund, 1985) that have provided general descriptions of age-related changes in the understanding of words and concepts, little is known about children's knowledge of content domains. It is necessary to gather detailed data concerning just what children of different ages know about selected areas of knowledge. Hayes' (1984; Hayes & Ornstein, 1985) examination of the understanding of 3, 5, and 7 year olds concerning the common domains of animals and cartoon characters represents an example of the type of information that needs to be obtained in a variety of areas. In addition, it is necessary to deal seriously with the issue of how to characterize children's knowledge of these domains. Within each area, it would be useful to specify existing concepts in terms of nodes of varying types, interconnecting links (type, number, strength), cohesiveness of the overall network, and processes of access; moreover, this analysis must be carried out developmentally. It is thus essential to go beyond the characterization of the knowledge of single subjects at a single point in time to the generation of representations across a variety of ages and domains.

The documentation of the details of the structure of the knowledge base in and of itself is not sufficient to explain age-related differences in remembering. In addition, the mechanisms by which these differences in the knowledge base operate to influence memory performance must be specified. At present, the bulk of the studies in the area are correlational in nature. For example, an association between expert/novice status in a particular area and differential patterns of recall of this material does not constitute an explanation of how such differences arise. The critical issue is that of how experts are able to use their better structured knowledge in the service of remembering. Similarly, it is necessary to explore why variations in stimulus properties of meaningfulness, typicality, and familiarity are associated with different levels of memory performance. Moreover, in all of these studies, but particularly in the contrast between experts and novices, the possible involvement of motivational and interest factors must be considered.

Comparable evidence concerning mediational mechanisms is necessary in studies inspired by the Piaget and Inhelder (1973) demonstrations. A general correspondence typically is obtained between children's understanding and more-or-less immediate memory of a stimulus (e.g., Liben, 1975a,b), but a detailed specification of the linkage between schemata and performance would be desirable. This is especially necessary in examining the issue of long-term improvements in memory that are predicted by Piaget and Inhelder; such improvements are not always obtained (see e.g., Liben 1975a,b), and when they are observed, they are not uniformly related to the hypothesized changes in structure (see, e.g., Maurer, Siegel, Lewis, Kristofferson, Barnes, & Levy, 1979).

Ornstein and Naus (1979; see also Naus & Ornstein, 1983) have suggested that one of the ways by which knowledge influences memory performance is via the mediation of particular memory strategies, and they have called for the joint investigation of strategies and knowledge. Although not developmental in nature, evidence consistent with this view has been reported by Voss and colleagues (Chiesi, Spilich, & Voss, 1979; Spilich, Vesonder, Chiesi & Voss, 1979) in their studies of adult experts and novices in the game of baseball. These investigators report that strategies such as chunking, information monitoring, and selective attention can be influenced by the subjects' knowledge of the area. Chi (1985) also has recently proposed that domain-specific strategies may account for the recall differences associated with network complexity in the Chi and Koeske (1983) dinosaur study. However, her proposal must be viewed as speculative in that particular strategies are neither defined nor measured. In order for the mediation-by-strategy position to be useful, the relevant strategies must be defined and related precisely to different degrees of underlying knowledge. Thus, it is necessary to examine specific deliberate memory strategies that are used by children of different ages when they are trying to remember different sets of materials, and these strategic activities need to be related to developmental changes in the contents and structure of the knowledge base.

These definitional issues are of considerable importance for understanding the influence of knowledge upon memory performance. However, even without their resolution, the interest in knowledge effects that has been generated by initial studies of the knowledge base is encouraging systematic developmental research. For example, based upon a consideration age-related changes in associative structure, and a view of automatic functioning within the knowledge base, Bjorklund and colleagues (1985; Bjorklund & Jacobs, 1984, 1985; Bjorklund & Zeman, 1982, 1983) have argued that prior to adolescence, children's organizational activities cannot be viewed as strategies. They suggest that the effects of the knowledge base upon young children's memory performance are involuntary or automatic (Hasher & Zacks, 1979; Naus & Halasz, 1979; Schneider & Shiffrin, 1977; Shiffrin & Schneider, 1977), requiring little of the child's attention or planful behaviors. Age-related changes in memory performance are seen as reflecting directly corresponding differences in the facility with which relations in semantic memory are activated by children of different ages. With increasing language experience, semantic categories are proposed to become better established, thus increasing the ease with which relations among items within a category are automatically activated. This increased efficiency in the processing of category information results in elevated levels of organization in memory that are viewed as automatic activations of relations within a well-established conceptual system. This automatization is viewed as freeing up additional processing capacity for other cognitive activities.

Regardless of whether one agrees with Bjorklund's (1985) interpretation of the organizational literature, his arguments place the knowledge base in a central position in the explanation of age-related changes in strategy use. In Section IV, literature that can be viewed as addressing the interaction of knowledge and memory strategies is presented. Studies of children's rehearsal and organizational strategies are examined to demonstrate the manner in which the current state of the knowledge base may affect the utilization of a deliberate mnemonic technique. Bjorklund's (1985) position is discussed more fully in Section IV,B.

IV. Effects of the Knowledge Base on Memory Strategies

In this section, particular attention is paid to the potential dependence of memory strategies upon the current status of information available in the knowledge base. The influence of the knowledge base is discussed both in terms of immediate or current performance, as a child attempts to remember something, as well as in terms of the long-term consequences of experiences that involve remembering.

A. CONCURRENT PERFORMANCE EFFECTS

This section addresses the manner in which the information available in a child's knowledge base can affect his or her deliberate attempts at remembering at any given point in time. In order to consider these influences, it may be helpful to differentiate clearly between two possible features of knowledge: the contents of the knowledge base and the ease with which information is retrieved from this system. These two aspects of the knowledge base are implicit in Chi and Koeske's (1983) account of a young child's knowledge concerning dinosaurs and in Chi's (1985) speculation concerning the manner in which the system may change with age and experience. It should be indicated, however, that the current literature does not routinely permit a ready differentiation between effects that may be due to the contents of the system, i.e., the number and type of interconnections, and the speed of gaining access to stored information.

Because the addition of interconnections in the system may shorten the retrieval process, it is difficult to examine the contents of the knowledge base without a concurrent consideration of questions of access. This can be illustrated by a brief reference to studies that examine the consequences of age-related changes in category structure. For example, it is well established that there is a developmental progression in the utilization of superordinate information (see, e.g., Bjorklund, 1985, for an overview). As a general rule, with increases in age children make use of superordinate categorical relationships in an increasing variety of tasks. However, this type of outcome can be interpreted either in terms of the absence of superordinate concepts in the young child, or in terms of a slower, less efficient process of gaining access to this information, or both.

These problems notwithstanding, an attempt is made here to categorize existing research in terms of the contents vs access distinction, while recognizing that the placement of individual studies within this dichotomy may be somewhat arbitrary. It is hoped, however, that such a differentiation may prompt additional research in the area. In principle, it should be possible to establish conditions that would highlight one or the other of these aspects of system architecture. This goal might be most readily accomplished by examining developmental changes in children's knowledge of particular subject matter domains. For example, once children acquire an initial understanding of fundamental principles of chemistry, they may become increasingly facile in accessing information from their limited knowledge base prior to learning advanced aspects of the subject.

1. Changes in Knowledge Base Contents

In this section, the influence of age- and experience-related changes in the information available in the knowledge base is considered. These changes can be in the number or amount of interitem associations, as well as in the types of relationships that are available. Three areas of knowledge change and use are discussed: the addition of categorical information, increases in the number of associations that can be made to individual elements, and retrieving from highly articulated domains.

a. Associative to Hierarchical Changes.   Studies involving a variety of different tasks suggest that hierarchical (i.e., superordinate) conceptual relations develop during the course of the preschool and elementary school years. Interitem connections among category exemplars seem to precede the development of strong subordinate–superordinate relationships. However, there is debate as to when hierarchical organization in the knowledge system first emerges.

Using a priming task in which children named pairs of pictures, McCauley, Weil, and Sperber (1976) demonstrated that associative priming facilitated the performance of both 5 and 7 year olds; in contrast, semantic (i.e., categorical) priming only facilitated the naming of the 7 year olds. The implication of these data, consistent with findings from the traditional class inclusion literature (e.g., Inhelder & Piaget, 1964), is that children below the age of 7 do not organize conceptual information in a hierarchical fashion. In contrast, investigators working with cued-recall tasks (e.g., Whitney & Kunen, 1983) have found some evidence for "modest" amounts of hierarchical organization by 5 year olds; however, age-related changes in the degree of such organization are evident. It would appear that variations in the task and stimulus materials clearly affect judgments of the categorical sophistication of young children. Nonetheless, there is a general trend toward increased use of categorical relationships with increases in age, a progression that is demonstrated nicely in a study by Bjorklund and de Marchena (1984). These investigators found that when presented materials that could be organized on either associative or categorical bases, the formation of groups based on category relations increased over the elementary school years.

Given findings of this kind, it might be expected that the basis of organization utilized in memory tasks such as free recall would vary as a function of the relative strengths of interitem (i.e., category example-to-category example) and example-to-category label links. In fact, some investigators have argued that much of the category clustering that is observed in the recall of preadolescent children primarily reflects strong associative connections among category exemplars in the knowledge base. For example, Lange (1973) noted that previous demonstrations of clustering in children of preschool and elementary school age (e.g., Rossi, 1964; Rossi & Rossi, 1965) involved the recall of stimulus materials that were both categorically and associatively related. When he presented 6 and 11 year olds categorical items that were not strongly interconnected, no evidence for above-chance clustering was obtained; only the 15 year olds in Lange's sample demonstrated a significant degree of clustering. These findings led Lange (1973, 1978) to suggest that much of what had been viewed previously as deliberate clustering in children's recall could perhaps more parsimoniously be interpreted as the more-or-less automatic activation of strong interitem associations in memory.

Recently, a number of investigators have provided additional evidence that is consistent with Lange's basic contention of the role of strong interitem connections in recall. Frankel and Rollins (1982) examined the clustering of 6 year olds and adults who were presented lists containing four categories, each with six exemplars. Focusing on the size of the category clusters present in recall, Frankel and Rollins (1982) reported differences in both the length and number of intracategory repetitions. The recall of the children was characterized by isolated category instances and pairs of category members. In contrast, the adults tended to recall strings containing four, five, and even six exemplars. This pattern of results is consistent with the view that the recall of the adults was mediated by categorical organization, whereas that of the 6 year olds reflected interitem associative linkages. Unfortunately, more definitive statements concerning Lange's position could not be made because the lists that were used by Frankel and Rollins (as is typically the case in this area) were composed of category members that were strongly related to each other, as well as to the category labels. This problem, however, was alleviated in Frankel and Rollins' (1985) experiment that was designed to provide a direct test of the matter.

To examine the claim of the associative basis of young children's clustering, Frankel and Rollins (1985) generated lists that varied in terms of the strength of associations between category exemplars. In addition, to explore flexibility in use of organization, the strength of the category relationships was also varied. The combination of these two variables yielded four list conditions: High Category Relatedness/High Interitem Associations (e.g., dog, cat, horse, cow, pig, bear); High Category Relatedness/Low Interitem Associations (e.g., tiger, elephant, cow, pig, bear, dog); Low Category Relatedness/High Interitem Associations (e.g., goat, deer, buffalo, hippopotamus, monkey, lamb); and Low Category Relatedness/Low Interitem Associations (e.g., beaver, walrus, alligator, camel, squirrel, giraffe).

With these materials, Frankel and Rollins (1985) reported that 10 and 16 year olds demonstrated considerable flexibility in recall. As can be seen in Fig. 3, these children evidenced high levels of clustering under conditions of either high category relatedness or high associative strength; in contrast, low levels of clustering were observed only in the condition in which both category relatedness and interim associations were low in strength. Consistent with Lange's (1973, 1978) hypothesis, a different pattern was found with 6-year-old children. These participants showed elevated clustering only

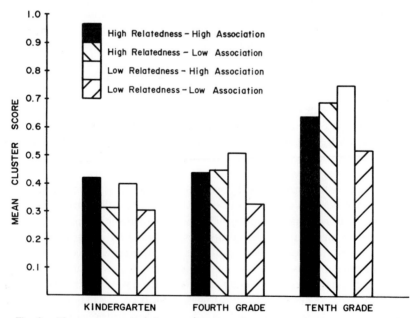

Fig. 3. Mean category clustering as a function of category relatedness and interitem association for 6, 10, and 16 year olds (kindergarten, fourth, and tenth graders). (From Frankel & Rollins, 1985.)

under conditions of high interitem strength. Thus, for 6 year olds, category relatedness was not critical for clustering. These findings were basically replicated by Schneider (1984), working with 8 and 10 year olds in Germany.

b. *Increases in Associative Connections.* With increases in age, children acquire a rich set of associations that link items in the knowledge base. Their increased understanding of lexical elements, in terms of interitem associations, nuance, etc., can easily be indexed in a crude fashion by calculating measures of meaningfulness (Noble, 1952), that is, by tabulating the numbers of associations that words can elicit. Because meaningfulness values increase with age (Emmerich, 1979), meaningfulness represents a stimulus parameter that is almost always confounded with age in developmental investigations of memory. Thus, although efforts are often made to guarantee that the youngest children in any experiment understand all of the selected stimulus materials, in most cases the stimuli are more meaningful for the older research participants. That meaningfulness values can affect recall performance has been demonstrated by Richman and colleagues (Chechile & Richman, 1982; Richman *et al.,* 1976). As discussed in Section III,A, when meaningfulness values were equated, age differences in recall performance were minimized.

If age differences in the associative structure of the knowledge base can be related to developmental changes in recall, what factors account for this relationship? One possibility is that as the knowledge base becomes more articulated, children are able to utilize the enriched associative structure in their deliberate attempts at remembering. This possibility was explored in an experiment by Tarkin, Myers, and Ornstein (1985). Children who were 8 years of age rehearsed aloud as they were presented either a high meaningfulness list or a low meaningfulness list. That is, although all of the words were known to the children, some participants rehearsed items that elicited many associations, whereas others rehearsed words that prompted fewer associations. The data indicated clear differences in rehearsal as a function of condition. The low meaningfulness group rehearsed fewer than two different items at each opportunity for rehearsal, whereas the high meaningfulness group included more than three items in each rehearsal set, a value characteristic of that of 11 and 12 year olds (cf. Ornstein & Naus, 1978).

These findings suggest that high-meaningful materials may facilitate rehearsal and recall because of an associative activation of the knowledge base. If it is assumed, as suggested above, that the words typically used in memory experiments may be functionally more meaningful for older children than for younger children, a potential mechanism underlying the developing tendency for joint rehearsal of several items may be identified. A form of associative priming may facilitate older children's retrieval of early list items and their inclusion in an active fashion in rehearsal with later list items. These data also imply that the effects of meaningfulness reported by Chechile and Richman (1982) and Richman *et al.* (1976) might have been mediated by unobserved changes in strategies.

c. Highly Articulated Domains. Conditions of expertise present unusual opportunities to examine the influence of a highly articulated knowledge base on memory performance. Within the context of specific domains of knowledge, experts and novices likely differ in much the same way as children of different ages are thought to differ vis-a-vis the stimuli typically used in experiments on memory development, i.e., in terms of the richness of connections in a semantic network and increased facility in gaining access to stored information. Articulation of the knowledge system may thus permit the expert to utilize domain information very effectively in the service of remembering. This issue is examined here in two types of investigations, one dealing with the rehearsal strategies of adult experts and novices in the game of soccer (Naus & Ornstein, 1985a), and the second describing children's organization and recall of the names of their classmates, a domain in which they are surely experts (Bjorklund & Zeman, 1982, 1983).

Naus and Ornstein (1985a) investigated whether the expected recall superiority of college-age experts in soccer, when asked to remember items concerning soccer, would be mediated by rehearsal strategies that differed from those of nonexperts. Soccer experts (defined by scores on a paper-and-pencil test, as well as by actual soccer-playing experience) and nonexperts were presented two different types of categorized lists to remember. One set of materials was composed of categorized soccer words (e.g., words describing the types of moves, plays, kicks, etc., that were possible in the game); the second set was constructed from typical taxonomic categories (e.g., Battig & Montague, 1969). For both lists, the items from each category were presented in a random, nonblocked fashion, and spontaneous overt rehearsal was recorded.

The non-soccer list served as a control condition and, as expected, with these materials the experts and novices did not differ in their rehearsal, trials to learn the items to a criterion, immediate recall, or 1-week delayed recall. However, differences in both rehearsal and recall were observed with the soccer list. Experts rehearsed in a more organized fashion than did the novices, by grouping together in their rehearsal more items from each category. In addition, the soccer experts recalled more on the immediate and delayed recall tests, and reached criterion in fewer trials. Recall data for the immediate test, as well as the organization-in-rehearsal findings, are presented in Fig. 4.

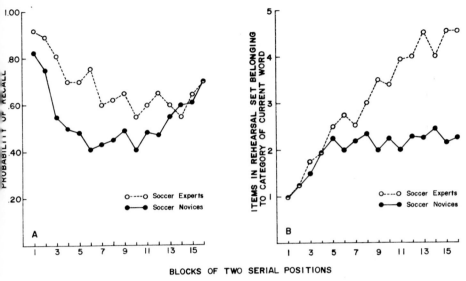

BLOCKS OF TWO SERIAL POSITIONS

Fig. 4. Mean proportion of "soccer" words recalled (A) and mean number of categorical items rehearsed together (B) by adult experts and novices, as a function of serial position. (From Naus & Ornstein, 1985a.)

These results suggest that extended familiarity with to-be-remembered materials may be critical for maximally efficient execution of active rehearsal techniques. The implication for an understanding of development is that age changes in knowledge about stimulus materials quite likely contribute to observed developmental differences in rehearsal technique. Moreover, Naus and Ornstein's (1985a) data on soccer experts, in combination with the findings of Tarkin *et al.* (1985) concerning children's rehearsal of high- and low-meaningfulness lists, raise the possibility that previous demonstrations of knowledge base effects (see Section III) may involve the operation of undetected memory strategies.

Another example of the effects of expert status on memory performance is seen in Bjorklund and Zeman's (1982, 1983) experiments on children's recall of their classmates. Children 7, 9, and 11 years of age were given two recall tasks, one involving recall of their classmates, and the other calling for recall of a set of taxonomic materials. Performance in the classmate recall task contrasted markedly with that in the category recall task in which typical age-related trends in both recall and clustering were observed. Recall of classmates was uniformly high and did not differ across age. Clustering, examined in terms of classroom groupings (e.g., assigned reading groups, seating patterns) and personal characteristics (e.g., race and sex of the children), was also very high and equivalent across the age range examined.

Clearly, the children who participated in Bjorklund and Zeman's (1982, 1983) research approached the classmate recall task as experts. When asked to recall from the very familiar and salient domain of friends-in-class, these children showed high levels of organization. They were able to utilize various dimensions inherent in this set of stimulus materials to perform in a fashion that contrasted markedly with their handling of the more traditional taxonomic materials. This contrast has led Bjorklund (1985; Bjorklund & Zeman, 1982, 1983) to suggest that the children's recall and organization was not mediated by deliberate memory strategies. Based in part on the results of metamemory analyses in which the children could not identify the bases of organization that were inherent in their own recall protocols, Bjorklund suggests that classmate recall is governed by an automatic retrieval of highly associated information from the knowledge base (cf. Lange, 1973, 1978).

2. Changes in the Accessibility of Information

As indicated in the introduction to Section IV,A, it can be difficult at times to distinguish between situations in which information may not be available in the knowledge base and cases in which available information cannot be easily accessed or retrieved. Some of the studies discussed above (especially in Sections IV,A,1,a and b) could be examined under the heading of possible changes in the accessibility of stored information. In fact, Bjorklund (1985; Bjorklund & de Marchena, 1984) discusses the age-related changes in the tendency to use hierarchical relations in terms of changes in the increased likelihood or ease of gaining access to these relations in the knowledge system. Nonetheless, from the point of view adopted here, these experiments seem best understood as examples of situations in which new information is being acquired.

In contrast, the experiments discussed in the following section provide clear examples of variations in the ease of gaining access to information that is available in the knowledge base. Two types of demonstration experiments are discussed here. First, differences in the activation of category and relational information are related to corresponding differences in strategy implementation. Then, some characteristics of memory tasks that can influence the likelihood of children's detection or recognition of category relationships are presented.

a. Ease of Activation of Information. Rabinowitz (1984) has examined this issue directly by focusing on age-related changes in the accessibility of available knowledge and in the consequent use of this knowledge for strategic purposes. Noting that production deficiencies (Flavell, 1970; Paris,

1978a) are typically discussed in terms of children's failures to utilize information that is available in memory, Rabinowitz (1984) suggested that many of these differences (as well as alternate preferences for the use of organizational dimensions; see, e.g., Worden, 1976) can be interpreted in terms of differential access to available information. Drawing upon research by Rosch and colleagues (e.g., Rosch, 1973; Mervis, Catlin, & Rosch, 1976) on category structure and typicality (see also Bjorklund, Thompson, & Ornstein, 1983), Rabinowitz (1984) suggested that children of different ages may differ in the accessibility of categorical information.

To examine these issues, Rabinowitz varied the representativeness of category exemplars employed in a free-recall task, as well as conditions that might affect the obviousness of the category structure. Representativeness was determined on the basis of the rankings of exemplars in the Posnansky (1978) category norms, with two levels (high and medium) being selected. Obviousness of the structure was varied by contrasting a standard free-recall condition with two other presentation conditions. In a repetition condition, designed to minimize attention to the list categories, single-item rehearsal of the currently presented item was requested; in contrast, in a category condition, designed to facilitate detection and use of categorical information, the items were presented in a blocked fashion and the participants were informed about the category structure as well as the beneficial consequences of grouping according to category.

Arguing that accessibility of categorical information determines its use in the context of recall, Rabinowitz (1984) predicted that performance with the high-representative list would be superior to that with the low-representative list, and that this should be enhanced under the category conditions of presentation. Performance under the standard and repetition conditions was not expected to differ. Data consistent with these predictions were obtained with the 8 and 11 year olds who participated in the experiment. Most importantly, the ability to take advantage of the category presentation condition was greater with the high-representative list than the low-representative list. Additional analyses suggested that this facilitation reflected greater efficiency with category entry and retrieval (i.e., use of category structure) under these materials.

Another example of variations in accessibility of categorical relations is reported in an experiment by Bjorklund and Ornstein (1976). Children 5 and 10 years old were asked to recall each of three sets of materials that varied according to the saliency of an available list structure. In contrast to a baseline condition with unrelated items, two other conditions called for the recall of categorical materials. These categorical materials, however, differed in terms of the representativeness of the category exemplars. On the basis of children's judgments of category typicality (see Bjorklund *et al.*, 1983), lists of high typical and low typical exemplars were generated. These were presented to the children either randomly or according to a blocked pattern that emphasized category relationships.

For the 10 year olds, recall of the category-typical items was superior to the recall of the category-atypical items which, in turn, was superior to the recall of the unrelated items. In contrast, the 5 year olds evidenced superior recall of the typical items (especially under conditions of blocked presentation), but did not differentiate between the atypical and unrelated items. Most importantly, and relevant to the task conditions discussed in Section IV,A,2,b, the use of category relationships in recall was clearly influenced by both category typicality and blocked presentation. Thus, in addition to age, clustering of the typical items was greater than that of atypical items, and the clustering of the blocked items was superior to that of randomly presented information. Access to categorical information was facilitated for the high-typicality materials, and blocked presentation served to underscore the common theme linking the items.

A consideration of differences in accessibility of information in the knowledge base may help to account for different patterns of sorting that have been obtained in experiments that have varied the nature of grouping instructions and the materials (Corsale, 1978; Corsale & Ornstein, 1980). In the initial study, Corsale and Ornstein (1980) gave 8 and 12 year olds several trials on a sorting task with relatively unrelated materials prior to a test of recall. The children were asked either to form groups that would help them to remember the words, or to sort on the basis of meaning. The 12 year olds sorted identically under these "remember" instructions and "sort-for-recall" instructions; under both conditions, the grouping pattern revealed the children's sensitivity to the underlying semantic relations that could interconnect the items. In contrast, the sorting patterns of the 8 year olds differed as a function of instructional condition. Consistent with previous experiments (e.g., Bjorklund, Ornstein, & Haig, 1977), the 8 year olds asked to group items in preparation for recall sorted in a seemingly random fashion; however, those who were asked to group on the basis of meaning sorted in an organized fashion similar to that of the 12 year olds. The recall data indicated that recall performance was always a function of the actual sorting pattern, regardless of intent to remember. Thus, 8 year olds instructed to form meaningful groups remembered more on the incidental test of memory than those asked to sort in preparation for recall.

The 8 year olds studied by Corsale and Ornstein (1980) seemed to have difficulties in responding in a strategic manner when given instructions to remember, but their performance with the meaning-based instructions suggested that they had the semantic information available in the knowledge base that would be necessary to group items in a highly organized fashion.

Consistent with Rabinowitz's (1984) analysis of production deficiencies (see Flavell, 1970; Ornstein & Corsale, 1979a; Paris, 1979a), it is possible to suggest that the recall instructions did not lead these children to gain access to semantic properties that might provide a basis for organizing the unrelated stimulus items. However, it seems likely that recall instructions might result in the use of active organizational efforts when 8 year olds are presented highly salient stimulus materials. The strong interitem associative properties of the stimuli likely elicit organizational activities in an automatic or obligatory fashion, even under instructions to remember (see Ornstein et al., 1985a).

Confirmation of this viewpoint is seen in Corsale's (1978) demonstration that when presented taxonomic stimulus materials in a sort/recall task, 8 year olds sorted spontaneously in a categorical fashion, even under instructions to remember. In a task similar to that used by Corsale and Ornstein (1980), Corsale (1978) asked 5 and 8 year olds to group items that "go together" or to group in preparation for recall. The list items were drawn from taxonomic categories, but the salience of the category exemplars was varied. One-half of the participants were given typical examples of the categories, whereas the others received atypical instances. With the typical category exemplars, the 8 year olds sorted in an organized fashion, forming taxonomic groupings under instructions to sort on the basis of meaning as well as instructions to generate groups that would facilitate remembering. Comparable patterns were observed when the 8 year olds were presented the atypical materials, although there was somewhat greater variability in the sorts under the recall instructions condition. In contrast, the 5 year olds sorted in a taxonomic fashion only with the highly salient list under instructions to group on the basis of meaning. The tendency of 8 year old children to use a task-appropriate strategy (i.e., the formation of semantically related groups when not explicitly instructed to do so) contrasts markedly with Corsale and Ornstein's (1980) 8 year olds who did not sort on the basis of meaning when presented relatively unrelated items under similar conditions. Interestingly, Corsale's (1978) 5 year olds presented taxonomic materials performed in a fashion that was somewhat similar to Corsale and Ornstein's (1980) 8 year olds given unrelated items.

One final demonstration of strategic deployment varying as a function of access of information in the knowledge base comes from the rehearsal literature. Naus and Ornstein (1985b) asked children who were 8 and 11 years of age to rehearse aloud while sorting to-be-remembered items into groups defined according to semantic (taxonomic) categories, "story" (thematic) categories, or randomly generated categories. An additional manipulation concerned whether the contents of each sorting group were visible after the placement of each item. In one condition, the children were given visual access to these sorts (words-visible condition), and in another condition, only the most recently sorted item in each group was visible (words-covered condition). The critical point for the present discussion was that when the children were sorting the words into meaningful groups (both semantic and story), they were able to include more items in their rehearsal sets than when the items were grouped into randomly defined categories; this pattern was somewhat more marked in the words-visible condition than in the words-covered condition. Further, as can be seen in Table II, the recall data paralleled the changes in rehearsal activity introduced by the differences in organization of the to-be-remembered items.

Naus and Ornstein's (1985b) experiment indicates that some presentation conditions facilitate access to interitem information in the knowledge base that can lead to a more efficient strategy, and, in turn, to greater recall. Here the nature of the joint grouping of the items leads to an accentuation of the underlying structure of the material. The only exception to this pattern is seen in the data of the 11 year olds given the randomly generated categories to sort under conditions of item availability. With the composition of the randomly generated categories visible during learning, the 11 year olds rehearsed these words more actively than the semantically constrained and narrative story items; further, the recall of the random cate-

TABLE II

Mean Number of Items Rehearsed Together and Mean Recall Probability[a]

	Items rehearsed	Recall probability
8 year olds		
Words-covered conditions		
Semantic	2.45	.55
Story	2.30	.54
Random	1.70	.40
Words-visible conditions		
Semantic	3.00	.68
Story	2.94	.65
Random	2.47	.54
11 year olds		
Words-covered conditions		
Semantic	3.86	.73
Story	4.08	.79
Random	3.33	.65
Words-visible conditions		
Semantic	3.84	.71
Story	4.66	.83
Random	7.01	.88

[a] From Naus and Ornstein (1985b).

gories actually exceeded that of the more highly structured lists. Naus and Ornstein suggested that these children might have "appreciated" the fact that active rehearsal techniques would be more valuable, in terms of generating an organizational plan, when items are randomly assigned to categories than when the categorical structure of the list is highly salient.

b. Ease of Detection of Relationships. The experiments described in the preceding section indicate that stimulus materials vary in terms of how readily semantic relationships can be activated and utilized in the service of a memory goal. However, in addition to these stimulus effects, certain experimenter-defined task conditions also influence the detection of underlying structure. Indeed, in the Rabinowitz (1984) and the Bjorklund and Ornstein (1976) studies discussed above, the blocking of items in terms of the categories served to facilitate the recognition of stimulus interrelationships. Also, in the sort/recall studies of Corsale (1978; Corsale & Ornstein, 1980), variations in the instructions clearly influenced the extent to which the children focused on interrelationships among the items. These are not knowledge base effects in the sense of demonstrating that differences in underlying knowledge influence current performance. Rather, these experiments call attention to variations in the conditions under which children come to utilize the information that is available in the knowledge system. In the present section, manipulations that serve to highlight the existing structure of information in the knowledge base are briefly reviewed.

Consistent with demonstrations that the blocked presentation of category exemplars can serve to facilitate a clustering strategy (e.g., Rabinowitz, 1984; Bjorklund & Ornstein, 1976; Kobasigawa & Orr, 1973), comparable effects can be shown in the rehearsal of taxonomic materials. Ornstein *et al.* (1975, experiment II) asked 8, 11, and 14 year olds to rehearse aloud while memorizing a list of items drawn from common taxonomic categories. One-half of the children were given the words in a random order, and the remaining children received blocked presentation.

The basic findings are presented in Fig. 5, in which both recall and rehearsal are displayed. The recall findings are basically similar to those obtained with unrelated words (discussed in Section II) and presented in Fig. 1. Under both blocked and random conditions, recall increased with age. As with unrelated materials, this increase was seen primarily in the initial and middle positions of the list. With both sets of materials, the progression from the rehearsal of isolated items to the grouping of several items in rehearsal was obtained. Inspection of Fig. 5 suggests that the salient organization created by the blocked presentation of the category instances facilitated active rehearsal and enhanced recall for the older children. Under blocked conditions, the 11 and 14 year olds were able to rehearse more

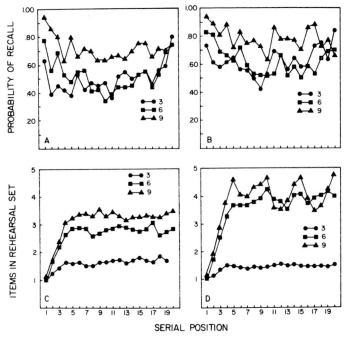

Fig. 5.   Mean proportion of related items recalled under random (A) and blocked conditions (B) of presentation, and mean number of different items in each rehearsal set under random (C) and blocked conditions (D) of presentation, as a function of serial position for 8, 11, and 14 year olds (third, sixth, and ninth graders). (From Ornstein et al., 1975.)

actively, and recall facilitation occurred. Additional analyses, similar to those described in connection with the Naus and Ornstein (1985a) experiment with soccer experts, demonstrated that blocking permitted the older children to rehearse category exemplars together. Thus, the blocked presentation of the items made the underlying organization more salient and facilitated the implementation of a more effective rehearsal technique than that used under random conditions.

The instructions provided by the experimenter also can influence the degree to which young subjects will attend to interrelationships among the stimulus materials, although instructional effects clearly interact with both age and the characteristics of the items to be remembered. These effects are readily illustrated in the context of the sort/recall experiments discussed above (e.g., Corsale & Ornstein, 1980). In general, when asked to sort relatively unrelated items so that the groups formed will facilitate remembering, adolescents and adults put words together on the basis of underlying meaning; younger children, in contrast, sort in a seemingly random pattern

(Bjorklund *et al.*, 1977; Corsale & Ornstein, 1980; Liberty & Ornstein, 1973).

To organize on the basis of meaning under these conditions, possible interrelationships among the stimulus items in the knowledge base must be accessed, and this does not seem to be done spontaneously by children of elementary school age. However, these children retrieve semantic interrelationships spontaneously under remembering instructions when the stimulus materials are clearly categorical and thus have a vivid structure. It is also apparent that young children can be encouraged to access semantic interrelationships, even with relatively unrelated stimuli. Thus, semantically constrained patterns of sorting are obtained when they are asked to group according to the patterns generated by older individuals (Bjorklund *et al.*, 1977; Liberty & Ornstein, 1973) or simply to group on the basis of meaning (Bjorklund *et al.*, 1977; Corsale & Ornstein, 1980).

B. DEVELOPMENTAL EFFECTS

The studies presented thus far deal with the impact of the knowledge base on the implementation of strategies for remembering in particular tasks. As such, mediation via strategies may be one of the most salient ways by which knowledge influences memory performance. Age differences in the contents and structure of the knowledge system, as well as in the ease of activation of stored information, appear to have major consequences for the types of strategic processing in which children can engage, thus contributing to age-related differences in memory performance. In addition, it is likely that the knowledge base can exert a long-term influence on the development of increasingly skilled memory techniques. Experience in remembering materials that are derived from a highly articulated domain in the knowledge base may lead to later applications of strategies more generally. It is quite likely that experience in remembering sets of interrelated items leads to the development of mnemonic routines that can be applied in a broad array of situations. Although expressed differently, this notion is present in current accounts of memory development presented by Bjorklund (1985) and Ornstein *et al.* (1985a).

As indicated in the discussion of the experiments on classmate recall (Section IV,A,1,c), Bjorklund and Zeman (1982, 1983) suggested that the clustering they obtained did not reflect the deployment of deliberate mnemonic strategies. Rather, they felt that the strongly overlearned associations among familiar classmates could be automatically activated. Consistent with the arguments of Lange (1973, 1978), Frankel and Rollins (1982, 1985), and Schneider (1984), Bjorklund and Zeman (1982, 1983) interpreted the classmate recall of preadolescents as being driven by associations in a nonstrategic fashion. Central to their thinking was the relative inability of the children in their samples to articulate the bases underlying their clustering.

Bjorklund (1985) has expanded this interpretation, by suggesting that age changes in memory performance prior to the adolescent years may primarily reflect developments in the structure and functioning of the knowledge system. Bjorklund (1985; Bjorklund & Jacobs, 1984) argues that associative interconnections are formed relatively early, and that these do not change significantly from the elementary school years through adulthood. He suggests (e.g., Bjorklund & de Marchena, 1984) that the critical age-related change is the activation of an increasingly broader set of categorical relationships that can be used subsequently to structure recall. For Bjorklund (1985), this greater ease in the activation of semantic relationships permits the use of increasing amounts of processing capacity (see Case, Kurland, & Goldberg, 1982) for the recognition of category relationships and the development of planful strategies. In fact, Bjorklund (1985) argues that strategies as deliberate memory endeavors may have at their foundation the accidental discovery of relationships during the process of recall. He feels that as children recall items in terms of their associative interconnections, they may notice strong interitem relationships, and be prompted by the recognition of these connections to search for other relationships.

Thus, for Bjorklund (1985), what begins as an automatic associative process leads to a deliberate activity. Support for this view is provided by Bjorklund and Zeman's (1982, 1983) analyses of the patterns of classmate recall and Bjorklund and Jacobs' (1985) examination of the recall of categories containing subsets of strongly associated items. In this latter study, children 13 and 15 years old were better able than younger subjects (9 and 11 years old) to use the recall of a pair of highly associated items as a prompt to recall other category members. From Bjorklund's (1985) point of view, these adolescents' abilities to use associated items to cue recall of other, weakly associated category items reflect their increased facility in the activation of categorical relationships. Automatic processes thus enter into Bjorklund's account in two ways: first in terms of an associative clustering that is observed with the young child, and second in terms of the older child's automated access to category information that facilitates the implementation of deliberate strategies.

The developmental consequences of the knowledge base have also been discussed by Ornstein *et al.* (1985a) who suggest that available knowledge has a significant impact on the emergence of particular memory strategies and on changes that may be observed in the "sophistication" of these skills. Ornstein *et al.* (1985a) discuss a broad continuum of mnemonic competence that ranges from the first tentative application of goal-directed memory efforts in various highly salient and supportive contexts, to the routine and efficient application of procedures in a broad variety of situations. Drawing upon demonstrations of early intentionality in memory (e.g., Baker-Ward *et al.,* 1984), as well as reports of children's strategies varying as a function of the saliency of the stimulus materials (e.g., Corsale, 1978; Corsale & Ornstein, 1980), Ornstein, Baker-Ward, and Naus suggest that initial attempts at remembering may be to some extent stimulus driven. Thus, in the sort/recall experiments (Corsale, 1978; Corsale & Ornstein, 1980), there may be a type of obligatory semantic encoding at work, an encoding that is forced to a degree by the strong associative links among the items. They suggest that when interconnections among the stimuli are very salient, there may be little that can be done to prevent organized sorting according to meaning, even in the face of a remembering-based instruction.

After experience in tasks that involve remembering information drawn from highly organized domains in the knowledge base, Ornstein *et al.* (1985a) speculate that children gradually transfer a strategic approach to settings in which the interitem connections may be less salient. Although firm data to support such a claim are lacking, Best and Ornstein (1985) have demonstrated that after experience in sorting categorical materials, 8 year olds will transfer a meaning-oriented sorting pattern to sets of unrelated items. Moving beyond a progression from highly salient to less supportive contexts, Ornstein *et al.* (1985a) speculate that further articulation of the knowledge system may facilitate the execution of more efficient strategies, as seems to be suggested by the meaningfulness data of Tarkin, Myers, and Ornstein (in preparation).

Ornstein *et al.* (1985a) view these contributions of the developing knowledge system in terms of a broader conceptualization of memory development. They suggest that once children employ mnemonic techniques effectively in a broad array of contexts, further improvement in strategic efficiency is possible as children become more facile in the execution of component parts of the strategies. They argue that with developmental advances in component skills such as retrieval (see Ornstein *et al.,* 1985b), the deployment of memory strategies comes to require less effort and becomes increasingly routinized or automatic (see also Case, 1978; Case *et al.,* 1982). Thus, consistent with the work of Guttentag (1984) on rehearsal, Ornstein *et al.* (1985a) suggest that with increases in age, the effort requirements of active and elaborative memory strategies are reduced.

The accounts of Ornstein *et al.* (1985a) and Bjorklund (1985) are similar in many respects. These positions stress the continuing impact of the information available in the knowledge base and its changing accessibility on children's memory processing. In different ways, the two points of view deal with automatic contributions to remembering, in terms of both mnemonic behaviors that may be elicited to some extent by stimulus materials in young children, and the growing routinization that is observed in later memorization attempts. As such, these positions are clearly developmental in orientation.

On the other hand, there are differences between the views that may reflect different conceptions of strategies and tasks. Bjorklund (1985) argues that the young child may not be behaving in a strategic fashion, i.e., that the memory task is not a deliberate one for the preadolescent. In contrast, Ornstein *et al.* (1985a) suggest that tasks of remembering involve both deliberate and automatic factors, and that the behavior of the young child is in fact strategic. Their argument in part stems from clear demonstrations of intentional mnemonic behavior in preschoolers (e.g., Baker-Ward *et al.*, 1984; see also Wellman, 1985). They feel that children's behavior is deliberate if it is motivated specifically by a request (either self- or other-generated) to remember, and that it is not necessary (and probably unlikely in many situations) for the child to be able to articulate the basis of a strategy. Once initiated, Ornstein *et al.* (1985a) feel that the strategic efforts of the child may be facilitated by the automatic execution of certain components of the task, and that with the articulation of the knowledge system and practice in remembering, the entire sequence may become automated, particularly under some task conditions.

Additional work is necessary to articulate further the Bjorklund (1985) and Ornstein *et al.* (1985a) positions, and to probe further their similarities and differences. Both frameworks are speculative, and in the process of evaluating them, the contributions of the expanding knowledge base to the development of memory will need to be studied in detail.

V. Summary

In this article, the importance of examining the linkage between knowledge and strategic factors in children's memory has been suggested. Indeed, it has been argued that a more complete analysis of the development of remembering in children requires a consideration of the operation of memory strategies in the context of the growing knowledge base. The effects of the knowledge base were analyzed in terms of concurrent influences on the use of strategies and long-term consequences for the development of increasingly skilled memory processing.

The available evidence suggests that age-related changes in the contents of the knowledge system, as well as increases in the ease with which information can be accessed, contribute to the strategies that are used by children of different ages, and influence the development of efficient modes of processing. Continued research on the concurrent effects of the knowledge base should provide a more complete account of children's memory than that currently available, taking into consideration knowledge of the materials, understanding of the task demands, as well as overall strategic abilities. Similarly, research on the long-term developmental effects of the knowledge base on memory strategies should facilitate an understanding of the mechanisms by which memory processing becomes more efficient and less effortful. Ideally, studies that examine these issues should be longitudinal in scope (Ornstein *et al.*, 1985a), but even cross-sectional research that explores the interrelationships between strategies and knowledge will facilitate an understanding of the development of memory in children.

ACKNOWLEDGMENTS

This article is dedicated to the memory of David A. Grant, who directed the graduate training of PAO at the University of Wisconsin and with whom MJN worked as an undergraduate.

Preparation of the article was supported in part by Grant HD 08459 from the United States Public Health Service. A draft of this article was completed while the first author was at the University of Haifa, on a Kenan leave of absence from the University of North Carolina. Additional support in the form of a Fulbright–Hays Travel Award, and an Einstein Visiting Fellowship from the Israel Academy of Sciences and Humanities is gratefully acknowledged. Much appreciation is expressed to Hayne W. Reese and Scott G. Paris for their significant contributions to the revision of the article.

REFERENCES

Anderson, J. R. (1976). *Language, memory, and thought*. Hillsdale, NJ: Erlbaum.

Anglin, J. M. (1977). *Word, object, and conceptual development*. New York: Norton.

Baker-Ward, L., Ornstein, P. A., & Holden, D. J. (1984). The expression of memorization in early childhood. *Journal of Experimental Child Psychology, 37*, 555–575.

Bartlett, F. C. (1932). *Remembering*. London and New York: Cambridge Univ. Press.

Battig, W. F., & Montague, W. E. (1969). Category norms for verbal items in 56 categories: A replication and extension of the Connecticut category norms. *Journal of Experimental Psychology Monographs, 80*, 1–46.

Belmont, J. M., & Butterfield, E. D. (1977). The instructional approach to developmental cognitive research. In R. V. Kail & J. W. Hagen (Eds.), *Perspectives on the development of memory and cognition*. Hillsdale, NJ: Erlbaum.

Best, D. L., & Ornstein, P. A. (1985). *Children's generation and communication of mnemonic organizational strategies*. Submitted.

Binet, A., & Henri, V. (1894). La mémoire des phrases (Mémoire des idées). *L'Année Psychologique, 1*, 24–59.

Bjorklund, D. F. (1985). The role of conceptual knowledge in the development of organization in children's memory. In C. J. Brainerd & M. Pressley (Eds.), *Basic processes in memory development: Progress in cognitive development research*. New York: Springer-Verlag.

Bjorklund, D. R., & De Marchena, M. R. (1984). Developmental shifts in the basis of organization in memory: The role of associative versus categorical relatedness in children's free-recall. *Child Development,* **55**, 952–962.

Bjorklund, D. F., & Jacobs, J. W., III. (1984). A developmental examination of ratings of associative strength. *Behavior Research Methods, Instruments and Computers,* **16**, 568–569.

Bjorklund, D. F., & Jacobs, J. W., III. (1985). Associative and categorical processes in children's memory: The role of automaticity in the development of organization in free recall. *Journal of Experimental Child Psychology,* **39**, 599–617.

Bjorklund, D. F., & Ornstein, P. A. (1976). *Young children's recall and organization of materials differing in list structure.* Unpublished manuscript, University of North Carolina at Chapel Hill.

Bjorklund, D. F., Ornstein, P. A., & Haig, J. R. (1977). Developmental differences in organization and recall: Training in the use of organizational techniques. *Developmental Psychology,* **13**, 175–183.

Bjorklund, D. F., & Thompson, B. E. (1983). Category typicality effects in children's memory performance: Qualitative and quantitative differences in the processing of category information. *Journal of Experimental Child Psychology,* **35**, 329–344.

Bjorklund, D. F., Thompson, B. E., & Ornstein, P. A. (1983). Developmental trends in children's typicality judgments. *Behavior Research Methods and Instrumentation,* **15**, 350–356.

Bjorklund, D. F., & Zeman, B. R. (1982). Children's organization and metamemory awareness in their recall of familiar information. *Child Development,* **53**, 799–810.

Bjorklund, D. F., & Zeman, B. R. (1983). The development of organizational strategies in children's recall of familiar information: Using social organization to recall the names of classmates. *International Journal of Behavioral Development,* **6**, 341–353.

Borkowski, J. G., & Cavanaugh, J. C. (1979). Maintenance and generalization of skills and strategies by the retarded. In N. R. Ellis (Ed.), *Handbook of mental deficiency.* Hillsdale, NJ: Erlbaum.

Bransford, J. D., & Franks, J. J. (1972). The abstraction of linguistic ideas: A review. *Cognition: An International Journal of Cognitive Psychology,* **2**, 211–249.

Bransford, J. D., Nitsch, K. E., & Franks, J. J. (1977). Schooling and the facilitation of knowing. In R. C. Anderson, R. J. Spiro, & W. E. Montague (Eds.), *Schooling and the acquisition of knowledge.* Hillsdale, NJ: Erlbaum.

Brown, A. L. (1975). The development of memory: Knowing, knowing about knowing, and knowing how to know. In H. W. Reese (Ed.), *Advances in child development and behavior* (Vol. 10). New York: Academic Press.

Brown, A. L. (1979). Theories of memory and the problems of development: Activity, growth, and knowledge. In L. Cermak & F. I. M. Craik (Eds.), *Levels of processing and memory.* Hillsdale, NJ: Erlbaum.

Brown, A. L. (1982). Learning and development: The problems of compatibility, access and induction. *Human Development,* **25**, 89–115.

Brown, A. L., Bransford, J. D., Ferrara, R. A., & Campione, J. C. (1983). Learning, remembering, and understanding. In J. H. Flavell & E. M. Markman (Eds.), *Handbook of child psychology: Vol. 3. Cognitive Development.* New York: Wiley.

Butterfield, E. C., Siladi, D., & Belmont, J. M. (1980). Validating theories of intelligence. In H. W. Reese (Ed.), *Advances in child behavior and development* (Vol. 15). New York: Academic Press.

Case, R. (1978). Intellectual development from birth to adolescence: A neo-Piagetian interpretation. In R. Siegler (Ed.), *Children's thinking: What develops?* Hillsdale, NJ: Erlbaum.

Case, R., Kurland, D. M., & Goldberg, J. (1982). Operational efficiency and growth of short term memory span. *Journal of Experimental Child Psychology,* **33**, 386–404.

Cavanaugh, J. C., & Borkowski, J. G. (1979). The metamemory–memory "connection": Effects of strategy training and maintenance. *Journal of General Psychology,* **101,** 161–174.

Cavanaugh, J. C., & Perlmutter, M. (1982). Metamemory: A critical examination. *Child Development,* **53,** 11–28.

Chase, W. G., & Simon, H. A. (1973). The mind's eye in chess. In W. G. Chase (Ed.), *Visual information processing.* New York: Academic Press.

Chechile, R. A., & Richman, C. L. (1982). The interaction of semantic memory with storage and retrieval processes. *Developmental Review,* **2,** 237–250.

Chi, M. T. H. (1977). Age differences in memory span. *Journal of Experimental Child Psychology,* **23,** 266–281.

Chi, M. T. H. (1978). Knowledge structure and memory development. In R. Siegler (Ed.), *Children's thinking: What develops?* Hillsdale, NJ: Erlbaum.

Chi, M. T. H. (1981). Knowledge development and memory performance. In M. Friedman, J. P. Das, & N. O'Connor (Eds.), *Intelligence and learning.* New York: Plenum.

Chi, M. T. H. (1985). Interactive roles of knowledge and strategies in development. In S. Chapman, J. Segal, & R. Glaser (Eds.), *Thinking and learning skills: Current research and open questions* (Vol. 2). Hillsdale, NJ: Erlbaum, in press.

Chi, M. T. H., & Koeske, R. D. (1983). Network representation of a child's dinosaur knowledge. *Developmental Psychology,* **19,** 29–39.

Chiesi, L., Spilich, G. J., & Voss, J. F. (1979). Acquisition of domain-related information in relation to high and low domain knowledge. *Journal of Verbal Learning and Verbal Behavior,* **18,** 257–273.

Cofer, C. (1973). Constructive processes in memory. *American Scientist,* **61,** 537–543.

Collins, A. M., & Loftus, E. F. (1975). A spreading activation theory of semantic processing. *Psychological Review,* **82,** 407–428.

Corsale, K. (1978). *Factors affecting children's use of organization in recall.* Unpublished doctoral dissertation, University of North Carolina at Chapel Hill.

Corsale, K., & Ornstein, P. A. (1980). Developmental changes in children's use of semantic information in recall. *Journal of Experimental Child Psychology,* **30,** 231–245.

Emmerich, H. J. (1979). Developmental differences in ratings of meaningfulness, concreteness, and picturability. *Developmental Psychology,* **15,** 464–466.

Flavell, J. H. (1970). Developmental studies of mediated memory. In H. W. Reese & L. P. Lipsitt (Eds.), *Advances in child development and behavior* (Vol. 5). New York: Academic Press.

Flavell, J. H., & Wellman, H. M. (1977). Metamemory. In R. W. Kail & J. W. Hagen (Eds.), *Perspectives on the development of memory and cognition.* Hillsdale, NJ: Erlbaum.

Frankel, M. T., & Rollins, H. A. (1982). Age-related differences in clustering: A new approach. *Journal of Experimental Child Psychology,* **34,** 113–122.

Frankel, M. T., & Rollins, H. A. (1985). Associative and categorical hypotheses in the free recall of adults and children. *Journal of Experimental Child Psychology,* in press.

Guttentag, R. E. (1984). The mental effort requirement of cumulative rehearsal: A developmental study. *Journal of Experimental Child Psychology,* **37,** 92–106.

Hagen, J. W., Jongeward, R. H., & Kail, R. V. (1975). Cognitive perspectives on the development of memory. In H. W. Reese (Ed.), *Advances in child development and behavior* (Vol. 10). New York: Academic Press.

Hasher, L., & Zacks, R. T. (1979). Automatic and effortful processes in memory. *Journal of Experimental Psychology: General,* **108,** 356–388.

Hayes, K. N. (1984). *Exploring the young child's knowledge base: Content and organization.* Unpublished doctoral dissertation, University of North Carolina at Chapel Hill.

Hayes, K. N., & Ornstein, P. A. (1985). *Age changes in children's knowledge: Animals and cartoon characters.* Submitted.

Inhelder, B., & Piaget, J. (1964). *The early growth of logic in the child.* New York: Norton.

Istomina, Z. M. (1975). The development of voluntary memory in preschool-age children. *Soviet Psychology,* **13** 5–64.

Jenkins, J. J. (1974). Remember that old theory of memory? Well forget it! *American Psychologist,* **29**, 785–795.

Kail, R., & Bisanz, J. (1982). Information processing and cognitive development. In H. W. Reese (Ed.), *Advances in child development and behavior* (Vol. 17). New York: Academic Press.

Klahr, D., & Siegler, R. S. (1979). The representation of children's knowledge. In H. W. Reese & L. P. Lipsitt (Eds.), *Advances in child development and behavior* (Vol. 12). New York: Academic Press.

Kobasigawa, A., & Orr, R. (1973). Free recall and retrieval speed of categorized items by kindergarten children. *Journal of Experimental Child Psychology,* **15** 187–192.

Lange, G. (1973). The development of conceptual and rote recall skills among school age children. *Journal of Experimental Child Psychology,* **15,** 394–407.

Lange, G. (1978). Organization-related processes in children's recall. In P. A. Ornstein (Ed.), *Memory development in children.* Hillsdale, NJ: Erlbaum.

Liben, L. S. (1975a). Evidence for developmental differences in spontaneous seriation and its implications for past research on long-term memory improvement. *Developmental Psychology,* **11,** 121–125.

Liben, L. S. (1975b). Long-term memory for pictures related to seriation, horizontality, and verticality concepts. *Developmental Psychology,* **11,** 795–806.

Liberty, C., & Ornstein, P. A. (1973). Age differences in organization and recall: The effects of training in categorization. *Journal of Experimental Child Psychology,* **15,** 169–186.

Lindberg, M. (1980). The role of knowledge structures in the ontogeny of learning. *Journal of Experimental Child Psychology,* **30,** 401–410.

Mandler, G. (1967). Organization and memory. In K. W. Spence & J. T. Spence (Eds.), *The psychology of learning and motivation* (Vol. 1). New York: Academic Press.

Maurer, D., Siegel, L. S., Lewis, T. L., Kristofferson, M. W., Barnes, R. A., & Levy, B. A. (1979). Long-term memory improvement? *Child Development,* **50,** 106–118.

McCauley, C., Weil, C. M., & Sperber, R. D. (1976). The development of memory structure as reflected by semantic-priming effects. *Journal of Experimental Child Psychology,* **22,** 511–518.

Mervis, C. B., Catlin, J., & Rosch, E. (1976). Relationships among goodness-of-example, category norms, and word frequency. *Bulletin of the Psychonomic Society,* **7,** 283–284.

Moely, B. E. (1977). Organizational factors in the development of memory. In R. V. Kail & J. W. Hagen (Eds.), *Perspectives on the development of memory and cognition.* Hillsdale, NJ: Erlbaum.

Naus, M. J., & Halasz, F. (1979). Developmental perspectives on cognitive processing and semantic memory structure. In L. S. Cermak & F. I. M. Craik (Eds.), *Levels of processing in human memory.* Hillsdale, NJ: Erlbaum.

Naus, M. J., & Ornstein, P. A. (1983). The development of memory strategies: Analysis, questions, and issues. In M. T. H. Chi (Ed.), *Trends in memory development research (Contributions to human development)* (Vol. 9). Basel: Karger.

Naus, M. J., & Ornstein, P. A. (1985a). *An investigation of the effects of expertise upon mnemonic strategies.* In preparation.

Naus, M. J., & Ornstein, P. A. (1985b). *An analysis of active rehearsal in children's memory: The effects of item retrieval and organizational structure,* in preparation.

Nelson, K. (1978). Semantic development and the development of semantic memory. In K. E. Nelson (Ed.), *Children's language* (Vol. 1). New York: Gardner.

Noble, C. (1952). An analysis of meaning. *Psychological Review,* **59,** 421–430.

Norman, D. A., & Bobrow, D. G. (1976). On the role of active memory processes in perception and cognition. In C. Cofer (Ed.), *The structure of human memory.* San Francisco: Freeman.

Norman, D. A., Rumelhart, D. E., & the LNR Research Group. (1975). *Explorations in cognition.* San Francisco: Freeman.

Ornstein, P. A., Baker-Ward, L., & Naus, M. J. (1985a). The development of children's mnemonic skill. In F. Weinert & M. Perlmutter (Eds.), *Memory development: Universal changes and individual differences* (tentative title), in press.

Ornstein, P. A., & Corsale, K. (1979a). Process and structure in children's memory. In G. Whitehurst & B. Zimmerman (Eds.), *The functions of language and cognition.* New York: Academic Press.

Ornstein, P. A., & Corsale, K. (1979b). Organizational factors in children's memory. In C. R. Puff (Ed.), *Memory organization and structure.* New York: Academic Press.

Ornstein, P. A., Medlin, R. G., Stone, B. P., & Naus, M. J. (1985b). Retrieving for rehearsal: An analysis of active rehearsal in children's memory. *Developmental Psychology,* **21,** 633–641.

Ornstein, P. A., & Naus, M. J. (1978). Rehearsal processes in children's memory. In P. A. Ornstein (Ed.), *Memory development in children.* Hillsdale, NJ: Erlbaum.

Ornstein, P. A., & Naus, M. J. (1979). *Effects of the knowledge base on children's memory processing.* Paper presented at the meetings of the Society for Research in Child Development, San Francisco, April.

Ornstein, P. A., Naus, M. J., & Liberty, C. (1975). Rehearsal and organizational processes in children's memory. *Child Development,* **26,** 818–830.

Paris, S. G. (1975). Integration and inference in children's comprehension and memory. In F. Restle, R. Shiffrin, J. Castellan, H. Lindman, & D. Pisoni (Eds.), *Cognitive theory* (Vol. 1). Hillsdale, NJ: Erlbaum.

Paris, S. G. (1978a). Coordination of means and goals in the development of mnemonic skills. In P. A. Ornstein (Ed.), *Memory development in children.* Hillsdale, NJ: Erlbaum.

Paris, S. G. (1978b). The development of inference and transformation as memory operations. In P. A. Ornstein (Ed.), *Memory development in children.* Hillsdale, NJ: Erlbaum.

Paris, S. G., & Cross, D. R. (1983). Ordinary learning: Pragmatic connections among children's beliefs, motives, and actions. In J. Bisanz, G. L. Bisanz, & R. Kail (Eds.), *Learning in children: Progress in cognitive development research.* New York: Springer-Verlag.

Paris, S. G., Newman, R. S., & McVey, K. A. (1982). Learning the functional significance of mnemonic actions: A microgenetic study of strategy acquisition. *Journal of Experimental Child Psychology,* **34,** 490–509.

Perlmutter, M., & Lange, G. (1978). A developmental analysis of recall–recognition distinctions. In P. A. Ornstein (Ed.), *Memory development in children.* Hillsdale, NJ: Erlbaum.

Piaget, J., & Inhelder, B. (1973). *Memory and intelligence.* New York: Basic Books.

Posnansky, C. J. (1978). Category norms for verbal items in 25 categories for children in grades 2–6. *Behavior Research Methods and Instrumentation,* **10,** 819–832.

Pressley, M., Borkowski, J. G., & O'Sullivan, J. (1985). Children's metamemory and the teaching of memory strategies. In D. L. Forrest-Pressley, G. E. MacKinnon, & T. G. Waller (Eds.), *Metacognition, cognition, and human performance.* New York: Academic Press.

Pressley, M., Levin, J. R., & Ghatala, E. L. (1984). Memory strategy monitoring in adults and children. *Journal of Verbal Learning and Verbal Behavior,* **23,** 270–288.

Puff, C. R. (Ed.). (1979). *Memory organization and structure.* New York: Academic Press.

Rabinowitz, M. (1984). The use of categorical organization in free recall: Not an all-or-none situation. *Journal of Experimental Child Psychology,* **38,** 338–351.

Richman, C. L., Nida, S., & Pittman, L. (1976). Effects of meaningfulness on child free-recall learning. *Developmental Psychology,* **12,** 460–465.

Rosch, E. (1973). On the internal structure of perceptual and semantic categories. In T. E. Moore (Ed.), *Cognitive development and the acquisition of language.* New York: Academic Press.

Rosch, E. (1975). Cognitive representations of semantic categories. *Journal of Experimental Psychology: General,* **7,** 573–605.

Rossi, E. (1964). Development of classificatory behavior. *Child Development,* **35,** 137–142.

Rossi, E. L., & Rossi, S. I. (1965). Concept utilization, serial order and recall in nursery school children. *Child Development,* **36,** 771–778.

Rundus, D., & Atkinson, R. C. (1970). Rehearsal processes in free recall: A procedure for direct observation. *Journal of Verbal Learning and Verbal Behavior,* **9,** 97–105.

Schneider, H., & Shiffrin, R. M. (1977). Controlled and automatic human information processing: I. Detection, search, and attention. *Psychological Review,* **84,** 1–66.

Schneider, W. (1984). *The role of conceptual knowledge, strategy knowledge, and specific mnemonic context in the development of organizational processes in memory.* Unpublished manuscript, Max Planck Institute for Psychological Research, Munich.

Shiffrin, R. M., & Schneider, W. (1977). Controlled and automatic human information processing: II. Perceptual learning, automatic attending, and a general theory. *Psychological Review,* **84,** 127–190.

Siegler, R. S. (1983). Information processing approaches to development. In W. Kessen (Ed.), *Handbook of child psychology Vol. 1. History, theory, and methods.* New York: Wiley.

Spilich, G. J., Vesonder, G. T., Chiesi, H. L., & Voss, J. F. (1979). Text processing of domain-related information for individuals with high and low domain knowledge. *Journal of Verbal Learning and Verbal Behavior,* **18,** 275–290.

Tarkin, B., Myers, N. A., & Ornstein, P. A. (1985). *The effects of stimulus meaningfulness on children's spontaneous rehearsal strategies.* In preparation.

Tulving, E., & Donaldson, W. (Eds.). (1972). *Organization of memory.* New York: Academic Press.

Wellman, H. M. (1985). The early development of memory strategies. In F. Weinert & M. Perlmutter (Eds.), *Memory development: Universal changes and individual differences* (tentative title), in press.

Whitney, P., & Kunen, S. (1983). Development of hierarchical conceptual relationships in children's semantic memories. *Journal of Experimental Child Psychology,* **35,** 278–293.

Worden, P. E. (1976). The effects of classification structure on organized free recall in children. *Journal of Experimental Child Psychology,* **22,** 519–529.

EFFECTS OF SIBLING SPACING ON INTELLIGENCE, INTERFAMILIAL RELATIONS, PSYCHOSOCIAL CHARACTERISTICS, AND MENTAL AND PHYSICAL HEALTH

Mazie Earle Wagner and Herman J. P. Schubert

BUFFALO, NEW YORK

Daniel S. P. Schubert[1]

CASE WESTERN RESERVE MEDICAL SCHOOL
AND CLEVELAND METROPOLITAN GENERAL HOSPITAL
CLEVELAND, OHIO

[1]Present address: Department of Psychiatry, Cleveland Metropolitan General Hospital, Cleveland, Ohio 44109.

149

I. Introduction

The purpose of this review is to assess and synthesize research findings concerning the effects of child spacing on intelligence, interfamily relations, psychosocial characteristics, and health. We shall suggest strategic and theoretically significant areas for further investigation and hope to encourage future research with the final goal of increasing our knowledge regarding personality and health. The effects of birth spacing is the least researched of sibling constellation variables, although several research groups have recently added interesting findings of spacing effects on intrafamily relations. In 1965, Sampson, reviewing over 200 references on ordinal position, mentioned only three regarding sibling spacing (Koch, 1954, 1960; Lasko, 1954). His review did not include physical health, thereby excluding a considerable number of definitive early studies on effects of sibling spacing. Difficulty in obtaining spacing data probably contributes to the limited number of relevant studies. Bibliographies, as well as school, work, and military histories, are likely to include sibship size, ordinal rank, and even sex of siblings, but not spacing between siblings.

Of over 3000 studies concerning effects of sibling constellation variables (D. S. P. Schubert, Wagner, & Schubert, 1976, 1984), only about 100 even minimally refer to effects of spacing. Studies have been located for spacing effects on intelligence, academic achievement, and success in other areas, as well as for a variety of personality characteristics and 30 on morbidity, mortality, and longevity. Before describing these studies, we point out overall methodology and research pitfalls likely in such investigations.

A. A METHODOLOGICAL NOTE

Errors in methodology in the general area of sibling constellation effects abound to trip the inexperienced researcher. Sibling spacing effects is no exception and has several pitfalls all its own, i.e., the first two mentioned below. The remaining errors are shared in their negative effects by other sibship variables.

1. *Spacing interval size.* Unfortunately, researchers in the area of spacing effects have used a considerable variety of spacing intervals. Close spacing may mean up to 18 months, more frequently 2 years or less (Koch, 1954, 1960; Schubert, Wagner, & Schubert, 1983), and sometimes up to 4 years (Rosenberg, Goldman, & Sutton-Smith, 1969). Sometimes three spacing intervals are used (Koch, 1954; Lasko, 1954), and frequently only two. Koch used, and recommended, spacing intervals of less than 2 years, 2–4 years, and 4–6 years. Lack of consistency between researchers can lead to non-comparable results, making comparisons of findings spurious.

In addition to spacing between siblings, spacing between marriage and the birth of the first child should be included in studying interval effects, as should be the age of parents, especially the mother, at the birth of the first child. Subgroups would include illegitimates, those premaritally conceived, the early married conceived, and those born 2 years or more after marriage.

2. *Spacings preceding and following the proband.* Spacing of siblings before and after the subjects under study have been combined by some authors who ignore the fact that having a close older sibling may, and sometimes does, have different effects from having a close younger. Effects of pre- and postintervals may be combined if, and only if, they are found very similar.

3. *Sibship size.* Of the sibship and demographic variables, sibship size is the one most related to birth interval because of the limitations of the human fertility span. The latter, divided by the number of offspring, results in narrower overall spacing in large sibships. However, narrow spacing may, and does, occur in sibships of two (SS2s) and three (SS3s) because it is preferred by some women who wish to get the tasks of baby-tending completed. This group includes those who wish to return to the work force and those who incorrectly assume that close spacing has more positive effects.

Child spacing effects have most frequently been researched for sibships of two. Indeed, authors seem to find weaker sibling interval effects for SS2s than for larger sibships (Nuttall & Nuttall, 1975) and one reported that the quality of the effect changes from SS3s to SS4+s (Wagner, Schubert, & Schubert, 1985). Results from SS2 studies, although indeed very important in their own right, cannot accurately be generalized to larger sibships. Apparently, sibship size should be held constant in studies of spacing effects, but this control, except for SS2s, is infrequently used.

4. *Sex of proband.* Combining the two sexes is a frequent methodological error. Indeed, if no differences exist, the sexes may be combined to increase reliability. However, the effect of spacing interval is not always the same for the two sexes; in fact, it is diametrically opposite for some vari-

ables (Koch, 1954; Rosenberg *et al.,* 1969). Obviously when the latter is the case, lack of findings may be attributable to an averaging out of effects. Sampson (1965) unequivocally argued for separation of the sexes in sibling constellation research. Yet some authors combine the two sexes, without examining their data for sex differences. Also, some authors have erroneously generalized from findings regarding males to the two sexes.

5. *Sex of sibling.* Not separating data by sex of sibling can also lead to confusion of results. A near older sister, for instance, has a greater effect on a boy's positive reaction to the female than does a near older brother (Bigner, 1974b). Or, if spacing has no effect for one sex but does for the other, the differences may be attenuated for the combination to lessen significance. Several authors (Jordan, Whiteside, & Monaster, 1982; Kidwell, 1981; Koch, 1954) highly recommend separating data by sex of sibling.

6. *Ordinal position.* Ordinal position of the proband may also be held constant in studying the effects of spacing interval. The interval following a firstborn is likely to be shorter than those following "laterborns." Further, an eldest with a close like-sexed sibling may be more affected than the third or fourth with a similarly close-spaced like-sexed younger sibling. Other authors (Jordan, Whiteside, & Manaster, 1982; Keane, 1976; Kidwell, 1981; Sampson, 1965) along with the present writers have emphasized the use of at least four ordinal subgroups: "onlyborns," eldests, "middleborns," and youngests.

7. *Era of birth.* Spacing interval size varies considerably by era of birth (Berglin, 1980; Ford, 1981). With such variation, the effects of any one specific size cannot be assumed to remain constant. For instance, any specific interval of the mid-1930s cannot be expected to have the same effect as that same interval during the mid-1940s.

8. *Socioeconomic status.* Sibship size effects have been shown to vary considerably with socioeconomic status (Belmont, Wittes, & Stein, 1979; Kennett & Cropley, 1970; Page & Grandon, 1979). With the close relationship between family size and spacing interval, effects of the latter might also be expected to vary with socioeconomic status. However, Suchindran and Lingner (1977), using the 1965 National Fertility Survey for women married 1955–1959, found no significant difference in birth interval for the second and third spacing for different socioeconomic levels (first spacing here is that between marriage and the birth of the firstborn). However, the effects of a specific interval size might still vary with socioeconomic status. They did find, however, that blacks had significantly narrower spacing than whites.

9. *Use of select samples.* The sample used to determine sibling spacing effects must be randomly chosen from the general population. Generalizing from clinical, college, or other select groups is unwarranted and leads to

erroneous conclusions. Results from volunteer samples, including questionnaire data, are suspect until it is demonstrated that the characteristics under investigation do not differentiate volunteers from nonvolunteers (Rosenthal & Rosnow, 1970).

10. *Sibling spacing*. And a final caveat. We should not omit that, in studies of sibship variables other than spacing (family size, ordinal position, and sex of sibling), sibling spacing itself should be controlled. As Strude and Ota (1982) stated in their study of Type A coronary-prone behavior patterns related to ordinal position and family size, "Spacing between siblings may have contributed to the family size effects since children are more closely spaced in large families" (p. 321).

We have tried to make the point that arbitrarily focusing on one aspect of the sibling constellation picture, without accounting for the effects of the other sibship variables, gives a distorted and inaccurate picture. Indeed it is most difficult for researchers to avoid all the differences inherent in sibling constellation research. However, understanding the pitfalls gives direction to our review. Now that the stage is set, we turn next to the conceptual organization of our procedure.

B. CONCEPTUAL ORGANIZATION

As in general for research on sibling constellation variables, research on spacing effects is much more abundant for intelligence and academic achievement than for other aspects of personality or for mental and physical health. Berglin (1980) listed 13 authors who "have suspected that length of sibling interval before or after a propositus could influence his reactions and development and form part of his epidemiological background" (p. 28). These authors reported from 1925 to the 1980s and in both Europe and America, mostly regarding intelligence. Our conceptual organization, therefore, is to begin with intelligence.

This review of sibling spacing effects on intelligence will be divided by age of propositi, starting with very young children, followed by preadolescent children and adolescents, and finally college students and other young adults. When research is available, older adults will be included. For these age groupings, we first describe results regarding sibships of two (SS2s), concerning whom much more research has been done than on larger sibships. The latter is the subsequent topic. A summary is attempted for each subtopic and for intelligence as a whole. The discussion of effects on intelligence is followed by reviews regarding effects of spacing on academic achievement, success other than academic, and creativity.

Our second major subdivision is the relation of birth interval and interfamilial exchange. Included are subtopics of age at "dethronement" (removal from status as youngest child), and parent–child, parent–parent, and child–child differences in interfamilial relations as related to size of sibling interval. We start with the immediate behavioral changes at the birth of a younger sibling on children of various ages at dethronement. Studies are available for effects on the older child's behavior both during the mother's pregnancy and at various intervals following the second's birth, with some detailing of the mother's behavior changes as well. Practically all these studies are for SS2s. Related topics to follow are reviews of parent–child relations, parent–parent relations, and sibling–sibling relations during this early age level. Sibship interactions studied include prosocial behavior (affinity), rivalry, jealousy, identification (cross-joining), and imitation, most of which are affected by sibling interval size.

Studies of spacing interval effects on *personality*, unearthed via an exhaustive review of the literature, were also found for a variety of additional measures, though none was investigated for all age levels nor for both small and larger sibships. Personality characteristics included are (1) the need to achieve, self-esteem, ego strength, and superego; (2) social skills, communication, popularity, and leadership; (3) gender role; (4) general adjustment, anxiety, fearfulness, need to affiliate, and dependency; and (5) major psychiatric disorders: alcoholism, delinquency, depression, and schizophrenia.

Our last review topic is physical health. Effects on rates of spontaneous abortion, prenatal and perinatal morbidity and mortality, and illness during infancy and early childhood comprise one of the larger and more carefully done areas of investigation of effects of birth interval. A final, short section covers spacing effects on longevity.

II. Effects of Sibling Spacing on Intelligence

The effect of spacing on intelligence is one of the better researched areas for sibling spacing. However, the relevant studies are largely limited to sibships of two (SS2s), middle-class suburban samples, and children. Obviously, SS2s cannot be safely generalized to larger families nor can middle-class suburban samples be generalized to lower socioeconomic levels or to inner city urban families.

A.   YOUNG CHILDREN FROM SS2s

We start with young children in SS2s. The research of Helen Koch (1954, 1956a,b, 1960) is among the earliest and was well planned. She studied 360 5- and 6-year-old SS2s, who were middle-class, white, urban children from intact families. She consistently dichotomized her results by sex, reporting all her findings separately for boys and girls. They were further separated by ordinal position, sex of sibling, and spacing interval. The latter were spacings of 2 years or less, 2–4 years, and 4–6 years. Thus distributing her 360 cases, with 15 in each cell, she held era, socioeconomic status, race, and family size constant; and she studied sex, spacing interval, ordinal position, and sex of sibling. Koch investigated not only intelligence, but also many personality factors and academic achievement; most of the latter results will be reviewed at appropriate places herein.

Koch felt that the homogeneous groupings she used were quite necessary, and noted that her findings may be limited to her age sample. Others have found that sibships of two (Ernst & Angst, 1983; Nuttall & Nuttall, 1975; See Section II,C) and upper middle-class subjects (Kennett & Cropley, 1970) show fewer sibling constellation effects than larger sibships and subjects from the lower social classes; therefore, perhaps, her findings should not be generalized beyond young middle-class children from SS2s. Koch also noted that her sibship data were largely gathered from school records and that miscarriages, stillbirths, and even early infant deaths were likely omitted. Such happenings are more likely during the widely spaced interval. Further, forcing her data to 15 cases per cell possibly led to going farther afield for additional cases, especially for the largest age spacing category. Such wider search might well change the social class and child-rearing patterns to a different universe. The differences in father's occupation and census tract levels could be real rather than artifactual.

To study effects of sibling spacing on intelligence, Koch used Thurstone's Primary Mental Abilities Test. On the verbal subtest, for six of the eight sex–birth order categories the highest averages were from the intermediate spacing subgroup (2–4 years). For the remaining two categories, $\underline{F}$1F and $\underline{F}$2M, the highest averages were within the short and long interval subgroup, respectively; that is, the categories of near-spaced older sister of two girls and far-spaced younger brother with an older sister were highest, though neither of these showed any large amount of superiority. According to Koch's data, then, the 2- to 4-year interval group showed the highest verbal scores for SS2s, especially for boys.

For the quantitative subtest, the direction of difference was, as for the verbal, that highest scores were shown by the 2- to 4-year interval group. The differences were small, and again some indications were present that close spacing is more advantageous for girls and wide spacing more for boys. For the perceptual speed subtest, the results were fairly inconsistent and the differences small. For girls with a sister, close spacing was advantageous; for boys with a brother, the wide spacing seemed better. For the space subtest, the differences were also small and inconsistent. The spacing interval most frequently showing advantage, as for the other tests, was that of 2–4 years. Narrow spacing was best for the younger girl, the older girl with a sister, and the younger boy with a brother.

Overall, for Koch's SS2 middle-class children, the intermediate spacing (2–4 years) most frequently showed advantage, with some advantage for the girls of close spacing and for the boys of wider spacing. Findings for verbal ability were more consistent than for the other subtests. Regardless of sex of sibling, firstborn males had higher intelligence than secondborns only when the firstborn was less than 4 years older. SS2 brothers showed no difference in IQ when spaced 4 years or more. Adler (1924) stated that spacing of over 4 years in SS2 sibships made them both virtually onlyborns.

Douglass, Ross, and Simpson (1968) studied 4123 middle- and working-class children in three age groups: 8, 11, and 15. They were born in 1946 in sibships of two. Boys with 2–4 years spacing tested higher than those with either longer or shorter birth intervals; differences were not clear for the girls. They found verbal scores were more sensitive to spacing than were nonverbal (e.g., space, math) scores, and that spacing effects were established by age 8. Their findings confirm Koch's on both counts.

Feiring and Lewis (1980) studied 21 firstborn infants who had no sibling by age 48 months (wide spaced), 35 who had a sib between 24 and 36 months, and a group (number not given) who had siblings between 12 and 24 months of age. The last group, with the shortest spacing, did the most poorly on the Bayley Infant Test. Kamin, Kubinger, and Schubert (1981) studied the medical reports of 402 children. Firstborns with a spacing interval of over 3 years had higher IQs than did those with less spacing to the second child.

McKenna, Null, and Ventis (1979) followed parents and both children for SS2s. Wide spacing and late marriage clearly led to higher IQs. Wide spacing (33 months and over) for firstborns was accompanied by higher vocabularies than nearer spacing (24 months or less); differences were greater for boys than for girls. Secondborns also had higher vocabularies when widely spaced, though the differences were not as great as for the firstborns.

Chittenden, Foan, Zweil, and Smith (1968) studied 128 pairs of siblings, using the first and second in the same family. Subjects were above average in socioeconomic status, white, suburban fourth and fifth graders (ages 10–12) and seventh and eighth graders (ages 13–15). The firstborns were superior to secondborns, and the superiority was greater when the two were closely spaced. The authors postulated that this superiority of the close-spaced elder was attributable to the greater handicapping of the secondborn in the close-spaced pairs. The difference between the first and second increased with age. The subjects were not separated by sex in these calculations.

Bigner (1974a) studied the thinking of 24 boys and 24 girls from SS2s, white, middle-class, 12 each with an older brother and with an older sister. Intervals were 12–20 months and 20–48 months. The more closely spaced younger children were more concrete in thinking than the more widely spaced, and more detailed in describing the older.

Rosenberg *et al.* (1969) replicated Koch's SS2 subgroups with 69 boys and 45 girls, average age 9 years. Overall, the older was superior in IQ to the younger. Spacing had no significant overall effect, although five of the eight sib–sex subgroups showed higher IQs for the wider spaced. Older children with a younger brother and girls with an older brother had higher IQs when closely spaced. Their spacing intervals, however, were unusual: 1–3 and 4–6. Also, the numbers in the respective cells varied from 15 to 3 cases, an average of 5 cases for the wider spacing. Obviously, with such small numbers the differences are unreliable. They do suggest that the sex of the sibling and the sex of the proband interact with spacing interval. And again, girls seem to be less affected by the spacing interval than boys. The unusual spacing intervals used here make comparisons difficult, although close spacing seems to be disadvantageous.

In summary, the variety of spacing interval sizes makes comparison of studies difficult, and the identification of any specific interval almost impossible. Lack of separation of the two sexes and combining the older and younger sibling further becloud the issue as does absence of control of sex of sibling. In spite of these design flaws, the evidence fairly conclusively indicates that an interval of less than 24 months between middle-class children makes for risk of lower IQ for both the older and younger children, especially for boys but for girls also. Spacings of 24–48 months, 30 months and over, and 48 months and over have been found most advantageous, leaving the precise division of greatest advantage unclear. For nonverbal abilities, spacing effects are infrequent. When children are spaced 4 or more years apart, intellectual differences diminish, both children perhaps developing more like "onlyborns."

B.   YOUNG CHILDREN FROM LARGE SIBSHIPS

We turn now to the few studies on effect of sibling spacing on young children from sibships of three or more. Douglas *et al.* (1968), in their investigation of 4196 children, specifically reported effects of spacing interval on SS3s. Those with narrow spacing had lower vocabulary and reading scores than the more widely spaced. For tests of nonverbal abilities they found no differences between spacing interval subgroups.

Berbaum and Moreland (1980) studied Outhit's data regarding 259 children from 51 unbroken families, with ages ranging from 3 to 30 years, and an above-average socioeconomic level. Spacing, parents' education, ordinal rank, and lastborn handicap (Breland, 1974; Zajonc, 1976) accounted for 51% of the variance in their prediction formula.

Dandes and Dow (1969) investigated the effects of spacing and family size on intelligence. They tested 184 children in grades 1–7 (ages 6–13). Children from larger and more closely spaced sibships had lower mean IQ than those from smaller and more widely spaced sibships. Dandes and Dow, along with Waldrop and Bell (1966; Section IV,B), were concerned with family density, a composite of spacing and family size.

Oldman, Bytheway, and Horobin (1971) calculated a family growth rate, while holding sibship and socioeconomic level constant. Their subjects were a subsample of all children born in Aberdeen, Scotland in 1 year, and were tested at age 7. They found that firstborns conceived before marriage had the lowest IQs. Nonverbal IQs were negatively related to family growth rate. The authors did not state whether spacing itself influences IQ or is merely an indicator of other social and biological variables that affect IQ.

Marjoribanks (1978) studied 500 11-year-old Australian children. Although he did not divide the sexes, he found cognitive ability positively related to spacing interval for both the older and younger child, especially in mathematics and word knowledge. For the younger child, cognitive ability also increased with age spacing. Age spacing to adjacent siblings was not related to birth order differences in achievement measures. Birth order/age spacing differences were not investigated for the different sibship sizes.

Lancer and Rim (1984), using the Ravens Matrix and a group intelligence test, studied 1985 sixth grade children (average age 12 years) and their 795 older siblings, also tested in sixth grade. They found large family size and close spacing to be associated with lower intelligence, with this effect greater on verbal than on nonverbal tests and in lower and middle socioeconomic levels than in higher levels.

Finally, Brackbill and Nichols (1982) used data from clinics of 12 affiliated hospitals. Their subjects were 47,000 pregnant women who were clinical patients from urban areas and their 53,000 children. The children were tested at age 4 with the Binet and at age 7 with the Wechsler and the Wide Range Achievement Test. Boys and girls were not separated in their calculations nor was any account taken regarding sex of sibling. They included the 47% blacks and the 45% whites, excluding the 8% of other races. The socioeconomic status of the whites was somewhat lower than that of the blacks, and both were slightly higher than for racially similar age-matched United States populations. The investigators stated that "Although a significant birth interval effect was found in all 6 analyses (2 each for blacks and whites for IQ's and one each for achievement), in only 1 analysis did longer intervals appear to reduce parity effects'' (p. 196). Unfortunately, even with this large number of cases, the sexes were not separated and attention was not paid to sex of sibling and sibship size. Clinical samples are likely to be nonrandom and selected, and, therefore, even with more careful grouping, differences between spacing groups would not have been similar to populations selected at random.

In summary, as with SS2s, narrow spacing places children from larger sibships at risk of lower IQs and poorer verbal knowledge. Also, as with SS2s, nonverbal ability is less affected by sibling spacing, although one researcher did find mathematical ability decreased as spacing interval decreased. Several researchers found the composite of family density inversely related to intellectual ability. Spacing effects were not reported separately for the two sexes in the above section on larger families, adding to confusion of results.

C. PREADOLESCENTS AND ADOLESCENTS

We start the present section with Nuttall and Nuttall (1975) because they extensively studied both SS2s and SS5 and over (SS5 + s). Their subjects were 13- to 16-year-old white, middle-class, suburban school children, with spacing data on 80 SS2s and 155 SS5 + s. Spacing intervals were 18 months or less, 19–30 months, and over 30 months. The sexes were not separated. Parents were solicited through newspaper advertisements (permitting volunteer error). The children were assembled on Saturdays, in competition with extracurricular activities (also inviting volunteer error).

For SS2s, the Nuttalls found no differences in intelligence between near, intermediate, and far-spaced groups, for spacing both to the next younger and to next older sibling. However, for the combined sibships (i.e., SS2 and SS5 +), probands with the shortest interval (18 months or less) averaged a significantly lower IQ (109) than those with the largest interval (30 months and over; mean IQ 120), for intervals both to the next younger and to the next older sibling.

Specifically for the large sibships (SS5 +), Nuttall and Nuttall reported that probands with far spacing (30 months and over) to the next older sibling were significantly higher in IQ than were closer spaced. Those 18–30 months separated (actually also a fairly short interval) from the next older averaged lower IQ than both those nearer and farther spaced. Spacing, then, of 30 months or more to either older or younger sibling is advantageous to intelligence. The Nuttalls added, ''The greater the interval to the next older sibling, the more intelligent, happy-go-lucky, controlled and affected by feeling the younger is" (1979, pp. 10–11). Since the sexes were combined and the numbers were small, the lack of spacing effects for SS2's should be viewed with caution.

Kidwell (1981) examined the records of 1700 tenth-grade boys (mean age 16 years) and found that the most advantageous spacing was 5 years and over, and the next was the very narrow interval of 1 year or less. The most negative was 2–3 years.

Breland (1974) exhaustively examined the records of National Merit Scholarship applicants including 670 randomly selected 1962 participants, 1147 randomly selected high-scoring 1962 participants, and almost the entire 1965 sample. The 1965 sample consisted of 794,509 eleventh-grade students (mean age 17) from 17,608 high schools. Such samples would be somewhat truncated at the lower end of the intelligence continuum. From a fairly exhaustive study of these large samples, Breland concluded, "Where a sibling followed closely in age (24 months or less), the verbal scores were significantly depressed. But where the age spacing was far (3 years or more), the same depression did not occur" (p. 1014). Breland reported no similar effects on the older child. Both sexes showed the negative effects of close spacing on the younger child, especially for the youngest. The study indicates no consistent differences related to sex of siblings. Breland supported Faris' (1940) "isolation hypothesis" (that children isolated from other children in early development are verbally advantaged). Further supporting this hypothesis, Record, McKeown, and Edwards (1970) had reported that twins reared together had on the average almost the lowest IQ of all sibling constellation subgroups and twins reared apart had scores similar to nontwins. Breland's data also showed that twins averaged almost the lowest IQ of all sibship subgroups.

Breland's data also support the conclusion that differences are attributable to family size per se and not to family size differences due to socioeconomic factors such as father's education, mother's education, and family income, nor to family size differences due to mother's age, nor to combinations of these variables. After breaking down his analysis of the total examination into parts, he concluded that the major portion of the findings was attributable to an advantage in verbal ability rather than in mathematical and other aptitudes.

Finally, several studies on clinical and delinquent subjects do not, on the surface, seem to support the more general finding of higher intellectual ability for those widely spaced than for those more closely spaced. Romanoff (1976) found that among 790 Jewish adolescent boys sent to a clinic for career counseling, those with nearer spacing to siblings had higher IQs than firstborns. This indeed is the reverse of the usual findings reported above. Schaefer (1977) examined the Wechsler Vocabulary and Block Design scores of 100 black juveniles awaiting a court hearing. He found that spacing to neither older nor younger sibling was related to these Wechsler scores, although vocabulary was related to family size. These findings suggest that abler, more widely spaced children were less frequently in need of counseling or delinquent (see also Section II,D regarding Schoonover, 1959; Galbraith, 1982; Velandia, Grandon, & Page, 1978).

In summary, despite ever-present flaws and variations in design, the evidence indicates that for preadolescents and adolescents, especially in the larger sibships, those with wide spacing to either an older or a younger sibling are intellectually advantaged.

D. COLLEGE STUDENTS AND OTHER YOUNG ADULTS

The most investigated sample in the area of sibship constellation variables is that of the 200,000 19-year-old Netherlands inductees born 1945–1948. This complete all-male sample was administered the Ravens Progressive Matrices, a comparatively culture- and environment-free intelligence test. In most research on this sample, family size, ordinal position, and socioeconomic level (measured as manual, nonmanual, and farmers) were homogeneously grouped. Sibling spacing effects were studied for two series of SS2s; 538 pairs of brothers and 521 unrelated first- and secondborns. Neither birth-order effect on intelligence nor actual level of ability was influenced by the length of interval between the first and second sibling. There was a positive difference in favor of firstborns whose mothers were older at their births, with a similar effect on the intelligence of the secondborns (Belmont, Stein, & Zybert, 1978). We have not been able to find a study on these data specifically of the effects of birth spacing for larger sibships.

However, Zajonc (1976) and Zajonc and Markus (1975) did use the Netherlands sample to develop their confluence model. The purpose of the model is to explain the relationship of sibship size, birth order, and sibling spacing to intellectual ability. They theorized that long birth intervals give older children the benefits of being in a small family, for a longer period of time and during an early phase of growth (which is more sensitive to environmental effects) and having a higher average level of intelligence for the family. They also suggested that the younger child also benefits from a postponed birth, thus arriving in a more mature family. They considered close spacing to be less detrimental to the older child, with the lastborn being especially disadvantaged. However, Zajonc reported (1976) that widely spaced youngests do not show this additional disadvantage in intellect.

Four researchers have tested college students; three combined the sexes, whereas the fourth did not. Obviously, combining the sexes attenuates their findings in that females seem less affected by spacing than males. However, because of college students' lack of representativeness (of the general population) for intelligence, scholastic achievement, and academic interest, the very areas being researched for sibling spacing effects, the samples are obviously greatly truncated at the lower levels of these variables, thus seriously limiting generalization. If narrow spacing reduces IQ, academic achievement, and interest, fewer such narrow-spaced individuals would be expected in these college samples. Such attenuation would be expected to minimize expected differences in IQ, college interest,—and sibling spacing.

Schoonover (1979) used sibling pairs of college students. Numbers varied from 33 to 60 pairs for various comparisons. The sexes and pre- and post-intervals were combined, and her subgroups were not separated for family size nor for ordinal position. In addition, selected for college attendance, the samples were truncated in intelligence, academic achievement, and interest in college. She found no difference by birth interval for intelligence or achievement, which absence, in a fashion, is the goal of selecting students for college attendance.

Galbraith (1982) compared the intelligence of about 15,000 college applicants at Brigham Young University, mostly Mormon in religion, for sibling spacing effects. The average sibship size is larger than for most other American university populations. Data presented indicate that firstborns were present in considerably larger numbers than lastborns. A part of this excess might be expected from the rapidly growing Mormon population with their emphasis on large families. However, that all is due to population growth is unlikely (Price & Hare, 1969). The relatively small representation of youngests indicates some of the truncation indicated above, since lastborns are fairly uniformly found to be less verbally intelligent and less likely to attend college. The combining of the sexes and the truncation for intelligence, academic achievement, and interest in higher education probably largely account for his finding no relation between intellectual development and sibling spacing. The very factors intended to be studied are diminished by the college selection process.

The third study on spacing effects on intelligence using college students as subjects is that by Velandia *et al.* (1978). Their statistically very sophisticated research investigated a sample of over 38,000 college applicants from Colombia, South America. This sample represents about 5% of the population from which it was drawn. The sexes were combined in their result. Measures of intelligence included verbal ability, mathematical aptitude, and abstract reasoning. Their results differed in many regards from the general finding that intellect decreases with family size. Probands from sibships of three and four surpassed those from sibships of one and two in mental ability, although eldests surpassed younger siblings. Subjects in the top quartile in socioeconomic level showed reduced overall ability, and those in the lowest quartile did not show the decrement with ordinal position. In the lowest quartile, the third child was superior to the first and second. Socioeconomic level swamped ordinal rank and family size in its effects, even though the authors suggested that they really included only an upper "elite" segment of the socioeconomic distribution. Their data on sibling spacing do not agree with those from the Holland sample, in part because, as they noted, the family size of their sample was so large. Another reason for the lack of similarity probably is the very considerable selection of their sample (5%).

Rosenberg and Sutton-Smith (1969) tested 353 male and 658 female college sophomores, all SS2s, with a 2:1 ratio of nonmanual to manual socioeconomic level. They used two ways of classifying spacing intervals: (1) 0–3 years and 4–6 years and (2) 0–2 years, 3–4 years, and 5–6 years. Koch's eight categories by ordinal position, sex of propositus, and sex of sibling were compared for verbal, quantitative, and total American College Entrance Examination scores.

They concluded, as Koch did in 1954, that wide spacing facilitates male cognitive functioning and close spacing facilitates female functioning. The improvement of cognitive functioning by closely spaced girls is attributable largely to those with sisters. Firstborn boys were superior to secondborn boys, with the greatest difference for those spaced 2 years apart or less, which was particularly caused by the depressed intellect of the secondborn boy. They hypothesized that this is due to the latter's not escaping from overwhelming competition. Spacing effects were greater on the verbal section of the test. They noted that "Results clearly imply that there are age differences, family size differences, and most probably SES differences cutting across the simplicity of sibling status effects upon intellectual functioning" (p. 667).

The results of a study by Davis, Cahan, and Bashi (1977) might illuminate the Velandia *et al.* study. Davis *et al.* studied Israeli children, dividing them by origin of parents into those from Europe, America, and South Africa from those from North Africa and Asia. They found for the former the usual effect: the eldest tested higher than the second, who in turn fared better than the third. For the North African–Asian group, however, the first was poorer than the second, the fourth was abler than the third, the fifth than the fourth, etc. For the North African–Asian group, the parents had no school education and did not assist their children with school work. However, the older helped the younger. This study indicates the effect on sibship effects of socioeconomic level, here parental education.

The conclusion of the present authors regarding the relation of sibling spacing to intellect at the young adult level is that (1) results regarding college students for effects of sibling spacing cannot be generalized beyond the specific university, (2) more methodologically sound studies are needed in this area, and (3) indeed the one study with appropriate methodology indicates that sibling spacing is positively related to intelligence.

E. THE EMINENT, GIFTED, AND CREATIVE

Three studies dealt with the relation of sibling spacing to eminence and giftedness and four on creativity. Roe (1953) studied 64 eminent scientists, 39 firstborns and 25 lastborns. She reported an average age interval of the laterborns to next older of 5 years, a very wide average spacing indeed.

Allen (1955) used mailed questionnaires to gather data and received usable returns from 316 Methodist ministers. These he divided by success into quartiles. The upper quartile derived from the smallest sibships and had the largest spacing to the next older sibling, with both mother and father better educated.

Hayes and Bronzaft (1979) sent questionnaires to 850 members of an academic honors society (Phi Beta Kappa), and received 559 (66%) usable returns. For SS2s, 19.5% were spaced by 1–2 years; 41.9%, 3–4 years; 22.7%, 5–6 years; and 15.7%, 7 years or over. Over one-third (38.4%) were spaced over 4 years. This percentage is larger than among average SS2s. Here, as for Allen (1955), one cannot be certain that those widely spaced do not more frequently answer questionnaires. Interaction between answering questionnaires and sibship variables is possible (Rosenthal & Rosnow, 1970).

Creativity is a fairly complex concept and the various authors have used different measures. Brim (1958) used Koch's data (1954a,b, 1956), with the same spacing intervals that Koch used (Section II,A). For originality, Brim found that younger children, both boys and girls, with either a brother or sister less than 2 years older were low on this measure. Children with a like-sexed sibling over 2 years older were high on originality: girls significantly so for a spacing interval of 2–6 years, and boys, for an interval of 4–6 years. All others, including all with opposite-sexed siblings over 2 years older, showed no difference.

Kaltsounis (1978) compared nine sets of four brothers in grades 3, 4, 5, and 6 who were a little over a year apart in age. The second brother performed significantly better on Thinking Creatively with Pictures and Words, Form A. Cicirelli (1967) compared 80 SS2 eighth graders and 140 from larger sibships. Among the SS2 children, the highest creativity scores were of boys with close brothers and girls with close sisters for fluency and flexibility. Datta (1968) found that boys with a distant older brother were low in creativity.

Summarizing the findings on measured creativity is difficult for several reasons: the measures are not consistent, the spacing intervals are not the same, and the ages of the subjects vary widely. The sex of the sibling indeed seems to affect creativity as much as and perhaps more so than spacing. However, age spacing does play a role with probable overall disadvantage to a closely spaced younger cross-sexed sibling or a widely spaced youngest boy.

F. NONINTERSIBLING SPACING MEASURES

Under the preceding four sections, we have discussed effects of intersibling spacing. Another frequently used spacing measure is the distance between marriage and the birth of the first child, with subdivision being illegitimacy, conceived before marriage, conceived soon after marriage, and born 2 or more years after marriage. A second measure of nonintersibling spacing is the age of parents at the birth of their child. Third, returning to intersibling spacing, we will briefly note those born with intersibling spacing approaching zero (twins) and those with infinite intersibling spacing (onlyborns); and finally intersibling spacing of non-blood-related children reared together (adoptives).

1. Space between Marriage and Birth of First Child
The interval between marriage and the birth of the first child is included as a sibling interval by some authors. Davidson (1970), using 1965 census data, found that the longer the period between marriage and the birth of the first child, the smaller the sibship size, as was also true for the interval between the first and second child. Ford (1981) interviewed 9800 women, aged 15–44, who had offspring. She found spacing varied by year of marriage. Women married in 1960–1964 more frequently had a first child within 12 months than those married in 1970–1973, and more often had a second in the following 18 months. Blacks, Hispanics, and Catholics more frequently marry early and have more closely spaced children. Better educated women, those who are farm born, and Hispanics less frequently have a child within 7 months after marriage. Norton (1980) estimated that 10% of firstborns are born before marriage. Blacks, low social class women, and those who later divorce more frequently have children before marriage. Illegitimates are especially handicapped in ability and personality, as are those born a short interval after marriage. Similarly, studies show that planned children are advantaged in intellect versus unplanned.

Embedded in the consideration of birth before marriage, premaritally conceived, planned versus unplanned births, and close spacing in many cases is the wantedness versus unwantedness of the child. Matecjek, Dytrych, and Schüller (1978) compared children born after the mother had twice requested abortion with a control group whose mothers had not requested abortion. Both groups were tested at various ages. The former were less able, made poorer use of their intelligence, and overall were much more poorly adjusted. As parents increasingly are able to choose when to have their children, many findings regarding effects of family size and sibling spacing will become outdated.

2. Age of Parents at Child's Birth

Three researchers have studied age of parent at child's birth for average samples, and six for gifted and eminent samples. McKenna *et al.* (1979) studied age at marriage, which obviously is related to age of parents at birth of children. They concluded that age at marriage has wide effects on children's intelligence, personality, self-esteem, etc. They stated that age at marriage has an importance close to that of child spacing. The older the parents and the more widely spaced the children, the abler are the children.

Belmont *et al.* (1978), in their study of male Netherlands inductees (Section II,D), reported that both the older and younger siblings in SS2s whose mothers were older had higher IQs. Roberts and Engel (1974), in an examination of 7110 children, found IQs increased with age of both the mother and father at the child's birth, to a maximum of 25–35 years for the mothers and 24–44 for the fathers.

Regarding age of parents at birth of gifted children, Albert (1980) studied 25 mathematically gifted boys and 25 with IQs of 150 and over. Mothers averaged 27.2 years and fathers 30.5, both over the normal average age. Terman (1925) and Freeman (1979) also reported parents of gifted as older than the norm.

Visher (1948) reported a median age of 35 for fathers and 29 for mothers of 906 top American scientists, including many Nobel prize winners. Goertzel, Goertzel, and Goertzel (1978) wrote, "Like many other parents of gifted, they [the parents of their 300 eminents] were not in early youth when their eminent children were born" (p. 22). Many of these parents stayed intellectually and physically active well into their 80s and 90s. Yoder (1894) pointed out that a child born to parents in their prime of life has better chances of greatness. He studied 50 great men and reported an average age of 37.8 for 39 fathers at the birth of their illustrious children, and 29.8 for 25 mothers. He quoted Galton's finding that at the births of 100 English men of eminence, their fathers averaged 36 years of age and their mothers 29 years.

Other things being equal, parents older at the birth of their children are likely to have abler offspring.

3. Spacing between Non-Blood-Related

Obliquely related to the topic of spacing effects on intelligence are the intellects of adoptives. In the only published study of spacing of adoptives, Grotevant, Scarr, and Weinberg (1977) reported that spacing is not related to intelligence among adoptives. Even when children are adopted very close to their births, one cannot be certain that their adoptive parents respond to and treat them in the same manner as they would their own children. Adoptive parents are never blind to the status of their adopted children and many may not have the same faith and belief in them, and perhaps even confer less love.

4. Zero Spacing

Regarding twins, who have a near zero spacing, Breland (1974) and Zajonc (1976) reported that these most closely spaced of children rate in verbal facility very close to, if not at, the bottom of all ordinal groups. Indeed, others have for a long time (e.g., Davis, 1937) reported the low linguistic skill of twins. Also reported (Record *et al.,* 1970) is that twins reared apart from birth have almost the same verbal skills as singleborns in the same birth order. However, for a clinic population, Brackbill and Nichols (1982) did not confirm this finding for twins whose co-twin died at birth. Twins, on the average, have lower birth weight, are more often prematurely born, and more frequently have physical handicaps at birth, all of which may contribute to their lower IQs.

5. Infinite Spacing

Onlyborns are, as it were, infinitely spaced. They rate higher in all measures of language ability than all other children (Davis, 1937). Wanted onlyborns rated higher than wanted "nononlies," who rated higher than unwanted nononlies, who rated higher than unwanted onlyborns (Matecjek *et al.,* 1979). Even when illegitimates and unwanteds are included, onlyborns have higher intelligence than all except SS2s and the eldest of SS3s (Belmont & Marolla, 1973). How much of this superiority is attributable to advantaged physiology (see Section V), how much to lack of emotional disturbance and competitive rivalry produced by near siblings (see Sections III and IV), and how much to their greater access to parental time, attention, support, and interest and to greater amounts of hidden educators (trips with parents, nonschool training, etc.) is not clear (Blau, 1981).

G. ACADEMIC ACHIEVEMENT AND ADULT SUCCESS

In this discussion of sibling spacing effects on general achievement, we will follow the same order as for intelligence: SS2s and younger subjects, then larger sibships, followed by older subjects and occupational success.

Reading success, as a measure of academic achievement, will be discussed first.

1. Reading Ability

Several authors have specifically studied the effects of spacing on reading ability. As noted above, Douglas *et al.* (1968) found that narrow spacing led to lower scores in reading. Levinson (1963), with spacings of up to 30 months and 31 months and over, found that wide spacing produces extremes in reading ability in the younger, with no spacing effects for the older. In neither study were the subjects separated by sex, nor by sex of sibling. Cicirelli (1967), with 80 sixth graders from SS2s and 140 from various larger sibship sizes, found that reading and arithmetic were enhanced for like-sexed siblings close in age. Cicirelli emphasized the danger of generalizing from SS2s to larger sibships and emphasized the interaction of the effects of spacing and sex of siblings.

Melican (1978) studied 5924 high school students and found that the effect of spacing varied from sibling size to sibling size and from one achievement measure to another (see the next subsection). Spacing to the next younger added significantly to the prediction of reading and composition scores for SS3s. Spacing did not add significantly to any SS2 measure nor to the prediction of reading for SS5s. Melican did not separate by sex in his compilations, nor by socioeconomic level, nor by sex of sibling. Certainly, with 5924 subjects, at least the sexes might have been separated in this study. With some authors finding that girls and boys are affected differently by spacing and the fairly accepted superiority of girls in things verbal, these authors might well have separated the sexes in their calculations, and perhaps also by sex of sibling. It is not clear, further, that spacing to the preceding child was separated from that to the child following the subject studied. With these variations in methodology, findings might be expected to vary, not really solving the problem under investigation. For instance, failure to separate the two sexes may actually cancel out, or at least greatly minimize, actual differences.

Farley (1978) studied 1186 junior high school students in two small cities in Ohio. He correlated months of spacing to the next younger sibling and school performance. His correlations were not statistically significant. With the number of cases Farley had, the sexes might have been separated, and family size held constant. He did not study spacing to next older child.

Schoonover (1979) found no significant differences by birth spacing on college achievement. Subjects were not separated for sex, family size, ordinal position, nor spacing preceding and following the index subject. As noted above (Section II,D), any college sample is not a random sample, but rather is curtailed at the lower end of ability and interest in academic pursuits. In fact, Nuttall and Nuttall (1975) found that subjects with a wide gap to the next younger significantly more often planned to attend college, especially for SS2s. They found no similar spacing effects for college plans for the next older. Spacing to the next older was related to placing greater importance on getting a job, with higher occupational aspirations in other than intellectual occupations.

2. Academic Success

Academic success and spacing have not been studied in young children. Nuttall and Nuttall (1975, see Section II,B) studied children 12–16 years of age, 80 SS2s and 156 SS5 + s. The sexes were not separated. Spacing effects generally were greater for the SS5 + s, greater for boys than for girls, and significantly in favor of those more than 18 months separated.

Melican (1978) and Melican and Feldt (1980, see Section II,C) studied 5924 high school students. The size of the spacing between children was found, in selected instances, to be related to achievement, in sibships of three or more. Results were not consistent for every sibship size nor for every position in the birth sequence, and varied from achievement measure to achievement measure. Increased spacing to the next younger was significantly related to prediction of quantitative abilities and to reading. Spacing to the next older was significantly related to prediction of quantitative and composite measures in sibships of three, but not to any measure for sibships of two and four. The relations were sometimes linear, and sometimes curvilinear. Inspection of the tables presented indicates that where spacing was not predictive, ordinal rank was, and vice versa. Unfortunately the sexes were not separated in this large study, because such separation would have permitted evaluation of interactions between sex of subject and specific abilities, and might have yielded more significant differences.

3. Adult Success

One additional study may be included here. Olneck and Bills (1979) compared 346 pairs of adjacent brothers for test ability, school achievement, occupational status, and earnings. The average differences on these measures did not vary systematically with age spacing. Their comparison groups were not homogeneously grouped for ordinal position nor for pre- and postspacing. They suggested that sibship size has a greater effect than spacing.

Koch (1954) found for her 5- and 6-year-old SS2s that the wider the spacing between siblings, the greater the number of interests. As the gap widened to an older brother, the younger brother showed more curiosity, enthusiasm, "planfulness," and interests. Widely spaced younger brothers with a sister also had wider interests.

Perhaps related to achievement are occupational interests. Nuttall and Nuttall (1975) found that a wide spacing to the next younger led to higher plans to attend college, especially for SS2s. No similar spacing effect to the next older was found for college plans. However, a small gap to the next older, especially for those who were the second child in the family, made getting a job important and made occupational success a high aspiration. Such children rated athletic success as very important.

Reilly (1976) investigated vocational preferences of 171 male and 202 female eighth graders (average age 13–14 years). All subjects were English speaking and children from sibships of one through four, with families intact to child's age 6, mostly from the next to lowest socioeconomic level. No significant relation was found between spacing interval and vocational choice.

Finally, the section on spacing interval among the gifted, eminent, and creative (Section II,E) is relevant here. For these high achievers in intellect and occupation, the widely spaced were overfrequently represented. Several of these achievement studies were flawed by use of mailed questionnaires, however, in that volunteers may select in the same manner that IQ and achievement do.

A summary of the research on sibling spacing effects on academic achievement and success in other areas is made almost impossible by less than optimal methodology for the majority of the investigators. Researchers who separated for sibship size did not for sex of the propositus. The spacing before the subject was frequently combined with that following. Samples were grossly truncated in the very measures being examined. For the dependent variable (achievement) verbal, mathematical, and science fields were combined and the sexes were combined, although males and females are widely believed to differ in their success in these fields. Also volunteers were used in several studies, although volunteers differ in some of the areas from nonvolunteers, slanting results in a specific direction. In spite of all these flaws of design, as one reads the research the hypothesis still seems tenable that with tighter design, spacing interval size is related to achievement, academic and otherwise. For several of the studies that had a large number of subjects, one wishes the authors would go back and make the appropriate subgroupings and redo their analyses. Unfortunately, most of the studies are quite old and unearthing the data and redoing the analyses would be quite difficult.

H. GENERAL SUMMARY: INTELLIGENCE, ACHIEVEMENT,
AND SUCCESS

1. Almost uniformly, available research indicates a risk of lower IQ for those spaced 24 months or less, with some suggestions that such risk may extend to longer intervals, especially for boys.

2. Spacing effects seem greater in larger sibships.

3. Boys are usually more affected by the spacing interval than are girls.

4. Verbal ability is more affected by spacing than nonverbal.

5. Firstborns are possibly more affected than laterborns.

6. Regarding reading and school achievement, findings are inconsistent, with some indication of negative effects of close spacing. As the research design improved in adequacy, the results pointed more clearly to negative effects of close spacing.

7. Gifted children are overfrequently more widely spaced especially for the younger child, but for the older also.

8. Eminents are very frequently born to older parents.

9. Twins, the closest spaced of all, averaged the lowest IQs.

10. Koch (1960) suggested that her data on 5 and 6 year olds may not be wholly generalizable to older children; and, indeed, some of the data on preadolescents and adolescents do suggest an increase of wider spacing effects with increase in age. Added years of experience at a specific constellation position might well compound effects. No one has done a longitudinal study to see whether, as the sample increases in age, specific effects change.

11. However, all this does not mean that every child who has close siblings will do more poorly than those with more widely spaced brothers and sisters. Indeed, many other factors affect the development of intelligence and achievement.

III. Sibling Spacing Effects on Family Interactions

As per our outline, we now turn to sibling spacing effects on family interactions: dethronement, and child–parent, parent–parent, and child–child relations. In each of the four subdivisions we will start with the smallest sibship size and progress to larger sibships and from youngest move to older children.

A. EFFECTS OF AGE AT "DETHRONEMENT"

Researchers almost uniformly find negative effects on the firstborn at the birth of the subsequent child, and the shorter the interval the greater the negative effects on the "displaced" older. Cameron (1963) wrote that children, especially if 4 years or less of age, universally show signs of hostility, anxiety, competitiveness, and regression at advent of a younger sib.

Henchie (1963) found that the probability of disturbance over the birth of a sib was greater the younger the child at "dethronement." Of his subjects under 3 years, 89% showed disturbance as contrasted with 11% of those over 6. These older children's reactions to the younger tended to deteriorate as the baby grew to the stage of disrupting play as a toddler. Legg, Sherick, and Wadland (1974) studied 29 children for reactions to the birth of a sibling. Children who were younger at dethronement frequently regressed to requesting bottle feeding, with interference of toilet training. Older children at dethronement frequently showed some forward movement in ego functioning, with later difficulty with the toddler fighting over possessions.

Nadelman and Begun (1981) found that SS2 firstborns in their youngest dethronement group (age less than 40 months) showed a greater increase in toilet accidents and need for help in doing things after the birth of the second child than did those 40 months or over. They suggested that this greater vulnerability of children younger at displacement may be attributed to physical immaturity, lesser grasp of reality, and greater separation fears. In a subsequent article, Nadelman and Begun (1982) reported that all firstborns, both immediately before and shortly after the birth of the second, showed disturbance. Boys showed greater withdrawal and more toilet accidents; girls showed more immaturity of behavior. Boys closely spaced by less than 40 months showed the greatest negative effects, and firstborn girls least.

Thomas, Birch, Chess, and Robbins (1961) found that firstborns showed more disturbance at the birth of a new sibling than did laterborns. They found that 18 months is a critical age for a child's dethronement. The father's involvement with the older child improved ability to tolerate the mother's lessening of attention. Trause (1978) studied the reactions of 37 firstborn, white, middle-class children, age 1–3.5 to a 2- to 6-day separation with mother's hospitalization. Both children who visited the mother and those who did not showed more problems after the mother's absence. Nonvisiting children showed more negative behavior at the time of the mother's discharge.

Mahler and Bergman (1956) and Mahler, Pine, and Bergman (1967) suggested that children aged 15–30 months go through a stage of separating the self from the mother and especially fear loss of the mother's love. They saw the child at this time engaged in individualization with increased separation anxiety. Stendler (1964) wrote, "Arrival of a new child is more traumatic when the first is still very dependent on the mother" (p. 144). The researchers in the field agree that the introduction of a new baby into the home is fairly uniformly hard on the older children at least up to 4 years of age, but especially so when the child is younger than 4 years. But how about the newcomer?

McCall (1984) studied 80 subjects, ages 2.5 to 67 years, from the Fels Longitudinal Study. Subjects, following the birth of a sibling, dropped 10 IQ points compared with onlyborns and 5.8 IQ points compared with lastborns. These differences were no longer significant at age 17 years.

White (1974, 1975) has done much observation of young children and has written considerably. He wrote, "To have an older sibling at home who is two almost invariably means receiving hatred from time to time. The older child, in his distress, may actually attack the baby" (1974, p. 9). All this, White pointed out, is quite different from the blissful acceptance of the first. Except for White, few researchers have written about the very early effects of close spacing on the second child. The interaction of young siblings is described below (Section VII,D). We now turn to the parent-child interaction, especially (1) the early mother–child interaction as related to sibling spacing, but also (2) the parent–child interaction for older children.

B. PARENT–CHILD INTERACTIONS

1. Early Parent–Child Interaction

Bowlby (1952) wrote that when a child experiences loss of maternal love deeply and frequently between ages 6 and 18 months, normal attachments become extremely difficult. Provence and Lipton (1963) studied institutionalized infants. Spitz (1945) studied children separated from their mothers because of her imprisonment. These, along with Ribble in her *Rights of Infants* (1943), described the intensity of lack of development of infants early deprived of mothering. Despite flawed methodology, especially in the studies prior to 1950, the consistency of findings is noteworthy.

Lasko (1954) elaborated comparisons of early mother–child interaction as related to spacing between children. Forty-six mothers were rated for behavior of children pairs at the same age. Her comparison produced a considerable amount of data. Closely spaced children benefited from more rational and understanding treatment than did those more widely spaced. However, the second child with 2 years or less spacing to next was at marked disadvantage compared to a like-spaced third child who was treated more warmly. The second was treated more restrictively, with more friction with the mother. With a spacing of 3 years or less a radical change appeared in treatment of the second child at the advent of the third child. No such change appeared when the second child was 4 years old at displacement. Generally, the mother found it easier to meet the needs of both children when they were more widely spaced. The earlier displaced generally suffered more from lack of warmth.

Judd and Lewis (1976) observed 190 mothers with their 12-week-old infants. They studied spacing between the infant and an older child for spacings of 9–18 months, 1.5–2.5 years, and 2.5–3.5 years. The mother vocalized more to the infant who was 9–19 months younger and to the older, treating the two babies alike and thus retarding the development of the older child.

For spacings between 18 months and 4 years, the older was too old to be treated as an infant and too young to care for itself. This period is the most difficult period for the mother. For spacings of 4 years or more, the older children take considerable care of themselves.

Lewis and Kreitzberg (1979) found that spacing effects were significantly related to the mother's behavior, such that very close and very widely spaced infants received more maternal attention than did the middle spaced. Their subjects were 193 3-month-old infants with mother and older sibling. Kendrick and Dunn (1982) reported that confrontation between mother and child increased when the first was close in age to the second. The sex of the sibling dyad also influenced the interaction of the triad. Gregg and Elmer (1959) reported on 146 families in which infants and very young children were referred from accidents and child abuse. With two or more small children of short birth interval, accidents and abusive injuries were more common.

For the early mother–child relations, we see again that the 4-year interval seems overall more advantageous than shorter intervals. We turn now to spacing effects on later parent–child relations.

2. Parent–Child Relations by Spacing for Older Children

Nuttall and Nuttall (1975), with 13- to 16-year-old subjects (Section II,C), found that closely spaced firstborns (up to 18 months) felt their mothers used the most firm discipline. In the SS2s, the closely spaced younger child felt least accepted by both parents, and felt that the father was more lax in discipline than did those middle spaced (18–30 months).

Kidwell (1981) studied over 1700 tenth-grade (average age 15–16) boys for their perception of parent relationships. For the best relationships, the spacing was the widest (5 years) and the narrowest (1 year or less), with spacings of 2–3 years being the most negative. Having a male sib most emphasized the above relationships. Boys with closest sibling a girl viewed their parents as most punitive.

In 1978, Kidwell studied 381 onlyborns and 1256 eldests, aged 13–18, with spacings of less than 2 years, 2–3 years, etc. She felt perceptions were more important than actuality. She found no consistent pattern for the girls. For boys, those in the 2- to 3-year spacing group had poorer relationships, as reported by both sexes, with both the father and mother, than other firstborns. Boys spaced under 2 years were next poorest, and those spaced by 3 years and over best. Also, adolescent onlyborns reported the most positive affect, both sexes and for father and mother, more so than other firstborns, in warmth and enjoyment for both parents and respect for the father. Parenthetically, Kidwell consistently argued for homogeneous grouping of subjects by family size, ordinal position, and sex of sibling.

Scheinfeld (1983) interviewed 33 mothers of black sons of very low income status. The mother's treatment of and attitude toward her son was highly correlated with the academic achievement of the son. One wonders whether some of the more positive treatment was due to wider spacing.

Overall, a spacing of 2–3 years seems to make for poorest parent–child relations both for very young children and for older children as well. However, the negative effects of the 2- to 3-year spacing is closely followed by those for shorter intervals. The best relations are for children spaced by over 4 years, including onlyborns who have no siblings. These differences are sharper for boys than for girls, in line with the generally weaker effect of spacing interval on girls. Good parent–child relations seem beneficial to the achievement of the child and some evidence indicates they can be improved with training (Eyberg & Robinson, 1982).

C. PARENT–PARENT RELATIONSHIPS

Regarding effects on the mother, Knox and Wilson (1978) found mothers with a second child closely spaced were more frequently tired at the end of the day and had less time for their husbands. Deacon and Firebaugh (1975) found mothers were affected by spacing of their children as to time spent on housework and in community participation. Clausen (1966) stated that a number of children fairly close in age, with the turmoil of interacting children, places a burden on the mother. Hurley and Palonen (1967) found a significant inverse relation between child density (a composite of number and closeness) and marital adjustment. Bell, Johnson, McGillicuddy-Delise, and Sigel (1980), in a review of this area, stated that the number and spacing of children are perpetrators of normative stress in young families. Increasing family size and sibling density creates more demands on the parents' finite time and energies.

We see here too that the researchers argued for wider spacing of children to improve family relations and reduce stress. However, Christensen (1968) gleaned that how well a couple matched the number and spacing of their children to their desires determined marital success rather than actual number and spacing.

D. INTERSIBLING RELATIONS

Possibly the most important, and certainly the most investigated of interfamilial relations, is that of sibling interaction, with rivalry comprising more of these investigations than all the others. Other variables studied for their relation to sibling spacing are prosociability, imitation, agonism, aggression, and trait oppositeness.

1.   Very Young Children

The researchers Abramovich, Corter, Lando, and Pepler have published a series of papers. In their first paper (Abramovich, Corter, & Lando, 1979), they studied verbal aggression and nurturant behavior in 34 child pairs of SS2, preschool, same-sex siblings. Their closely spaced boys, 2 years or less, engaged in more verbal aggression than did those more widely spaced (2.5–4 years); girls showed the opposite pattern. Firstborn girls in both narrowly and widely spaced pairs engaged in more positive and nurturant behavior than did the laterborns, acting like little mothers. Suomi (1982) in his study of primates found that older sisters groomed and cared for youngers, especially sisters. The older female siblings who had this opportunity seemed to know better how to care for their own offspring.

Pepler, Abramovich, and Corter (1981) observed 28 pairs each of same-sex and cross-sexed SS2 dyads for two 1-hour periods. The spacing intervals were up to 2 years and 2.5–4 years. Same-sex closely spaced pairs responded more negatively to prosocial approach and cross-sexed closely spaced submitted more frequently to agonism. Neither sex of dyad nor spacing interval had any effect on imitative behavior. In fact, spacing did not have much effect on patterns of cooperation, aggression, and imitation for these preschoolers.

Corter, Abramovich, and Pepler (1982), with 32 mixed-sex dyads together in the laboratory, found more prosocial behavior initiated with wide spacing, 2.5–4 years. Widely spaced older SS2s were more prosocial; closely spaced youngers were least prosocial. Sex had no effect on prosociability. Agonistic acts were more frequent in mother's presence, but were not affected by sex, spacing, or age among these SS2, middle-class sibling dyads.

Abramovich, Corter, and Pepler (1980) again observed preschool cross-sexed SS2 dyads spaced 2 years or less and over 3 years. Results were very similar to like-sexed dyads. For the intervals studied, they reported little effect of spacing on agonism or on prosocial and imitative behavior. For the studies performed by this team, interactions of children spaced 4 years or over unfortunately were not included.

In these studies of quite young children, close spacing of boys, especially in like-sexed pairs, seems to lead to more aggressiveness, consistent with findings listed below for older children. The finding that closely spaced girls are less aggressive in contrast to the findings that closely spaced boys are more aggressive emphasizes the need to study the sexes separately to avoid cancelling out the effects of spacing.

2.   Latency and Preadolescent Children

First, we consider the effects of sibling–sibling relationships other than rivalry and/or jealousy in latency and preadolescent children. Cicirelli (1974) studied the helping effects of near- and far-spaced eldest children on their younger siblings. His subjects were 180 pairs of SS2 dyads from 22 schools. The older child aided the younger. Children aided by a sibling 4 years older used inferential style more than those aided by a 2-year-older sibling. The younger children were more willing to accept help and profited more as a result of aid when it was given by a sibling 4 years older than from a close sibling.

Minnett, Vandell, and Santrock (1983) videotaped SS2 7–8 year olds as they interacted with siblings 4–12 years old in cooperative, competitive, and neutral situations. Spacings were 1–2 years and 2–4 years. Widely spaced firstborns were more likely to praise and teach siblings; widely spaced secondborns were more positive in behavior and affection than their closely spaced counterparts. Girls praised and taught; boys engaged in more neutral behavior. Like-sexed sibs were more likely to cheat and to be aggressive and dominant then cross-sexed siblings. Children's experience of sibling relationships varies systematically with sibling status.

Pfouts (1980) compared 37 boys, aged 5–16 years, of white, upper-middle class SS2s, for spacing interval effects. She found that an interval of 2 years or less was associated with more negative feelings to each other, and to the father, and of the younger sibling to the mother. She made the point, confirming Bigner's finding, that power relations between sibs are negatively related to spacing.

Koch (1956a), in her study of SS2 5 and 6 year olds, reported that eldest boys spaced 2–4 years from a younger sibling were relatively more jealous, quarrelsome, exhibitionistic, loud, and insistent on rights than with other spacings. In general, children spaced 4–6 years apart with a male sibling were relatively higher on competitiveness, leadership, and tendency to insist on rights as compared to those with sisters. Widely spaced children with a male sibling were higher on aggressiveness than with a sister. Closely spaced girls were higher on aggressiveness than closely spaced boys. The younger of two brothers, as the spacing increased, showed more aggressiveness, curiosity, enthusiasm, and "planfulness," with more interests. Comparing younger boys with brothers to those with sisters, the spacing effect increased to significance by 4 years for aggression, enthusiasm, ambition, tenacity, and number of interests.

Black and Sturge (1979) reported that all children with a sibling less than 4 years younger showed some disturbance: aggression, depression, etc. Boys with a close older sibling, especially with a sister, were more "sissy." Firstborns with a sibling less than 3 years younger were more affiliative. Hoffman (1976) concluded that close spacing gives excellent opportunity for cross-joining to become extremely rich. Both conflict and affinity, the poles of ambivalence, can flourish and are especially cross-joined in monozygotic twins.

One author, Tesser (1980), reported on the effect of inequality of ability on the relation of spacing to identification and friction of siblings. Using 513 university students as subjects, he found that identification decreased and friction increased with close spacing when the subject reported that his/her sibling performed better on important dimensions. When the subject himself performed better than his/her sib, the relationship to closeness in age was reversed for identification and was severely attenuated for friction. Pfouts (1976) presented similar data regarding unequally endowed siblings. Tesser saw this interrelation as related to the maintenance of self-esteem. Both Pfouts (1976) and Bank and Kahn (1982), in their reviews, similarly stated that close spacing of some siblings fosters identification and common interests. Bank and Kahn added, "yet by virtue of the closeness in age, they may collide and struggle with each other more frequently" (p. 27). They continued, "Narrow spacing can force siblings into contact, dependence and competition and heighten mutual influence. The earlier and more prolonged, the more intense and the more fraught with difficulty, conflict, and ambivalence" (p. 88).

Suomi (1982) reported that for primates the smaller the age difference, the more absolute the time they spent in interaction and in mutual play activities with siblings. White (1980), after years of observing children, remarked that he could think of no advantages of having close siblings, but that when more widely spaced they seemed to enjoy each other even though they played together infrequently. We now turn to the relation of spacing specifically to sibling rivalry and jealousy.

3. Sibling Rivalry

Intersib jealousy, competitiveness, and hostility seem to disturb parents greatly. Perhaps this is the reason that so many researchers have investigated this attribute of relation between siblings. Generally, children near in age and same sexed are seen as most hostilely competitive. Mahler *et al.* (1967) wrote that maximal sibling rivalry is present when the elder child is 15–22 months older than a younger sibling. Sewall, already in 1930, reported that jealousy was found for 50% of firstborns and was more likely to occur if the spacing was between 18 months and 3 years. Smalley, also in 1930, reported that jealousy was more likely to occur with like-sexed siblings, especially girls. Smalley had no data on spacing. Koch found for her SS2 5 and 6 year olds that girls with a younger brother and wide spacing were more jealous.

Tsukada (1979), in a review, concluded that as the interval decreased from 4 years to less spacing, sibling rivalry increased. He further stated that sibling rivalry impedes a child's adjustment to peers. He quoted Burgess and Locke (1953), Koch (1956b), and Toman (1969) to the effect that close spacing is associated with greater stress and conflict. White wrote (1975), "Close spacing not only makes for difficulty for the baby; it is also tough on the parents; but most of all it is hard on the slightly older child. . . . This has led me to recommend that parents space their children at least three years apart" (p. 16). Maybe 4 years would be even better, especially if the older child is a boy.

In summary, for family relations the probability of negative effects of close child spacing runs through all combinations: the early dethronement of the older child, and parent–child, parent–parent, and child–child relations. They appear from the time of birth into childhood, adolescence, and even young adulthood, and for parents into the middle years.

Although the pervasive effect of family size, with its obvious relation to birth interval, has not always been included, the large percentage of SS2 researchers and the considerable unanimity of results heighten the validity.

E. SUMMARY: INTERFAMILY RELATIONS

The review of the literature on sibling spacing effects on family interaction is divided into four possible points of contact: age at "dethronement," parent–child, parent–parent, and child–child, each strongly suggesting that the closely spaced are at risk of disadvantage.

1. The earlier the older child is displaced by the younger, up to 4 years, the harder the experience on the older, who may regress to an earlier stage of development, lose earlier learning, and show emotional disturbances.

2. Parent–child interactions with older children are often similar to their interactions with the younger with close spacing (which handicaps the development of the older); a harder time is meted out to the older when intermediately spaced; and relations are generally good with 4-year spacing. By age 4, children are better able to care for themselves, are less attached to the mother, and have more interests of their own.

3. Closely spaced older children feel parents have used harsh discipline; best relations were seen when the children were the most widely spaced (by 5 years); a 2- to 3-year spacing was related to the poorest relations between parent and children at age 15–16. Such effects were milder for girls than for boys.

4. Wider spacing of children left the parents less stressed and with better marital relations.

5. Wider spacing resulted on the average in better adjusted, happier children with more interests and better feelings toward each other, and with less cross-joining of affinity and conflict. Those spaced by 2–4 years were more quarrelsome, loud, exhibitionistic, and insistent on rights. Rivalry was found greatest between closely spaced same-sexed siblings. Girls as well as boys developed rivalry with close spacing. Recommended: 4-year interval.

IV. Sibling Spacing Effects on Personality

Of the four subdivisions of this review (intelligence and achievement, family interrelations, personality, and morbidity–mortality and longevity), personality is most complex, confused, and difficult to organize. Its large number of subdivisions, their interrelations, and the lack of clarity of definition of attributes are part and parcel of any review in the field. As an illustration of the slipperiness of the personality variables, conformity, à la the Asch (1948) experiment, is used for consistency of judgment with the group norm, yet the dictionary says "to be consistent with general rules." The two can be quite different. To this difficulty of definition needs to be added the aforementioned interactions of sibling spacing with family size, sex of proband and of sibling, and ordinal rank, as well as socioeconomic status and racial/cultural background. In view of these difficulties, we are allowing the studies available somewhat to dictate the subdivisions.

In this review of effects of child spacing on personality, we begin with (A) characteristics considered socially desirable. Here we include (1) the need to achieve (nAch), (2) need for affiliation (nAffil) and conformity, (3) self-esteem, ego strength, and internality, (4) social communications skills and prosocial behavior, and (5) gender role. Our second subdivision will be (B) emotional intrapersonal disturbances: dependency; depression; anxiety; fearfulness, including fear of death; and psychosocial maladjustment. And finally, the third subdivision is (C) the grossly negative disorders that disrupt the self and society: delinquency and criminality, alcoholism and drug abuse, suicide, and the psychiatric disorders of psychotic depression and schizophrenia.

A. SOCIALLY DESIRABLE CHARACTERISTICS

1. The Need to Achieve

The need to achieve (nAch) would seem, in United States culture, to be a fairly fundamental subdivision of personality. Indeed, researchers would seem to feel so, as indicated by the number contributing studies of the effect of spacing of siblings on this characteristic.

Koch (1960), in her study of SS2 5 and 6 year olds, did not use the term nAch, although the terms she did use clearly describe nAch in its various aspects. She reported that narrow-spaced firstborn boys, regardless of sex of sibling, were more passive, less aggressive, and had fewer interests. Wide-spaced firstborn boys were most aggressive and enthusiastic, but less intense, quarrelsome, and jealous, especially than middle-spaced (2–4 year) boys. The younger of SS2 boys, regardless of sex of sibling, as the distance to the older increased, showed more ambition, enthusiasm, and tenacity. This difference became significant by the 4-year interval. Middle-spaced firstborn boys were more jealous, quarrelsome, exhibitionistic, loud, and insistent on their rights, and were high strivers.

Regarding girls, Koch found both the older and the younger were more enthusiastic and dawdled less when widely spaced than when closely spaced. Generally, with widening of spacing, social effectiveness and expansiveness increased. Middle-spaced girls—and boys—were more defensive and struggled more aggressively to be the center of the stage.

Regarding tenacity, Koch (1956b) reported that the closely spaced younger of two boys exceeded a closely spaced younger boy with an older sister. For girls the relationship was in the reverse position: closely spaced older girls with a brother were more tenacious than those with a sister. The interaction of sex of index case with spacing is thus supported. To illustrate the interaction of sex of sibling, Koch reported that older girls with a brother spaced by up to 4 years were higher on tenaciousness and dominance than elder girls with a sister. At 4- to 6-years spacing, secondborn girls were also dominant and tenacious.

Elliott and Elliott (1970) found that wide birth spacing led to higher aspirations (nAch) of younger siblings, if the next older was an achievement-oriented eldest. If the older sibling was not an eldest, no relation with spacing was found. Their subjects were 206 sibling pairs, but not all were SS2s.

Gunderson (1969) administered the Edwards Personal Preference Schedule to 219 Navy enlistees who volunteered for Antarctic service, all males. Those with a close brother had high nAch; those with an older sister had high need for Abasement, and those with neither a close brother nor close older sister had high need for Order.

Hornbostel and McCall (1980) administered the EPPS to 120 SS2 college students. Those spaced by 24 or more months had higher average nAch than those more closely spaced. This higher nAch was especially high both for those widely spaced to a sister and for widely spaced females. Sibling competition, which is usually found stronger among closely spaced sibs of the same sex, seemed to inhibit nAch. Spacing increased nAch for firstborns and inhibited it for secondborns, i.e., for postspacing vs prespacing. As college students, this sample would seem to be selected for IQ, socioeconomic level, interest, and possibly nAch for educational pursuits, with consequent reduction of generalizability of findings.

Strumpfer (1973), with 158 male and 160 female undergraduates as subjects, all from SS2s, found no significant relation of nAch to density, family size, sex, nor ordinal position in his dyads.

Nuttall and Nuttall (1975) studied SS2s and SS5s, age 13–16 (see Section II,C). They did not separate the sexes, which as we see from immediately above may have cancelled out differences. They found that the younger of two closely spaced siblings (less than 18 months difference) had higher aspirations and were more self-sufficient. For these, getting a job was more important than education. The closer to the next younger, the more excitable, controlled, and tense the older child was.

In summary, despite the potpourri of ages of sample, variety of sibship sizes and spacing intervals with one or both sexes used, full range of socioeconomic educational backgrounds, and inadequate methodology, several generalizations seem to show through, although most need further cross-validation: (1) the second child, especially when a boy and closely spaced to a brother, is likely to be highly driven to succeed, but not through education, verbal, or science avenues; (2) wide spacing of a younger when his older brother (an oldest child) is himself highly motivated increases likelihood of nAch in the younger; (3) wide spacing to an older sister on the average increases motivation; (4) wide spacing to the second for an eldest makes for likelihood of especially high nAch; and (5) as usual, spacing has greater effects on the male than on the female. Generally, the data on spacing effects on nAch are more provocative than conclusive.

2. Need to Affiliate (nAffil) and Conformity

Three authors have contributed papers on the relation of sibling spacing to nAffil when under stress. All used young adults as subjects.

Cornoldi and Fattori (1976) compared 32 pairs of firstborns, 17–19 years of age. Firstborns having a sibling less than 3 years younger showed greater nAffil and nSuccor (need for succorance) than firstborns not having a close sibling. Their findings are consistent with Koch's finding (see Section VI,A,1 on nAch) that closely spaced eldest boys were more passive. Waldrop and Bell (1964) also found that close spacing increased dependency in young boys. Cornoldi and Fattori theorized that by age 3 individuation is completed, and that this age is an important dividing line.

Miller and Zimbardo (1968) compared the effects of sibling spacing of 2 years or less versus 5 years or more on nAffil. They concluded that nAffil is least important for closely spaced lastborns, i.e., not more than 3 years younger than their penultimate predecessor. NAffil is most important for a youngest who is 5 years or more junior to the next older. The eldestborn are midway in nAffil between closely spaced and widely spaced youngests. To describe their findings they quoted Helmreich, Kuiken, and Collins (1968), "Firstborns and widely-spaced lastborns are highly similar, and both are significantly different from small-interval youngests" (p. 470).

Sterner (1973) used 201 Navy enlisted men as subjects. As a stress test they were shown bloody and mutilated bodies of highway accidents. They were given the choice of waiting alone or in a group. Weak nAffil was shown by low-esteem closely spaced laterborns. Such laterborns had negative relations to peers and to older brothers. If a low-esteem closely spaced had an older brother close in age, he (1) reported a history of negative and competitive interaction and (2) avoided affiliation. With positive feedback, such low-esteem closely spaced laterborns shifted to be affiliative.

In summary, then, closely spaced firstborns and widely spaced lastborns average highest nAffil and closely spaced laterborns and youngests average low nAffil. Perhaps somewhat related to this is a study by Croake and Hayden (1976). Their subjects were 90 SS2 university students and their respective siblings, all from unbroken homes. They studied trait dissimilarity. Close male sibs were frequently opposite. Increased instances of oppositeness were found when sibling intervals were limited to 2–3 years, as contrasted with 4–5 years for submission–dominance. Females did not show such trait oppositeness on any of their scales. Such trait oppositiveness for the males might well have developed out of early negative intersibling relations.

3. Self-Esteem, Ego Strength, and Internality

The present subsection covers self-sufficiency, feelings of capability, ego strength, and internality (the feeling that circumstances are controlled by the individual rather than by outside influences such as luck, or the stars), in addition to self-esteem.

Nuttall and Nuttall (1975) studied SS2 and SS5+ white suburban adolescents, 13–16 years of age. Those spaced 18–30 months to the next younger felt least capable but worked harder and were more obedient. Those closely spaced (up to 18 months) to the next older had highest aspirations and highest feelings of self-sufficiency. The closer the older child was to the next younger the more excitable, controlled, and tense the older child was. For the younger child, the greater the spacing to the next older, the more intelligent, happy-go-lucky, controlled, and affected by feeling he was.

Howarth (1980, 1982) found widely spaced SS2s were less afraid of being socially unacceptable and that eldest SS2s were highest on superego. McKenna *et al.* (1979) reported that firstborns of later marriages had highest self-esteem; closely spaced males were more ego defensive; and those closely spaced with earlier married parents were least conforming. They felt that both age at marriage and spacing of children were important influences.

Kidwell (1982), using both average spacing within the sibship and family size, studied self-esteem for the middleborn adolescent males with equal number of older and younger sibs. She found middleborns had lower self-esteem than either oldests or youngests and that those with narrower sibship spacing and larger sibships were lowest in self-esteem. Those whose sibs were all sisters had higher self-esteem than those whose sibs were mixed sex or all brothers.

Spock (1970) and Stone and Church (1973) both report that 2- to 4-year spacing is most threatening to the older child.

In a carefully controlled investigation, Bloom, Anderson, and Hazaleus (1984) studied 187 firstborn SS2 college students from unbroken homes for effects of spacing on trait anxiety (Anx) and internality–externality locus of control (IE). They found no significant differences in Anx nor in IE by sex of subject or spacing between siblings. They did find that close spacing had a significant positive effect on self-concept and on feeling nearer to one's positive self-goal than did either medium or 3-to 5-year spacing. The latter, those widely spaced, reported that others viewed them more positively than they did themselves as contrasted with those spaced by 2–3 years. Since these are all firstborn, the spacing studied is that following (i.e., age at dethronement), and not that preceding the cases studied. As with all samples of college students, caution must be made in generalizing to less well educated and possibly also lower socioeconomic samples. Further, before more widely generalizing, sibship sizes of more than two need to be investigated, since spacing effects seem to increase as family size increases.

Internality, one end of the internal–external continuum, is the feeling that one's success is controlled by oneself rather than by outside forces. Such feelings would seem to be related to self-esteem and ego strength. Hoffman and Toyber (1979) studied this continuum in 191 SS2 college students 18–22 years old. No SS2s were twins nor separated from an adjacent sibling by 15 years or more. They divided the spacing into 36 months or less and over 36 months. They used the Rotter Internal–External scale and Eysenck's Neuroticism scale. Widely spaced males were more internal than closely spaced males. No significant spacing differences were found for females, who were less internal than males. When the sample was divided for spacing at 45 months (the mean average spacing for the sample), widely spaced males were significantly more internal and widely spaced females were more external. They concluded that wide spacing was more favorable to male development than to female development. Here again was found that males and females cannot be combined in studying spacing effects.

In summary, firstborn males who are widely spaced or born of later marriages, especially when only sons, seem to average higher self-esteem and to be likely to feel more capable, more poised, more socially acceptable, and in general more in control of their situation than those nearer spaced. Wide spacing for the younger sibling also makes for greater poise and more feelings of security. Spacing seems to have an opposite effect on females.

4. Social and Communication Skills

Koch (1956a,b, 1960) presented her data for each sex-pair separately for her various findings (see Section II,A), without summarizing. In MF pairs (a younger sister with an older brother), wide spacing was associated with less quarrelsomeness and more popularity, enthusiasm, competitiveness, and leadership as compared with narrow spaced MFs. Widely spaced FMs were more enthusiastic. Widely spaced MFs, like MFs, were also less intense, quarrelsome, and jealous and more enthusiastic and responsible. With increase in spacing the younger brother with an older sister, FMs, had more expansiveness and social effectiveness. The younger of two boys (MM), especially when widely spaced, got on well with his mother and with teachers, and liked school. Only the elder of two boys MM did not benefit from greater spacing. He became less enthusiastic. Older sisters (FFs) identified with their sisters and were generally sociable, and liked their teachers and school, those closely spaced were especially high in these characteristics. Younger sisters (FFs) got on especially well with their sisters and her friends, were very feminine, were close to their mothers, and were responsive to their teachers, being inclined to tattle to her. These characteristics were especially strong when the two sisters were close in age.

The Nuttalls (1975) did not separate the sexes in their study of 13- to 16-year-old middle-class suburban SS2s and SS5 + s. They studied intervals of less than 18 months, 18–30 months, and over 30 months. Their middle-spaced group, which is still fairly narrow, were least involved socially. Girls spaced by over 30 months, their most widely spaced group, had more friends in school. They found that for SS2s separated by 18 months or less, the older was more authoritarian, and the younger more obedient, serious, and sober, more emotionally stable, and more careless of protocol. They felt that sibship size had more effect socially than spacing, and that the effects of spacing were greater in large sibships.

Newcomb (1976) had 44 second graders (average age 7 years) teach kindergarten children (average age 5 years plus). The spacing intervals for the second graders were up to 2 years older, over 2 years older, and no older sibling; and for younger, similarly, up to 2 years younger, over 2 years younger, and no younger sibling. Her measures of teaching ability were teacher's responsiveness, quality of explanation, teacher's willingness to wait, and transcript length.

Those with close (2 years or less) *younger* siblings were significantly poorer on teacher responsiveness ($p < .05$) and teacher willingness to wait ($p < .001$), as well as nonsignificantly poorer on the other two measures. Those without younger siblings (lastborns) were intermediate. The lastborns showed significant sex differences: these youngest girl teachers scored as high or higher than the widely spaced, whereas the boys scored the lowest of the three spacing groups on three of the teaching measures, with only willingness to wait being as high as the widely spaced.

For the child teachers with older siblings, again the more widely spaced were superior to those more closely spaced. However, only on the measure of willingness to wait were the differences significant (between $p > .05$ and

$p < .10$). Teachers with no older siblings (firstborns) were lowest in teaching skills.

Newcomb emphasized the need to hold interacting sibship variables constant in studying sibling spacing. She presented data indicating such interacting effect for sex of case, sex of sibling, and ordinal position. These data, however, were not significant due to the reduction of numbers as a consequence of the subdivisions. She further urged holding socioeconomic status and IQ constant.

Richer (1968) suggested that from 2 years of age on, the child gradually becomes aware of the value of his compliance with parental directions.

Overall, wider spacing of these children seems, on average, beneficial to their social skills and communication ability.

5. Gender Role

Koch (1960) found that SS2 younger girls who were widely spaced to an older brother (MF) were more tomboyish than more closely spaced girls with an older brother. Conversely, widely spaced older brothers with a younger sister (MF) had more feminine interests and friends and were more often rated as sissy by teachers than was found for other boys. Mid-spaced boys were more father allied, were more masculine, and preferred male playmates more than closely spaced boys. The widely spaced boy with an older sister (FM) had "feminine tinged values" (p. 116) which led to ineffectiveness with peers. The boys with an older sister (FM) were not as good fighters or cooperators as boys with an older brother (MM) at wide spacing. The interaction of sex of sibling with spacing is considerable here.

Bigner (1972) had as subjects white middle-class preschoolers: 105 each near and far spaced and 79 onlyborns. His spacing intervals were 12–20 months and 28–48 months. Boys with older brothers were more masculine; girls with older sisters, more feminine. Spacing had no effect except for males with a near older sister, who were more feminine. In a second study, Bigner (1974b) examined the attitudes of 576 SS2s aged 5–13 years. Close spaced MFs attributed more power to older brother than did more widely spaced MFs. Boys assigned more facilitation to a closely spaced brother and more interference to a closely spaced sister than those more widely spaced. Closely spaced FMs attributed more power to girls than did those more widely spaced.

Sutton-Smith (1968) found that close spacing in girls led to feminine sex role development, whereas wide spacing to male sex role development. Younger boys with an older brother were most masculine; younger girls with an older sister, most feminine.

The sex of the sibling in SS2s has considerable effect on gender role. Close spacing of siblings makes for conflict and estimates of high power; widely spaced sibs seem more compatible and have more appropriate gender role attitudes. As Bigner noted, when attitudes seem more cross-sexed such attitudes are not a subtraction of like-sexed interests and attitudes but an addition of cross-sexed interests, i.e., those with opposite-sexed siblings have broader interests, which holds for both sexes.

B. EMOTIONAL INTRAPERSONAL DISTURBANCES

1. General Adjustment

We turn now to the effect of sibling interval on psychosocial problems and general adjustment. In this section, as in other sections, we start with the younger subjects and progress to older ones. Again Koch, with 5- and 6-year-old SS2s, had the youngest group. And again, she reported for the different sex and sex-of-sibling combinations. With spacing under 2 years, secondborns more quickly recovered from emotional upset than firstborns. As the size of the spacing interval increased, firstborns recovered more like secondborns. Mid-spaced firstborn SS2 boys are quicker to anger than those closely spaced. The converse was found for secondborn boys. No differences were found for girls here. As spacing increased, boys with a same-sexed sib were more self-confident. Among boys, vacillation decreased as spacing interval increased. Firstborn girls, spaced 2–4 years, were rated by teachers as highest in seeking attention, having intense and nervous habits, more fault finding, and less cheerful, and the girls said they would be happier without their sibling. Firstborn boys spaced 2–4 years were more quarrelsome, teasing, intense, and slow to recover poise. For general adjustment, closely spaced older boys were more withdrawn, apprehensive, and passive; both mid-spaced boys and girls seemed more disturbed but with a ready-to-attack stance; girls were less affected by spacing than boys; and youngers tolerated close spacing better than firstborns.

Breslau (1982) compared 248 randomly selected children with 237 children, aged 6–18, who had a considerably disabled sibling. Younger male siblings, especially those with close age spacing to the disabled child, scored higher on psychological impairment than widely spaced older siblings. For girls, sibling spacing was not related to the psychological functioning of those with a disabled sibling.

Hendricks (1977) studied 62 black low-income mothers and their pre-adolescent children (29 boys and 33 girls). She found spacing, family size, and child density were poor predictors of stress. The mother's full-time employment was most productive of stress among the children.

Grinker, Grinker, and Timberlake (1962) studied "normal" young men. They found that the very well adjusted averaged 4.5 years to the next younger; the fairly well adjusted averaged 3.9 years; and the marginally adjusted averaged 2.2 years. The very well adjusted had the most brothers.

Howarth (1980) found among 170 women and 148 male undergraduates that those born to older parents were less impulsive.

The present authors (Wagner *et al.*, 1985) compare two groups of middleborn college freshmen women who were white, low-middle socioeconomic level, same educational level and year of birth, of whom 54 were SS3s and 84 SS4 + s. The spacing intervals were 30 months or less and over 30 months. Both the SS3 and SS4 + closely spaced showed more social maladjustment than their comparable widely spaced classmates. However, the SS4 + s were the more disturbed. Closely spaced SS3s tended to be more hysterical, naive, bland, and inflexible than SS3 widely spaced college women. SS4 + narrow-spaced women tended to have disturbed interpersonal relationships, including heterosexual and with women. They were also more anxious, with poorer communication skills than their wider spaced counterparts. Those with close spacing to both adjacent siblings were the most disturbed, generally lacking trust and being resentful. SS4 + women with near-spaced sisters fared worse than with near-spaced brothers. This study does suggest that family size, spacing, and sex of sibling all affect adjustment, even among females where such affects generally are weaker than among males. Generalization of these findings beyond female college students should be done with caution.

In summary for general adjustment, close spacing seems to have definite negative effects especially on firstborn males, but also on other ordinals and on women. Close spacing for secondborn boys in SS2s seems to have less negative, and possibly even more positive effects. Females seem to be less affected by spacing than do males, although with careful control of the many interacting variables, they too show differences. When sibship size is held constant, spacing differences stand out more clearly. Sex of proband should always be held constant.

2. Depression

Three authors have contributed research on effects of sibling interval on depression. As noted above, Koch (1960) found that closely spaced firstborn boys were more passive, withdrawn, and apprehensive. Waldrop and Bell (1964) found that high child density led to dependency as illustrated by children hanging onto their mother's skirts and by child-initiated contact with teachers. Such behavior was reported more for boys than for girls.

Finally, McKenna *et al.* (1979) studied SS2 white, middle-class children for effects of spacing and of age of marriage of their parents. They found that closely spaced firstborns averaged higher on depressions than those widely spaced for those whose parents had married early, but not for children of late-married parents. Further, laterborns with close spacing were less dependent than those widely spaced of early marriages. This research definitely suggests that age at marriage of parents is another variable that needs to be held constant; i.e., age at marriage and sibling spacing interact in their effects.

In summary regarding depression, firstborns, especially of early marriages, seem to be more at risk of depression when closely spaced than when more widely spaced. Such risk of depression seems not to hold true for laterborns.

3. Anxiety and Fear

Little has been done on the effect of sibling interval on anxiety and fear. Collard (1968) studied the speed with which children took a toy in a strange situation. Firstborns and those widely spaced to next younger sibling paused longer before taking a toy in an unfamiliar situation. Collard made the point, which had been made earlier, that youngests spaced 5 years or more to the next older sibling are more like firstborns than they are like youngests with a close next older.

Gladstein, Seider, and Kidd (1981), in their study of 300 sibships, found no significant difference in age separation or ordinal rank between stutterers and nonstutterers.

Templer (1970) and McDonald and Carroll (1981) examined death anxiety, which the latter felt is related to the need to achieve. Firstborns had higher death anxiety than laterborns, but only when the laterborn was less than 5 years younger than his next older sibling. When more widely spaced they do not have this fear.

These studies on anxiety and fear, as well as some on other topics, emphasize the interaction of spacing, ordinal position, and family size. Once more we see the interaction of a host of family characteristics upon each other. However, close spacing, especially for firstborns, seems to put such individuals at greater risk of fear, anxiety, and depression.

Walker, Johnson, and Goolishian (1973) studied 614 SS2s and 245 onlyborns, age 10 and over, all neuropsychiatric patients. They were all from intact families, white, and admitted between 1957 and 1968. Firstborn females spaced less than 2 years were overrepresented. Also, females spaced over 4 years were overrepresented among the schizophrenics. Widely spaced secondborns were overfrequently present among transient-personality disordered women. Both very wide and very narrow spacing seems disadvantaging among these highly disturbed samples.

Wilsnack (1972) studied spacing intervals among alcoholic women and control women. The alcoholic women were separated 3 years or more from their nearest older and/or younger sibling; nonalcoholic women were separated 3 years or less from their adjacent siblings. The alcoholic women showed greater separation from their adjacent younger sibling than from their adjacent older sibling (4.8 years vs 2.4 years), which was not true of the control women (3.0 vs 3.6 years). Here too atypically wide or narrow spacing seems to indicate a negative prognosis for these women.

Schubert (1966) compiled data on the family structure for 40 consecutively discharged chronic alcoholics: 39 males and 1 female of which 26 were white, 13 black, and 1 American Indian. Of these, 10 (25%) had a close older sibling and 14 (35%) a close younger sibling. Of these 7 had both a close older and younger sibling. Three were twins. Thus 20 (50%) may be considered closely spaced, significantly higher than for a control sample of medical ward patients. Schubert points out that 12 were father deprived and the mothers of 2 died before age 13. He suggests that parental deprivation was related to chronic alcoholism.

In summary, the theme of close spacing of these disturbed cases runs through the large majority of the studies presented here. Close spacing seems to be more disadvantaging to firstborns. Unusually wide spacing also seems to increase risk of disturbance, especially for women and for a lastborn child.

C. SUMMARY: PERSONALITY

Research on effects of sibling spacing on personality is handicapped by inadequate measures of the various facets of personality. The number of studies is few and of these many are less than best designed. Much of the research here is more suggestive (for further study) than conclusive.

1. Wide spacing generally leads to higher need to achieve for both sexes, except that the closely spaced younger son has a high need to achieve in other than academic and intellectual fields.

2. Closely spaced eldests and widely spaced youngests have higher need to affiliate.

3. Widely spaced males born to late marriages have high self-esteem, feel more in control, and feel better poised. The opposite seems true for females.

4. Regarding social skills, spacing effects are similar for males and females, but seem greater in large sibships than in small. Widely spaced children were found more popular, less quarrelsome and rivalrous, higher in leadership, and more authoritarian, responsible, and socially effective. The more widely spaced middleborn college women were found better socially adjusted.

5. Gender role interests seem more related to sex of siblings and ordinal position than to spacing interval.

6. The closely spaced older son is more passive, apathetic, apprehensive, and withdrawn, as well as more oral, in that he drinks more alcohol and

smokes more. Mid-spaced (24–36 months) boys and girls are more disturbed and have an aggressive stance. Girls are less affected than boys. Best adjusted young men were found widest separated; moderately well adjusted were intermediately spaced; and the poorest adjusted were most closely spaced to adjacent siblings.

7. Being closely spaced seems to increase risk of depression, apathy, fear (e.g., death anxiety), general anxiety, and poor social relations. Eldests seem more at risk as a result of close spacing than laterborns, and boys more than girls.

8. All areas of sibling interval effects are in need of further well-planned research, but the area of personality is in greatest need.

V. Morbidity, Mortality, and Longevity

Spacing effects on morbidity, mortality, and longevity have a long research history with many excellent studies, very large and representative samples, and sophisticated statistics. Of the over 100 references dealing with spacing, about 30 concern aspects of physical health. As with preceding subdivisions of this article, we start as in life with the youngest subjects—here perinatals—and continue through to longevity.

A. STILLBIRTH, PREMATURITY, AND LOW BIRTH WEIGHT

The effect of birth intervals on perinatals has been reviewed by James (1968). From his review, he found that for both short and long intervals premature infants were overrepresented. A high risk of perinatal mortality was also present for both short and overlong intervals, in that high risk of mortality is related to prematurity. From James's own data, stillbirth was related to both short and long intervals; neonatal death was associated more with short intervals.

Yerushalmy (1945) also noted that both long and short intervals were related to higher rate of stillbirth. James noted that lower socioeconomically rated women have both shorter birth intervals and higher neonatal mortality. Eastman (1944) put it that children conceived very early (i.e., before 6 months following a previous delivery) show a tendency to premature delivery, which he notes is related to stillbirth and neonatal death. Others have reported finding mortality and low birth weight to be related to short birth interval (Holley, Rosenbaum, & Churchill, 1969; Hughes, 1923; Woodbury, 1925; Yerushalmy, Bierman, Kemp, Connor, & French, 1956).

Selvin and Janerich (1971) studied single births in the state of New York between 1959 and 1967. They reported, as others have shown, that spacing increased with the mother's age, as did birth weight. Younger mothers have nearer spaced and lighter weight babies. By 1976, James argued that no necessarily causal relation existed between close spacing and stillbirth. "It is just that the women who are most prone to have stillborn infants have short birth intervals" (p. 131).

Two other researchers reported on factors obliquely related to neonatal health. Maccoby, Deering, Jacklin, and Kraemer (1979) studied 256 newborns and their placentas. For both sexes, firstborns had significantly more progesterone in umbilical blood than laterborns, and for females more estrogen. Laterborns who were closely spaced to a preceding older sibling had lower hormonal concentrations. By an interval of 4 years, testosterone had very measurably increased for males and progesterone for both sexes. The findings seem less definite for females. Results were discussed for possible effects of lower hormonal concentrations on psychological development.

Foster and Archer hypothesized (1979) that antibrain antibodies develop with parity, similar to Rh antibodies and the lower concentrations of sex hormones described by Maccoby *et al.*, and that such antibrain antibodies are stronger with narrow spacing and are reduced in concentration between births.

In summary, regardless of causes, infants who are closely spaced to the next older sibling are at greater risk of premature delivery, stillbirth, and perinatal death. Very long intervals are also related to increased stillbirth.

B. INFANT MORBIDITY AND MORTALITY

Woodbury, already in 1925, reported that infants born after short birth intervals had markedly a high rate of mortality from all causes. The rate decreased from 146.7/1000 for a 1-year interval, to 98.6/1000 for a 2-year interval, to 86.5/1000 for 3 years, and 84.9 for 4 years and over. Eastman (1944) argued, in agreement with James cited above, that fertile women have more fetal wastage, and that mortality is more related to family size than to spacing.

Three researchers attempted control of confounding variables. Wray (1971) reported that young mothers with closely spaced births showed an increase in deaths of neonates, which held true when socioeconomic status was held constant. Spiers and Wang (1976) matched variables of maternal age, race, mothers' education, and the number of previous live births. They found significantly higher rates of sudden infant death syndrome and neonatal deaths for short interval among cases than among control cases. They argued that short intervals between pregnancies exert influence on risk of death in infancy through the effects on birthweight. They estimated that infant mortality would be reduced by about 5% by elimination of short interval cases.

Acheson (1965) studied 3901 babies. Excluding stillborn and those who died prior to mother's discharge, 203 babies were rehospitalized. Multiple births had the highest rate of rehospitalization (6.6%) versus singletons (3.4%). Babies of mothers under 20 averaged 6.2 versus 2.5% for mothers at age 25. Young mothers (under 20) with a second and third child following closely after the first had babies with especially high morbidity. Illegitimate babies also had a high rate of rehospitalization. Waldrop and Bell (1966) found that infants born to mothers who had experienced a number of closely spaced pregnancies were more lethargic than those with more widely spaced previous pregnancies.

In summary, quite clearly closely spaced infants are disadvantaged healthwise over those more moderately spaced. Wide spacing also seems related to morbidity and mortality, though less so than close spacing. Ratner (1970) pointed out that nature's spacing of the lactating mother is between 16 and 24 months. He recommended the latter interval. The above data seem to indicate a preferred spacing of somewhat more than this interval, nearer 4 years.

C. CHILDHOOD HEALTH AND GROWTH

Morrison, Heady, and Morris (1959) studied English and Welch births. They wrote, "In all SES and mother age groups, the mortality rate is higher for the more closely spaced children. The third closely spaced child is at higher risk than the second" (p. 110), indicating that the risk is accumulative. They also found that firstborns born less than 1 year after marriage have higher mortality rates than firstborns born longer after marriage. Among preschoolers malnourishment was greater for the older with short spacing. Here the effect of short interval was greater on the first of a pair of siblings.

Wray and Aguirre (1969) also reported greater risk of protein calorie malnutrition for closely spaced children in Columbia, South America. Only-borns had clear advantage. An interval of over 3 years protected the older somewhat from such malnutrition.

Three studies provide data on the effects of spacing on height of children. Grant (1964) found that laterborns tended to be taller than their preceding sibling at age 6, if the spacing was less than 2 years as contrasted with those spaced more than 3 years. Wray and Aguirre (1969) found that British children from large sibships were shorter than those from smaller sibships. In addition, the preceding sibling tended to be shorter if the next younger followed by less than 2 years. The birth of a sibling acts as a check on the growth of the preceding child, particularly if the interval is less than 2 years. Russell (1976) investigated the height of Mayan children at 8 years of age. The height of male children significantly increased as spacing increased from 12–17 months to 30–36 months. In addition, sibship size was related negatively to height. The effect of sibling spacing on height was less evident for girls. There is little doubt that close spacing negatively affects the height of the preceding child, especially for males.

D. ADULTS DISEASES AND LONGEVITY

Regarding the health of adults, one author discussed the effect of sibling spacing on tension and related difficulties, another on coronary heart disease, and five on cancer (one each for breast cancer and Hodgkins disease, and three more general).

Mirra, Dole, and MacMahon (1971), with data from 86.4% of 10,051 college graduates and undergraduates, reported that subjects with siblings separated by 7 or more years had illnesses related to stress similar to actual onlyborns: high in nerve tension and nerve exhaustion and low in migraine. Oscherwitz, Krasnow, and Moretti (1969) compared 100 coronary heart disease patients (73 men and 27 women) with 200 non-coronary-disease subjects. The fathers of the former were older at the births of their propositi and the former included more laterborns.

Regarding cancer, Gutensohn, Johnson, and Cole (1975) reported that patients with Hodgkins disease (cancer) had fewer siblings than those free from this illness. Gutenson and Cole (1981) reported less Hodgkins disease among those with closely spaced siblings. It is suggested that older siblings carry the disease to their younger siblings; their absence allows individuals to carry susceptibility to Hodgkins disease to adulthood.

Mirra et al. (1971) reported that women who had a first pregnancy prior to age 20 had only about two-thirds the risk of breast cancer of those whose first pregnancy was at age 25 or over. Risk of breast cancer decreases as sibship size increased because those who have early pregnancies tend to have more children.

Duszynski, Shafer, and Thomas (1981) compared 30 male medical doctors with major cancer with 109 who were healthy. These were similar in age (year at medical school), education and occupation, and sex. All were white. Of the cancerous, 10 (34.5%) had a sibling younger by 2 years or less. Of the healthy doctors, 21 (19.3%) had similarly close younger siblings, $p < .10$. Differences in child trauma that showed direction toward cancer also included death of parent, death of sibling, and divorce of parents as well as the 2 years or less spacing to next younger sibling.

LeShan and Resnikoff (1960) and LeShan (1966), with subjects representing 200 families, found that 27% of 78 cancerous as contrasted with 9% of 235 noncancerous subjects were spaced by 10–23 months. Eldests seemed especially at risk of cancer when closely spaced. For those more widely spaced, the percentage who were cancerous was the same as or less than the percentage who were noncancerous.

We see here a variety of ways that lengthy sibling spacing affects risk of cancer: (1) early pregnancy (before age 20) seems to protect against breast cancer; (2) early exposure to a specific virus seems to reduce Hodgkins disease among young adults; and (3) overall close spacing seems to increase the risk of acquiring cancer.

Finally, for longevity, Beeton and Pearson (1901) compared 1784 pairs of male siblings and their parents. They found older siblings lived an average of 4 years longer than younger siblings; i.e., longevity decreased with birth rank and was greater in small sibships. However, the difference at age of death of older and younger differed with the size of spacing from a minus figure for 1 and 2 years difference to more than 4 years for those most widely spaced. Although most sibships were large in 1901, these differences may still have been contaminated by sibship size.

In addition to Beeton and Pearson, other researchers have consistently found that people who are followed by a relatively long interval to the next sibling experience a greater mean longevity than those followed by a short interval (Morrison *et al.,* 1959; Spiers & Wang, 1976; Wyron & Gordon, 1962; Yerushalmy, 1945).

In summary, the studies reviewed in this section, dating back to the turn of the century, are of high statistical quality, usually included large samples, and are amazingly consistent in their findings that close spacing is related to higher morbidity and mortality rates among perinatals, infants, young children, adults, and senior citizens. They indicate the following conclusions:

1. Short birth intervals to the next older child are specifically related to stillbirth, low birth weight, prematurity, sudden infant death syndrome, rehospitalization after mother's discharge, and reduced amounts of the hormones estrogen and progesterone at birth.

2. Longer than average birth intervals are also related to an increased risk of stillbirth, possibly related to very large family size or to intervening miscarriages or mother's illness.

3. Children closely spaced to a younger sib are at greater risk of malnutrition, reduced height, and death from a wide variety of causes.

4. Closely spaced adults are at greater risk of coronary heart disease, and when close to a younger sibling, of cancer. Women with a pregnancy prior to age 20 are at reduced risk of breast cancer.

5. Close spacing and large sibships seem to protect against Hodgkins disease, probably due to absence of early related infection with resultant immunity.

6. A full dozen researchers report wide spacing to the next younger as related to greater longevity, which is also negatively related to birth rank.

Breland (1974) and others have pointed out the lower intellectual performance of twins. Brackbill and Nichols (1982), who also found that both black and white twins had lower IQs, suggested that prenatal factors probably are implicated in their lower intellectual performance. The physiological handicaps found to be related to close spacing might well here also be implicated in the lower intelligence of closely spaced young children, preadolescents, and even older persons, as well as possibly also contributing to some mental disorders.

VI. Discussion and Conclusions

The findings on spacing effects are astonishingly consistent. Close spacing is more disadvantageous to perinatal, infant, and childhood health and to longevity of adults (Section V,D). It seems deleterious to intelligence and achievement (Section II,H), to good relations between children and parents, between children and their siblings, and even between the parents themselves (Section III,E), and to emotion and psychological adjustment (Section IV,D). Practically all areas should have their conclusions cross-validated with careful research design, holding constant demographic and all sibship constellation variables not being explored. With the consistency of findings of negative effects of spacing up to 24 months, and probably to 30 months, the chances seem high that similar effects will again appear, especially for boys but likely for girls too, and especially for verbal ability and morbidity and mortality, but also for many personality variables and psychosocial adjustment.

Psychologists have generally attributed the cause of negative effects of close spacing to limited finite parental time and reduced amount of hidden educators, and perhaps also to different socioeconomic status and cultural ideologies. Undoubtedly, these variables do have measurable effects. However, the careful studies of spacing effects on morbidity and mortality suggest the possibility that health factors are implicated in intelligence, achievement, personality, and adjustment. When the presence of a close younger sibling so strongly affects the older child as actually to reduce his height, one might suspect effects on intelligence and personality. And when having close older siblings actually increases the risk of prematurity and low birth weight, such physical disadvantages might well also affect intelligence, school achievement, and peer relations as indeed they are seen to do among twins, the most closely spaced of all children.

But to return to sociopsychological effects of close spacing, many variables not yet studied need attention. One such variable is wantedness (see Matecjek *et al.,* 1978). For instance, a comparison of firstborns who are illegitimate, whose parents waited at least a year before starting to have a child, and finally whose parents delayed their first child still longer might provide a continuum of wantedness. All the demographic and family constellation variables would need to be held constant.

That girls and boys are different in many respects and need to be studied separately should come as no surprise. Nonetheless, that the two sexes are so frequently differently affected by spacing interval is still a challenging question as to why. The suggestion that the short period before separation from the mother is extra difficult for the closely spaced child certainly has merits. However, the two sexes are not thought to encounter this task of development at different ages. The fact that the male child has the additional developmental task of identifying with the male may leave him more vulnerable to close spacing. Will the trend of increasing amount of nurturing by the father help the closely spaced male accomplish this task? And what effect will early fathering have on his closely spaced daughter? Attention by the father has been found to aid the adjustment of the closely spaced older. Sons of farmers show less effect of sibship size (Belmont & Marolla, 1973) and sons of ministers are frequently quoted as being well adjusted. Does the father being at home and spending more time with his sons aid in their double tasks of early male development and close spacing adjustment?

The inconsistencies of findings regarding wide spacing (over 4 years) leads to speculation that samples widely spaced are harder to come by and thus are not as controlled for socioeconomic status, ideology, etc., and that illness of the mother, spontaneous abortions, and family crises intervene during the spacing interval. More carefully controlled samples would be helpful to settle such inconsistency.

Researchers in the area of effects of sibling constellation variables have come a long way in their understanding of the necessity of holding constant all sibling variables except the one under investigations, as well as keeping constant such demographic variables as socioeconomic status, race, and ideology (see Section I,A). They understand that sex differences should be taken for granted until proven otherwise; that an onlyborn may well differ from other firstborns; that firstborns with one sibling differ from those with three, five, seven, or 10; that boys with sisters have a different perspective from those with all brothers, and that those closely spaced differ from those more widely spaced.

Carefully planned research regarding spacing effects, or indeed sibling constellation effects in general—especially with a novel twist—will add to our understanding of child development and individual differences. To paraphrase Goethe, Where you take hold of life you will find it interesting, an attitude also applicable to sibling effects. Especially insufficiently studied are lower socioeconomic levels, blacks, those with specific ideologies, and females. Also lacking is carefully planned research regarding spacing effects (as well as effects of sibship size, ordinal position, and sex of sibling) on personality, psychosocial characteristics, and mental health. Studies of false positives frequently lead to new insights.

And one more caveat: Differences refer to the likelihood or chance that they will be found in other similar samples. Such differences say how likely individuals will fit into the scheme; they do not say that all individuals will be in the plus or minus category. Nonetheless, significant differences do state the direction of safe betting.

REFERENCES

Abramovich, R., Corter, C., & Lando, B. (1979). Sibling interaction in the home. *Child Development, 50,* 997–1003.
Abramovich, R., Corter, C., & Pepler, D. J. (1980). Observations of mixed-sex sibling dyads. *Child Development, 51,* 1268–1271.
Acheson, E. D. (1965). Hospital morbidity in early life in relation to certain maternal and foetal characteristics and events at delivery. *British Journal of Social Medicine, 19,* 164–173.
Adler, A. (1924). *The practise and theory of individual psychology* (P. Radin, Trans.). New York: Harcourt.
Albert, R. S. (1980). Exceptionally gifted boys and their parents. *Gifted Child Quarterly, 24,* 174–180.
Allen, P. (1955). Childhood background of success in a profession. *American Sociological Review, 20,* 186–190.
Anderson, W. P., & Holcomb, W. E. (1983). Accused murderers: Five MMPI personality types. *Clinical Psychology, 39,* 761–768.
Asch, S. E. (1948). The doctrine of suggestion, prestige, and imitation in social psychology. *Psychology Review, 55,* 250–276.
Bank, S. P., & Kahn, M. (1982). *The sibling bond.* New York: Basic Books.
Beeton, M., & Pearson, K. (1901). Inheritance of the duration of life. *Biometrika, 1,* 59–89.
Bell, C. S., Johnson, J. E., McGillicuddy-Delise, A. V., & Siegel, I. E. (1980). Normative stress and young families: Adaptation and development. *Family Relations, 29,* 453–458.
Belmont, L., & Marolla, F. A. (1973). Family size and intelligence. *Science, 182,* 1096–1101.
Belmont, L., Stein, Z., & Zybert, P. (1978). Child spacing and birth order: Effects of intellectual ability in two-child families. *Science, 202,* 995–996.
Belmont, L., Wittes, J., & Stein, Z. (1979). Relation of birth order, family size, and social class in psychological function. *Perceptual and Motor Skills, 45,* 1107–1116.
Berbaum, M. L., & Moreland, R. L. (1980). Intellectual development within the family: A new application of the confluence model. *Developmental Psychology, 16,* 506–515.

Berglin, C. G. (1980). *Regular skewness of birth order distribution.* Göteborg: Scandinavian Journal of Social Medicine.

Berkowitz, G. S., & Kasl, S. V. (1983). The role of psychosocial factors in spontaneous preterm delivery. *Journal of Psychosomatic Research, 27,* 283–290.

Bigner, J. J. (1972). Sibling influence on sex-role preference of young children. *Journal of Genetic Psychology, 121,* 271–282.

Bigner, J. J. (1974a). A Wernerian developmental analysis of children's descriptions of siblings. *Child Development, 45,* 317–323.

Bigner, J. J. (1974b). Secondborns' discrimination of sibling role concepts. *Developmental Psychology, 10,* 564–573.

Black, D., & Sturge, C. (1979). The young child and his siblings. In J. Howells (Ed.), *Perspectives in the psychiatry in infancy.* New York: Brunner Mazel.

Blau, Z. S. (1981). *Black children, white children: Competence, socialization, and social structure.* New York: Free Press.

Bloom, E. J., Anderson, S., & Hazaleus, S. (1984). Personality correlates of age-spacing in firstborns. *Child Study Journal, 17,* 247–257.

Bossard, J. H. S., & Boll, E. S. (1960). *Families of size: Sociology of child development* (3rd ed.). New York: Harper.

Bowlby, J. (1952). *Maternal care and mental health.* Geneva: World Health Monograph.

Brackbill, Y., & Nichols, P. L. (1982). A test of the confluence model of intellectual development. *Developmental Psychology, 18,* 192–198.

Breland, H. M. (1974). Birth order, family configuration, and verbal achievement. *Child Development, 43,* 1011–1019.

Breslau, N. (1982). Siblings of disabled children: Birth order and age spacing effects. *Journal of Abnormal Child Psychology, 10,* 85–95.

Brim, O. G., Jr. (1958). Family structure and role learning. *Sociometry, 21,* 1–16.

Burgess, E., & Locke, H. (1953). *The family.* New York: American Book Co.

Cameron, N. (1963). *Personality development and psychopathology: A dynamic approach.* Boston: Houghton Mifflin.

Chittenden, E. A., Foan, M. W., Zweil, D., & Smith, J. R. (1968). School achievement of first- and secondborn siblings. *Child Development, 39,* 1223–1228.

Christensen, H. T. (1968). Children in the family: A relationship of number and spacing to marital success. *Journal of Marriage and the Family, 30,* 283–289.

Cicirelli, V. G. (1967). Sibling constellation, creativity, IQ, and academic achievement. *Child Development, 38,* 481–490.

Cicirelli, V. G. (1974). Relation of sibling structure and interaction to younger siblings' style. *Journal of Genetic Psychology, 125,* 37–49.

Clausen, J. A. (1966). Family structure, constellation, and personality. In M. L. Hoffman & L. W. Hoffman (Eds.), *Review of child development research* (Vol. 2, pp. 1–53). New York: Russell Sage Foundation.

Collard, R. R. (1968). Social and play responses of firstborn and laterborn infants in an unfamiliar situation. *Child Development, 39,* 325–334.

Cornoldi, C., & Fattori, L. C. (1976). Age spacing in firstborns and symbiotic dependence. *Journal of Personality and Social Psychology, 33,* 421–434.

Corter, C., Pepler, D., & Abramovich, R. (1982). Effects of situation and sibling status on sibling interaction. *Canadian Journal of Behavioral Science, 14,* 380–392.

Croake, J. W., & Hayden, D. J. (1976). Trait oppositeness in siblings: Test of Adlerian tenet. *Journal of Individual Psychology, 31,* 175–178.

Dandes, H. M., & Dow, D. (1969). Relation of intelligence to family size and density. *Child Development, 40,* 641–645.

Datta, L. E. (1968). Birth order and potential scientific creativity. *Sociometry, 31,* 76–88.

Davidson, M. (1970). Social and economic variations in child spacing. *Social Biology,* **17,** 107–113.

Davis, D. J., Cahan, S., & Bashi, J. (1977). Birth order and intellectual development: The confluence model in light of cross-cultural evidence. *Science,* **196,** 1470–1472.

Davis, E. A. (1937). *The development of linguistic skill in twins, singletons with siblings, and only children from age 5 to 10 years.* Minneapolis: Univ. of Minnesota Press.

Deacon, R., & Firebaugh, F. (1975). *Home management context and concepts.* Boston: Houghton Mifflin.

Douglas, J. W. B., Ross, J. M., & Simpson, H. R. (1968). *All our future—A longitudinal study of secondary education.* London: Peter Davies.

Duszynski, K. R., Shafer, J. W., & Thomas, C. B. (1981). Neoplasms and traumatic events in childhood. *Archives of General Psychiatry,* **38,** 327–331.

Eastman, N. J. (1944). Effects of the intervals between births on maternal and fetal outlook. *American Journal of Obstetrics and Gynecology,* **47,** 445–463.

Elliott, J. L., & Elliott, D. H. (1970). Effects of birth order and age gap on aspiration level. *Proceedings Annual Convention American Psychological Association,* **5,** 369–370.

Ernst, C., & Angst, J. (1983). *Birth order: Its influence on personality.* New York: Springer-Verlag.

Eyberg, S. M., & Robinson, W. A. (1982). Parent–child interaction training: Effects on family functioning. *Journal of Clinical Child Psychology,* **1,** 130–137.

Faris, R. E. L. (1940). Sociological causes of genius. *American Sociological Review,* **5,** 689–699.

Farley, F. S. (1978). Scholastic ability, birth order, family size, sibling age spacing and parental absence in 7th and 8th graders: An empirical study of the confluence model. *Dissertation Abstracts International,* **38,** (10A) 6008.

Feiring, C., & Lewis, M. (1980). *Children, parents and siblings: Possible sources of variation in behavior of firstborn and only children.* Paper presented at the American Psychological Association meeting, Montreal.

Ford, K. (1981). *Socioeconomic differentials and trends in the timing of births.* U.S. Dept. of Health and Human Services, National Center of Health Statistics.

Foster, J. W., & Archer, S. J. (1979). Birth order and intelligence: An immunological interpretation. *Perception and Motor Skills,* **48,** 79–93.

Freedman, R., & Combs, L. (1966). Child spacing and family economic position. *American Sociological Review,* **31,** 631–648.

Galbraith, R. C. (1982). Sibling spacing and intellectual development: A closer look at the confluence model. *Developmental Psychology,* **18,** 151–173.

Gladstein, K. L., Seider, R. A., & Kidd, K. K. (1981). Analysis of the sibship patterns of stutterers. *Journal of Speech and Hearing Research,* **24,** 460–462.

Glueck, S., & Glueck, E. (1950). *Unraveling juvenile delinquency.* New York: Commonwealth Fund.

Goertzel, M. G., Goertzel, V., & Goertzel, T. G. (1978). *Three hundred eminent personalities.* San Francisco: Jossey-Bass.

Gordon, J. E. (1969). Social implications of health and disease. *Archives of Environmental Health,* **18,** 216–234.

Grant, M. W. (1964). Rate growth in relation to birth rank and family size. *British Journal of Preventive Social Medicine,* **18,** 35–42.

Gregg, G., & Elmer, E. (1959). Infant injuries: Accident or abuse? *Pediatrics,* **44,** 434–439.

Grinker, R. R., Sr., Grinker, R. R., Jr., & Timberlake, J. (1962). Mentally healthy young males (homolites). *Archives of General Psychiatry,* **6,** 405–553.

Grotevant, H. D., Scarr, S., & Weinberg, R. A. (1977). Intellectual development in family constellations with adopted and natural children: A test of the Zajonc and Markus confluence model. *Child Development,* **48,** 1699–1703.

Gunderson, M. M. (1969). Relationships between expressed personality needs and social background and military status variables. *Journal of Psychology,* **71,** 217–224.

Gutensohn, N., & Cole, P. (1981). Childhood social environment and Hodgkins disease. *New England Journal of Medicine,* **304,** 135–140.

Gutensohn, N., Johnson, R. E., & Cole, P. (1975). Hodgkins disease, tonsillectomy and family size. *New England Journal of Medicine,* **292,** 22–25.

Hare, E. H., & Price, J. E. (1969). Birth order and family size: Bias caused by change in birth rate. *British Journal of Psychiatry,* **115,** 647–657.

Hayden, D. J. (1973). Trait oppositeness in siblings. *Dissertation Abstracts International,* **33,** B 3285.

Hayes, R. F., & Bronzaft, L. (1979). Birth order and related variables in an academically elite sample. *Journal of Individual Psychology,* **35,** 214–224.

Helmreich, R., Kuiken, D., & Collins, B. (1968). Effects of stress and birth order on attitude change. *Journal of Personality,* **36,** 466–473.

Henchie, V. (1963). *Children's reaction to the birth of a new baby.* University Child Development Report, University of London, Institute of Education.

Hendricks, L. E., Jr. (1977). The effect of family size, child spacing and family density on stress in low income black mothers and their preadolescent children. *Health Sciences, Mental Health* (Order No. 7807136).

Hinshaw, R., Pyeatt, P., & Habicht, J. P. (1972). Environmental effects on child-spacing and population increase in Highland Guatamala. *Current Anthropology,* **13,** 216–230.

Hoffman, J., & Toyber, E. C. (1970). Some relationships between sibling age spacing and personality. *Merrill-Palmer Quarterly,* **25,** 77–80.

Hoffman, L. (1976). Enmeshment and the too richly cross joined system. *Family Process,* **14,** 457–468.

Holley, W. L., Rosenbaum, A. L., & Churchill, J. A. (1969). *Effect of rapid succession of pregnancy* (Scientific Publication No. 185). Washington, D.C.: Pan American Health Organization.

Hollingshead, A. B., & Redlich, F. C. (1958). *Social class and mental illness: A community study.* New York: Wiley.

Hornbostel, L. K., & McCall, J. N. (1980). Sibling differences in need-achievement associated with birth order, child-spacing, sex, and sibling sex. *Journal of Individual Psychology,* **36,** 36–43.

Howarth, E. (1980). Birth order, family structure and personality variables. *Journal of Personality Assessment,* **44,** 299–301.

Howarth, E. (1982). Birth order and personality: Some empirical findings and a behavioral theory. *Personality and Individual Differences,* **3,** 205–210.

Hughes, E. (1923). *Infant mortality: Results of a field study in Gary, Indiana, based on births in one year* (Publication No. 1121). Washington, D.C.: Children's Bureau.

Hurley, J., & Palonen, D. (1967). Marital satisfaction and child density among university student parents. *Marriage and the Family,* **29,** 483–484.

James, W. R. (1968). Stillbirth, neonatal death, and birth interval. *Annals of Human Genetics,* **32,** 163–172.

James, W. R. (1976). Birth order, maternal age, and birth interval in epidemiology. *International Journal of Epidemiology,* **5,** 131–132.

Jordan, E. W., Whiteside, M. M., & Manaster, G. J. (1982). A practical and effective research of birth order. *Journal of Individual Psychology,* **38,** 253–255.

Judd, E., & Lewis, M. (1976). *Effects of birth order and spacing on mother-infant relations.* Paper presented at the Eastern Psychological Association, New York City.

Kaltsounis, B. (1978). Creative performance among siblings of various ordinal birth positions. *Psychological Reports,* **12,** 915–918.

Kamin, A., Kubinger, K. D., & Schubert, M. R. (1981). Sibling constellation and intelligence in behavior disordered children. *Zeitschrift für klinische Psychologieforschung und Praxis,* **10,** 98–109.

Kammeyer, K. (1967). Birth order as a research variable. *Social Forces,* **46,** 71–80.

Keane, W. M. (1976). Black mothers and their sons: Correlates and predictors of cognitive development from the second to the eighth year of life. *Dissertation Abstracts International,* **37,** 3081.

Kendrick, C., & Dunn, J. (1982). Protest or pleasure? The response of firstborn children to interactions between their mothers and infant siblings. *Journal Child Psychology and Psychiatry and Allied Disciplines,* **23,** 117–120.

Kendricks, L. R. (1978). The effects of family size, child spacing and family density in low income Black mothers and their preadolescent children. *Dissertation Abstracts International,* **38,** 5844.

Kennett, K. F., & Cropley, A. J. (1970). Intelligence, family size, and socioeconomic status. *Journal of Biosocial Science,* **2,** 227–236.

Kidwell, J. S. (1978). Adolescents' perceptions of parental affect: An investigation of only children vs firstborns and the effect of spacing. *Journal of Population,* **1,** 148–166.

Kidwell, J. S. (1981). Number of siblings, sibling spacing, sex, and birth order: Their effects on perceived parent–adolescent relationships. *Journal of Marriage and the Family,* **43,** 315–332.

Kidwell, J. S. (1982). The neglected birth order: Middleborns. *Journal of Marriage and the Family,* **44,** 225–235.

Knox, D., & Wilson, K. (1978). The difference between having one and two children. *Family Coordinator,* **27,** 23–25.

Koch, H. L. (1954). The relation of primary mental abilities in 5- and 6-year-olds in sex of child and characteristics of his sibling. *Child Development,* **25,** 209–223.

Koch, H. L. (1956a). Children's work attitudes and sibling characteristics. *Child Development,* **27,** 289–310.

Koch, H. L. (1956b). Sissiness and tomboyishness in relation to sibling characteristics. *Journal of Genetic Psychology,* **88,** 231–244.

Koch, H. L. (1960). The relation of certain formal attributes of siblings to attitudes held toward each other and toward their parents. *Child Development Monograph,* **25,** (4).

Lancer, J., & Rim, Y. (1984). Intelligence, family size and sibling age spacing. *Personality and Individual Differences,* **5,** 151–157.

Lasko, J. K. (1954). Parent behavior toward first and second children. *Genetic Psychology Monographs,* **49,** 97–137.

Legg, C., Sherick, I., & Wadland, W. (1974). Reaction of preschool children to the birth of a sibling. *Child Psychiatry and Human Development,* **5,** 3–39.

LeShan, L. (1966). An emotional life-history pattern associated with neoplastic disease. *Annals of the New York Academy of Science,* **136,** 180–193.

LeShan, L., & Resnikoff, M. (1960). A psychological factor apparently associated with neoplastic disease. *Journal of Abnormal and Social Psychology,* **60,** 439–440.

Levinson, P. (1963). The relationship between birth order and reading ability (doctoral dissertation, University of Pennsylvania). *Dissertation Abstracts International,* **24,** 2614.

Lewis, M., & Kreitzberg, V. S. (1979). Effects of birth order and spacing on mother–infant interactions. *Developmental Psychology,* **15,** 617–623.

McCall, R. B. (1984). Developmental changes in mental performance: The effects of birth of a sibling. *Child Development,* **55,** 1311–1321.

Maccoby, E. E., Deering, C. H., Jacklin, C. N., & Kraemer, H. (1979). Concentrations of sex hormones in umbilical cord blood: Their relation to sex and birth order of infants. *Child Development,* **50,** 632–642.

Mahler, M., Pine, P., & Bergman, A. (1967). *The psychological birth of the human infant.* New York: Basic Books.

Marjoribanks, K. (1978). Birth order and spacing between siblings and cognitive performance. *Psychological Reports,* 42, 115–123.

Matecjek, S., Dytryck, Z., & Schüller, V. (1978). Children from unwanted pregnancies. *Acta Psychiatrica Scandinavia,* 57, 67–90.

McDonald, R. T., & Carroll, J. D. (1981). Three measures of death anxiety, birth-order effects and concurrent validity. *Journal of Clinical Psychology,* 37, 674–677.

McKenna, V. V., Null, C. B., & Ventis, L. (1979). *Marital age and the spacing of children: Influence on children, parents, and family interactions* (Contract R01 HD 42844, NICHD). Washington, DC: U.S. Dept. of Health and Human Welfare, Center Population Research.

Melican, G. J. (1978). The effects of age spacing to next-younger and age-spacing to next older on academic achievement. *Dissertation Abstracts International,* 39, 3535.

Melican, G. J., & Feldt, L. S. (1980). The empirical study of the Zajonc-Markus hypothesis for achievement test score declines. *American Educational Research Journal,* 17, 5–19.

Miller, N., & Zimbardo, P. G. (1966). Motives for fear-induced affiliation: Comparison of interpersonal similarity. *Journal of Personality,* 34, 481–505.

Minnett, A. M., Vandell, D. L., & Santrock, J. (1983). The effect of sibling status on sibling interaction: Influences of birth order, age spacing, sex of child, and sex of sibling. *Child Development,* 54, 1064–1072.

Mirra, A. P., Cole, P., & MacMahon, B. (1971). Breast cancer in an area of high parity: SaoPaulo, Brazil. *Cancer Research,* 31, 77–83.

Morrison, S. L., Heady, J. A., & Morris, J. N. (1959). Maturity in the postneonatal period. *Archives of Diseases of Children,* 34, 101–114.

Nadelman, L., & Begun, A. (1982). The effect of the newborn on the older sibling: Mothers' questionnaire. In M. Lamb & B. Sutton-Smith (Eds.), *Sibling Relationships* (pp. 13–36). Hillsdale, N.J.: Erlbaum.

Newcomb, M. R. (1976). *Sibling Spacing and Communication Skills.* University of Oregon. University Microfilms International, 1979. Ann Arbor, Michigan.

Norton, A. J. (1980). Influence of divorce on traditional life-cycle measures. *Journal of Marriages and the Family,* 42, 63–69.

Nuttall, R. L., & Nuttall, E. V. (1975). *Family size and spacing in the U.S. and Puerto Rico* (Contract NICHD, 72-2033). Washington, DC: Center for Population Research, NICHD, U.S. Department of Health, Education and Welfare.

Nuttall, E. V., & Nuttall, R. L. (1979). Child spacing effects on intelligence, personality, and social competence. *Journal of Psychology,* 102, 3–12.

Oldman, D., Bytheway, B., & Morobin, G. (1971). Family structure and educational achievement. *Journal of Biosocial Science Supplement,* 3, 81–91.

Olneck, M. R., & Bills, D. B. (1979). Family configuration and achievement: Effects of birth order and family size in a sample of brothers. *Social Psychology Quarterly,* 42, 135–148.

Oscherwitz, M., Krasnow, S. O., & Moretti, L. (1968). The relationship of myocardial infarction to parental mortality and longevity. *Journal of Chronic Diseases,* 21, 341–348.

Page, E. B., & Grandon, G. M. (1979). Family configuration and mental ability: Two theories contrasted with U.S. data. *American Educational Research,* 16, 257–272.

Pepler, D. J., Abramovich, R., & Corter, C. (1981). Sibling interaction in the home: A longitudinal study. *Child Development,* 52, 1344–1347.

Pfouts, J. H. (1976). The sibling relationship: A forgotten dimension. *Social Work,* 21, 200–204.

Price, J. S., & Hare, E. H. (1969). Birth order studies: Some sources of bias. *British Journal of Psychiatry,* 115, 633–646.

Provence, S., & Lipton, R. C. (1967). *Infants in institutions: A comparison of their development during early life with family-reared children.* New York: International Universities Press.

Ratner, H. (1970). Child spacing II: Nature's subtleties. *Child and the Family,* **9,** 2-3.

Record, R. G., McKeown, T., & Edwards, H. H. (1970). An investigation of the difference in measured intelligence between twins and single births. *Annals of Human Genetics,* **84,** 11-20.

Reilly, J. Z. (1976). Birth order and vocational choice among eighth-grade pupils. *Dissertation Abstracts International,* **36,** 5159.

Ribble, M. A. (1943). *Rights of infants.* New York: Columbia Univ. Press.

Richer, S. (1968). The economics of child rearing. *Journal of Marriage and the Family,* **30,** 462-466.

Roberts, J., & Engel, A. (1974). *Family background, early development and intelligence of children 6-11 years.* Hyattville, MD: U.S. National Center of Health Statistics.

Roe, A. (1953). A psychological study of eminent psychologists and anthropologists and a comparison with biological physical scientists. *Psychological Monographs,* **67** (entire No. 352).

Romanoff, J. S. (1976). Birth order, family size, and sibling spacing as influences on intelligence and academic abilities of Jewish adolescents. *Dissertation Abstracts International,* **37,** 2086-2087.

Rosenberg, B. G., Goldman, R., & Sutton-Smith, B. (1969). Sibling age-spacing effects on cognitive activity in children. *Proceedings of the 77th Annual Convention, American Psychological Association,* pp. 261-262.

Rosenberg, B. G., & Sutton-Smith, B. (1969). Sibling age spacing on cognition. *Developmental Psychology,* **1,** 661-668.

Rosenthal, R., & Rosnow, R. L. (1970). *The volunteer subject.* New York: Wiley.

Russell, M. (1976). The relationship of family size and spacing to the growth of school children in Guatemala. *American Journal of Physical Health,* **66,** 1165-1172.

Sampson, E. E. (1965). Study of ordinal position antecedents and outcomes. In B. A. Maher (Ed.), *Experimental personality research.* New York: Academic Press.

Schaefer, W. M. (1977). Factors associated with intellectual development: Birth order and family size effects for a select population. *Dissertation Abstracts International,* **38**(4A), 2009-2010.

Scheinfeld, D. (1983). Family relationships and school achievement among boys in lower-income urban black families. *American Journal of Orthopsychiatry,* **33,** 127-143.

Schoonover, S. M. (1959). The relationship of intelligence and achievement to birth order, sex of sibling, and age interval. *Journal of Educational Psychology,* **50,** 143-146.

Schubert, D. S. P. (1966). *Family structure of alcoholics.* Unpublished manuscript.

Schubert, D. S. P., Wagner, M. E., & Schubert, H. J. P. (1976). One thousand references on sibling age-spacing, and sex of sibling. *JSAS Catalog of Selected Documents in Psychology,* **6,** 75 (Manuscript No. 1242).

Schubert, D. S. P., Wagner, M. E., & Schubert, H. J. P. (1984). An additional 2,000 references on sibling constellation variables: Ordinal position, sibship size, sibling age-spacing and sex of sibling. *Psychological Documents,* No. 4185.

Schubert, H. J. P., & Reiss, B. F. (1976). Unpublished data.

Schubert, H. J. P., Wagner, M. E., & Schubert, D. S. P. (1983). Child spacing effects: A comparison of institutionalized and normal children. *Journal of Developmental and Behavioral Pediatrics,* **4,** 262-264.

Selvin, S., & Janerich, D. T. (1971). Four factors influencing birth weight. *British Journal of Preventive Social Medicine,* **25,** 12-16.

Sewell, M. (1930). Two studies in sibling rivalry. I. Some causes of jealousy in children. *Smith College Studies of Social Work,* **1,** 6-22.

Smalley, R. E. (1930). Two studies in sibling rivalry: II. Influences of age, sex, and intelligence in determining attitudes of sibs toward each other. *Smith College Studies of Social Work,* 1, 23–40.

Spiers, P. S., & Wang, L. (1976). Short pregnancy interval, low birthweight, and the sudden infant death syndrome. *American Journal of Epidemiology,* 104, 15–21.

Spitz, R. A. (1945). Hospitalism: An inquiry into the genesis of psychiatric conditions in childhood. *Psychoanalytic Study of the Child,* 1, 53–74.

Spock, B. (1970). *Baby and child care.* New York: Pocket Books.

Stabeneau, J. R., Pollin, W., Roff, M., & Ricks, D. P. (Eds.). (1970). *Life history research* (Vol. 1). Minneapolis: Univ. of Minnesota Press, pp. 94–126.

Stendler, C. B. (1964). Possible causes of overdependency in young children. *Child Development,* 25, 125–147.

Sterner, G. A. (1973). Birth order and self-esteem as determinants of affiliative behavior under ego-threatening conditions. *Dissertation Abstracts International,* 33, 5501b.

Stone, L. J., & Church, J. (1973). *Childhood and adolescence: A psychology of growing persons.* New York: Random House.

Strude, M. J., & Ota, S. (1982). Type A coronary-prone behavior pattern: Relationship to birth order and family size. *Personality and Social Psychology Bulletin,* 8, 317–323.

Strumpfer, D. J. (1973). Failure to find relationships between family constellation and achievement motivation. *Journal of Psychology,* 85, 29–36.

Suchindran, C. M., & Lingner, J. W. (1977). On comparison of birth interval distribution. *Journal Biosocial Science,* 9, 25–31.

Suomi, S. J. (1982). Sibling relationships in nonhuman primates. In M. E. Lamb & B. Sutton-Smith (Eds.), *Sibling relationships* (pp. 329–356). Hillsdale, N.J.: Erlbaum.

Sutton-Smith, B. (1968). Modeling and reactive components of sibling interaction. In J. P. Hill (Ed.), *Symposium on Child Psychology,* Minneapolis, MN: Institute of Child Development.

Templer, J. (1970). The construction and validation of a death anxiety scale. *Journal of General Psychology,* 82, 165–177.

Terman, L. M. (Ed.) (1926). *Genetic studies of genius. Vol. I. Social and physical traits of 1,000 gifted children.* Stanford: Stanford Univ. Press.

Tesser, A. (1980). Self-esteem maintenance in family dynamics. *Journal of Personality and Social Psychology,* 39, 77–91.

Thomas, A., Birch, H. G., Chess, S., & Robbins, L. C. (1961). Individuality in responses of children in similar environmental situations. *American Journal of Psychiatry,* 117, 798–803.

Toman, W. (1969). *Family constellation: Theory and practice* (3rd ed.). New York: Springer-Verlag.

Trause, M. A. (1978). Birth in the hospital: The effects on the sibling. *Birth and the Family Journal,* 5, 207–210.

Tsukada, G. K. (1979). Sibling interactions: A review of the literature. *Smith College Studies on Social Work,* 49, 229–247.

Velandia, W., Grandon, G. M., & Page, E. B. (1978). Family size, birth order, and intelligence in a large South American sample. *American Educational Research Journal,* 15, 399–416.

Visher, S. S. (1948). Environmental backgrounds of leading American scientists. *American Sociological Review,* 13, 65–72.

Wagner, M. E., Schubert, H. J. P., & Schubert, D. S. P. (1979). Sibling constellation effects on psychosocial development, creativity, and health. In H. W. Reese & L. P. Lipsitt (Eds.), *Advances in child development and behavior* (Vol. 14, pp. 57–148). New York: Academic Press.

Wagner, M. E., Schubert, H. J. P., & Schubert, D. S. P. (1985). Family size effects: A review. *Journal Genetic Psychology,* 146, 65–78.

Waldrop, M. F., & Bell, R. Q. (1964). Relation of preschool dependency behavior and family size and density. *Child Development,* 35, 1187–1195.

Waldrop, M. F., & Bell, H. Q. (1966). Effects of family size and density on newborn characteristics. *American Journal of Orthopsychiatry,* 36, 544–550.

Walker, L. V., Johnson, D. L., & Goolishian, M. (1973). Ordinal position and psychopathology in two child families. *Texas Reports of Biology and Medicine,* 31, 777–790.

White, B. L. (1974). *Reassessing our educational priorities.* Paper presented at the Education Commission of the States Early Childhood Education Symposium, Boston.

White, B. L. (1975). *The first three years of life.* New York: Avon Books.

White, B. L. (1980). *Parents' guide to the first three years.* New York: Prentice Hall.

Wilsnack, S. C. (1972). Psychological factors in female drinking. *American Doctoral Dissertations,* **321.**

Woodbury, R. M. (1925). Causal factors in infant mortality: A statistical study based on investigation of eight cities. In *Children's Bureau Publication* (No. 142, pp. 60–68). Washington, DC: U.S. Government Printing Office.

Wray, J. D. (1971). *Populations pressures on families: Family size and child spacing.* New York: Population Council.

Wray, J. D., & Aguirre, A. (1969). Protein-caloric malnutrition in Candelaria. Vol. 1. Prevalence: Social and demographic factors. *Journal of Tropical Pediatrics,* pp. 76–98.

Wyron, J. B., & Gordon, J. E. (1962). A longterm prospective type field study of population dynamics in Punjab, India. In C. Y. Kiser (Ed.), *Family planning* (pp. 17–32). Princeton, NJ: Princeton Univ. Press.

Yerushalmy, J. (1945). On the interval between successive births and its effects on survival of the infant. *Human Biology,* 17, 65–106.

Yerushalmy, J., Bierman, J., Kemp, D., Connor, A., & French, F. (1956). Longitudinal studies of pregnancy on the Island of Kauai, Territory of Hawaii. *Journal of Obstetrics and Gynecology,* 71, 80–96.

Yoder, A. H. (1894). The study of the boyhood of great men. *Pedagogical Seminary,* 3, 134–156.

Zajonc, R. B. (1976). Family configuration and intelligence: Variations in scholastic aptitude scores parallel trends in family size and the spacing of children. *Science,* 192, 227–236.

Zajonc, R. B., & Markus, G. B. (1975). Birth order and intellectual development. *Psychological Review,* 82, 74–88.

Zucker, R. A., & VanHorn, H. (1972). Sibling social structure and oral behavior: Drinking and smoking in adolescence. *Quarterly Journal for Study of Alcoholism,* 33, 193–197.

INFANT VISUAL PREFERENCES:
A REVIEW AND NEW THEORETICAL TREATMENT

Martin S. Banks

SCHOOL OF OPTOMETRY
UNIVERSITY OF CALIFORNIA, BERKELEY
BERKELEY, CALIFORNIA

Arthur P. Ginsburg

AVIATION VISION LABORATORY
AEROSPACE MEDICAL LABORATORIES
WRIGHT-PATTERSON AIR FORCE BASE, OHIO

I. Introduction

The looking patterns of infants, young and old, are characterized by unmistakable tendencies to look longer at some stimuli as opposed to others. These so-called visual preferences were the object of intense study for many

ADVANCES IN CHILD DEVELOPMENT
AND BEHAVIOR, VOL. 19

years. Indeed, the study of preferences was for awhile all but synonymous with the study of early visual perception. Lately, however, interest in visual preferences has waned decidedly. Rise and decline of scientific interest in a phenomenon are, of course, not unusual. Phenomena often lose interest value because they have been explained to everyone's satisfaction, but this was not the reason in the case of preference research. Between 1967 and 1978, several theories of preferences were developed and debated, but none of them gained wide acceptance. Thus, an explanation of the rise and decline of preference research must be sought elsewhere. Let us indulge then in a brief historical review in an attempt to pinpoint reasons.

The modern era of preference research began with the late Robert Fantz's refinement of the visual preference paradigm. Fantz was most interested in determining if the percepts of sensorially inexperienced neonates were the "great blooming, buzzing confusion" pictured by William James or something more refined. Specifically, he asked whether young infants could differentiate visual stimuli on the basis of differences in form. In his experiments, infants were shown pairs of stimuli that differed only in form (e.g., Fantz, 1958, 1961). For example, a bull's-eye was paired with a grating of the same area, luminance, and contrast. If an infant looked repeatedly at one target rather than the other, Fantz reasoned that the targets had been discriminated on the basis of differences in their form. Even newborns exhibited reliable preferences among such stimuli (Fantz, 1963), so Fantz had demonstrated that visually inexperienced infants had at least a rudimentary capacity to detect and discriminate forms (or patterns). This work was exciting and fundamentally important, and it understandably spawned an enormous amount of research designed to characterize these early visual capabilities. In the process, however, the experimental question changed. More often than not it became, What aspects of visual stimuli determine infants' preferences? The pursuit of this question motivated numerous experiments in the 1960s and 1970s. For example, several researchers analyzed bull's-eyes and gratings in order to determine the differences that caused bull's-eyes to be preferred (Fantz, Fagan, & Miranda, 1975; Fantz & Nevis, 1967; Miranda, 1970; Ruff & Birch, 1974; Ruff & Turkewitz, 1975). Others sought the determinants of infants' preferences for checkerboards of various check sizes (Cohen, 1972; Fantz & Fagan, 1975; Greenberg & Blue, 1975; Karmel, 1969; Miranda & Fantz, 1971).

The proliferation of data naturally led to attempts at synthesis. Several theoretical accounts of early visual preferences followed including discrepancy theory (Kagan, 1970), complexity theory (Berlyne, 1960; Dember & Earl, 1957), contour density theory (Karmel, 1969), size and number theory (Fantz & Fagan, 1975), and neural substrate theories (Fantz *et al.,* 1975: Haith, 1978; Karmel & Maisel, 1975).

The discrepancy, complexity, and contour density theories were optimal level theories; that is, a moderate level of stimulation was assumed to be most preferred at each age and the optimal level was assumed to shift with age. Two of these theories—discrepancy and complexity—originated from the view that infants' information-processing capacity grows with age. They proposed that different levels of stimulus complexity provide optimal stimulation at different ages. To define complexity, discrepancy theory referred to the interaction between the stimulus and the infant's previous experience with it or related stimuli. Complexity theory referred more directly to the stimulus by defining complexity in terms of predictability (Haith, Kessen, & Collins, 1969), number of elements (Brennan, Ames, & Moore, 1966), or number of angles (Munsinger & Weir, 1967). The contour density theory originated from Karmel's post hoc analysis of checkerboard preferences. Contour density was defined as the total length of contour in a stimulus divided by the total area. According to this theory, different amounts of contour density were most preferred at different ages.

The neural substrate theories and, to some extent, the size and number theory were maximal level theories; that is, the highest available level of stimulation was assumed to be most preferred at all ages. The neural substrate models of Fantz *et al.* (1975), Haith (1978), and Karmel and Maisel (1975) stated that young infants' preferences are governed by the response rate of neurons in the central visual system. Patterns that match the size and shape of these neurons' receptive fields evoke greater activity and thereby attract or hold fixation. Finer patterns become more preferred with age because the receptive fields of such neurons become smaller. The size and number model was developed by Fantz and Fagan (1975) from a post hoc analysis of their preference data. According to this theory, stimuli with large elements are preferred over those with smaller elements, and stimuli with more elements are preferred over those with fewer. However, the relative importance of the two variables changes with age, size being most important in younger infants and number in older infants.

By the mid-1970s then, the developmental literature was filled with data and theories on infants' visual preferences; no more active area of research existed in the field of infant visual perception. If the rate of publication on the topic is used as an index, developmental researchers appear to have begun to lose interest in preferences shortly thereafter. What went wrong? We believe two things did.

First, progress in understanding the phenomenon had been slow at best. All of the preference theories proposed by 1978 had encountered some obvious difficulties. In each case, the theories could not account for some existing data. Welch's (1974) results were inconsistent with discrepancy theory (see also Thomas, 1971), and Karmel's (1969) and McCall and Melson's

(1970) results contradicted complexity theory. The contour density and size and number theories could not explain why pattern arrangement (Fantz *et al.*, 1975) and line thickness (McCall & Melson, 1970) affected preference. In retrospect, the fact that these models lacked predictive power is not surprising because they had some critical shortcomings involving the characterizations of both the stimulus and the infant. In regard to the stimulus, the relevant dimensions were either not defined rigorously enough to allow unambiguous predictions (discrepancy and complexity theories) or not defined with the richness required to incorporate a broad range of stimuli (contour density and size and number). In regard to the characterization of the infant, the theories were vague about what changes in the infant cause changes in preferences. The discrepancy and complexity theories did not specify how one could measure the child's current schema or level of information-processing capacity. The contour density and size and number models described the relevant mechanisms—the neural receptive fields proposed by Haith and others—but the dimensions of the mechanisms could not be determined at a given age because no way was (or is) available to measure them in human infants.

The second event that we believe led to the decline of preference research is the following. Many developmentalists seem to have turned to other research problems perhaps because they recognized that an explanation of the development of preferences might not enrich our general understanding of the development of visual perception. To illustrate this point, let us construct a hypothetical example. Suppose that we became convinced that complexity theory was an adequate account of young infants' preferences (this implies, of course, that complexity could be rigorously defined and that the optimal level of complexity could be determined at each age). What would such a theory tell us about the development of vision in some general sense? Our guess is that it would not tell us very much at all. For instance, one could not ascertain from such an account even very simple things such as whether a 3 month old can see pattern information that newborns cannot. Thus, such an account of preferences would probably not illuminate anything about early visual perception other than preferences. Indeed, researchers did become more concerned in the mid-1970s with questions about visual processing per se. Preferential looking was still measured, but it was now thought of as a response index of various capabilities including visual acuity (Dobson & Teller, 1978), contrast sensitivity (Atkinson, Braddick, & Moar, 1977a), color vision (Peeples & Teller, 1975), depth perception (Fox, Aslin, Shea, & Dumais, 1980), and cross-modal perception (Spelke, 1976).

Thus, the study of the determinants of infants' visual preferences reached an early retirement, and the field moved on to examine visual capabilities per se. Progress in understanding how various capabilities develop was remarkable, a fact that is documented in several recent reviews (Aslin, 1985; Banks & Salapatek, 1983; Teller & Bornstein, 1985; Yonas & Owsley, 1985). Starting 4 years ago, one of us realized that our improved understanding of the development of basic visual mechanisms could serve the construction of more useful models of early visual preferences (Banks & Salapatek, 1981). We expand those ideas in this article. In so doing, we resurrect the once lively debate about what determines infants' visual preferences at different ages. We propose a quantitative model of preferences based on linear systems techniques and test it against data from several well-known preference experiments. The model's predictions agree quite well with observed preferences for a variety of stimuli. The success of this model implies that infants' visual preferences are governed simply by a tendency to look at highly visible patterns. This account of early preferential looking is thus consonant with our understanding of how the growth of basic sensory mechanisms affects visual perception during the first months of life.

II. Linear Systems Analysis and Its Application

Before presenting our model of infant pattern preferences, we need to describe the engineering technique upon which it is based: linear systems analysis. Our discussion will be brief and conceptual. For more comprehensive and rigorous treatments, the reader is referred to Cornsweet (1970), Gaskill (1978), or Georgeson (1979).

Linear systems analysis is based on Fourier's theorem. This powerful theorem implies that any two-dimensional, time-invariant visual stimulus can be exactly described by combining a set of more basic stimuli. (We will consider only achromatic stimuli, that is, stimuli with contours defined by a difference in luminance rather than by a difference in hue.) These basic stimuli are sine wave gratings, examples of which are shown in Fig. 1. A sine wave grating is a pattern of light and dark stripes whose intensity varies sinusoidally with position. Sine wave gratings are specified by four parameters: (1) spatial frequency, the number of pattern repetitions (or cycles) per degree of visual angle; (2) orientation, the grating's tilt to the left or right of vertical; (3) phase, the grating's position with respect to some reference position; and (4) contrast, which is related to the difference between maximum and minimum intensities of the grating. [Formally, contrast is defined as $(I_{max} - I_{min})/(I_{max} + I_{min})$, where I_{max} refers to the peak intensity of a light stripe and I_{min} is the intensity of the least intense part of a dark stripe.] Fourier's theorem implies then that even a complex, two-dimensional visual stimulus, such as the picture of a face, can be described exactly by the com-

212   *Martin S. Banks and Arthur P. Ginsburg*

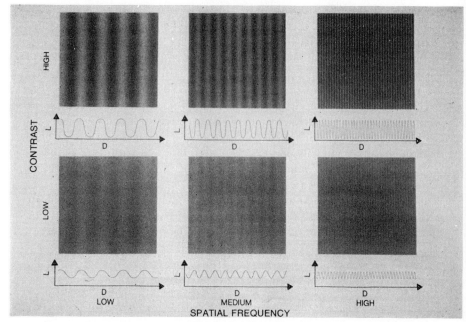

Fig. 1.   *Six sine wave gratings differing in spatial frequency and contrast. From left to right, the gratings increase in spatial frequency. From bottom to top, they increase in contrast. If the figure is held at arm's length, the gratings have spatial frequencies of 1.5, 3, and 12 cycles/degree.*

bination of a set of gratings of various frequencies, orientations, phases, and contrasts.

Figures 2 and 3 demonstrate this principle. They show how sine wave gratings can be added together to reproduce the checkerboard shown in the upper half of Fig. 2. The lower half is the Fourier or spatial frequency representation of the checkerboard, and is obtained by Fourier transformation of the pattern (Kelly, 1976, pp. 286–287). This particular representation is called an amplitude spectrum. It contains all the information necessary to specify the spatial frequency, contrast, and orientation of the checkerboard's constituent sine wave gratings. Phase is not represented in this type of plot. Each spot in the lower half of Fig. 2 represents a grating component. The spatial frequency of each component is indicated by the spot's distance from the center of the plot; the greater the distance, the higher the frequency. Contrast is represented by the area of the spot. Orientation is indicated by the angle between the horizontal axis and a line from the origin to the spot. According to Fourier's theorem, one can reconstruct the original checkerboard by adding together the grating components represented in the lower half of the figure. This process is called Fourier synthesis and

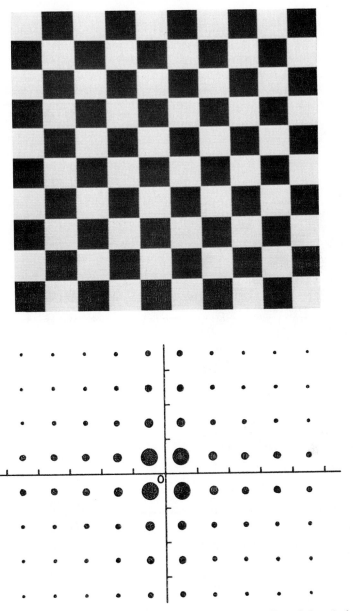

Fig. 2.   *A checkerboard and its spatial frequency components. Top: A 5 × 5 checker-board. Bottom: The spatial frequency representation (amplitude spectrum) of the checkerboard. Each spot represents an individual sine wave component. Spatial frequency is indicated by the spot's distance from the origin. Orientation is represented by the angle between the spot and the origin. Contrast or amplitude is indicated by the spot's area.*

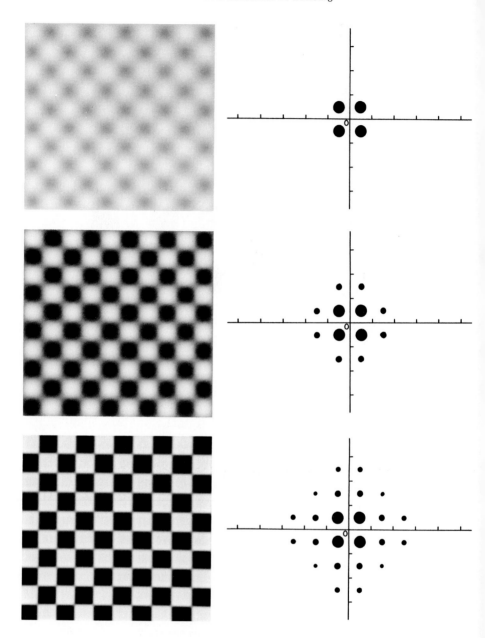

Fig. 3.   *Synthesis of a checkerboard. The graphs on the right are representations of the components that have been added to create the images on the left. From top to bottom in the figure, more and more spatial frequency components have been added. See text for details.*

is illustrated by Fig. 3. From top to bottom, more and more of the checkerboard's components are added until the original pattern emerges. In the two top panels, the four gratings of lowest frequency have been added; these components are called the fundamentals. The basic structure of the checkerboard has already emerged, but the shape of each check has not. The two middle panels show what happens when the next eight gratings are added; some of the individual checks have begun to take shape. Finally, the next 12 components have been added in the lowest two panels; the resulting pattern is virtually indistinguishable from the original checkerboard. If we added all of the remaining components to this image, the checkerboard of Fig. 2 would be reconstructed precisely.

To this point, we have discussed how Fourier's theorem allows one to describe any two-dimensional stimulus in terms of sine wave gratings of various spatial frequencies, contrasts, orientations, and phases. We turn now to the analysis of real systems by considering how Fourier's theorem and linear systems analysis can be used to characterize the image-forming quality of a camera lens. We will use some engineering terms throughout this section because they make the discussion simpler. The term *input* will refer to the stimulus presented to a lens (or a visual system), the term *output* to the image created on the camera's film (or the perceptual response of a visual system), and the terms *transmission* and *filtering* to what goes on in between. The application of linear systems techniques allows an optical engineer to characterize the quality of a camera lens completely. In other words, an engineer can use these techniques to predict the lens' output no matter what the input is. Because any input can be represented by a set of sine wave gratings, linear systems techniques involve the measurement of how sine wave gratings of various frequencies are transmitted by the lens. The index of this measurement is the modulation transfer function, which is the proportion of input contrast at different spatial frequencies that is transmitted by the lens onto the camera's film. Lenses transmit low spatial frequencies very well and high spatial frequencies rather poorly. Thus, the modulation transfer function of a lens is like a low-pass filter; the proportion of input contrast transmitted onto the film is nearly 1 at low frequencies and nearly 0 at high frequencies.

As we mentioned above, any input can be represented by the addition of various gratings. Thus, according to linear systems theory, the output of a linear system to any input can be represented by the addition of the responses to the input's constituent gratings. This statement is described more formally by the following equations:

$$A_0(f,g) = A_i(f,g) \cdot A_h(f,g) \qquad (1)$$
$$P_0(f,g) = P_i(f,g) + P_h(f,g) \qquad (2)$$

Equation (1) relates the amplitudes of the input and output sine wave grating components. $A_h(f,g)$ is the lens' two-dimensional modulation transfer function; it is the proportion of input contrast that is transmitted onto the film as a function of the spatial frequency in two dimensions (f and g). $A_i(f,g)$ is the amplitude spectrum of the input stimulus. Thus, the multiplication of the input's sine wave components, $A_i(f,g)$, by the appropriate weighting factor, $A_h(f,g)$, yields the amplitude spectrum of the output. Inverse Fourier transformation (the operation involved in Fourier synthesis) can then be used to synthesize the output, $A_0(f,g)$. Equation (2) relates the phases of the input and output spatial frequency components. Most optical systems and visual systems do not change the phase of a stimulus or its components during processing. Therefore, the phase transfer function of a system, $P_h(f,g)$, is generally zero, which implies that the output and input phases are identical. For this reason, we will disregard phase transfer functions and their effects henceforth.

Figure 3 can be used to illustrate how linear systems analysis is used to predict the output of an optical system to a particular input. Suppose that the modulation transfer function of the lens is a simple low-pass filter. That is, suppose that the lens transmits spatial frequencies lower than 2 cycles/degree (c/deg) perfectly and does not transmit higher spatial frequencies at all. In that case, Eq. (1) implies that the amplitude spectrum of the output contains all of the spatial frequencies of the original checkerboard except those above 2 c/deg. In other words, the output spectrum would be that of the top right graph in Fig. 3. One can then use inverse Fourier transformation to produce the predicted output. This is shown in the top left graph in Fig. 3. As can be seen, a lens that transmits only low spatial frequencies would produce a noticeably degraded version of the original checkerboard. The middle and bottom pairs of panels in Fig. 3 illustrate the outputs that would be obtained for modulation transfer functions cutting off at 4.5 and 7.2 c/deg, respectively.

Our real interest is the evaluation of visual systems, not optical systems, so we now turn to that topic. Linear systems analysis has been successfully applied for two decades or more to the investigation of visual performance (e.g., Cornsweet, 1970; Ratliff, 1965). According to linear systems theory, the output (perceptual response) associated with any input (two-dimensional, time-invariant stimulus) can be predicted if one knows the system's response to sine waves of various spatial frequencies. For the prediction to be precise, however, the visual system must satisfy certain conditions, a topic we return to below.

The contrast sensitivity function (CSF) is used instead of the modulation transfer function to represent the visual system's ability to detect and transmit information as a function of spatial frequency. The CSF is determined by measuring an observer's contrast sensitivity to sine wave gratings of various spatial frequencies. In practice, this is done by presenting gratings of a number of different spatial frequencies one at a time and determining the least contrast necessary for an observer to detect the grating at each of those frequencies. An example of a typical adult's CSF is shown in the lower portion of Fig. 4. Contrast sensitivity, the reciprocal of the minimum contrast required for detection, is plotted as a function of spatial frequency. Note that sensitivity is greatest for intermediate spatial frequencies (2–6 c/deg) and lower for low and high frequencies. The figure also presents a grating, varying in spatial frequency and contrast, to give the reader a feeling for what the CSF represents. The grating increases in spatial frequency from left to right and increases in contrast from top to bottom. The *physical* contrast of the grating is constant along any horizontal line in the photograph, but its *perceived* contrast is not. Clearly, the highest perceived contrast is for intermediate frequencies. Note the correspondence between your ability to detect the grating at different frequencies in the upper part of the figure and the CSF plotted in the lower part.

The CSF then is used in place of the modulation transfer function in Eq. (1) to predict the visual system's response to any pattern. There is a catch, however. The use of linear systems analysis requires that the system satisfy four conditions: linearity, isotropy, homogeneity, and state invariance. The mature visual system does not satisfy any of these assumptions exactly (Banks & Salapatek, 1981; Cornsweet, 1970); thus, the CSF cannot completely characterize how the adult visual system transmits two-dimensional stimuli. There is no compelling reason to expect that the infant visual system exactly satisfies these conditions either, but there are reasons to believe that they are more nearly satisfied in infants than in adults. For one thing, the infant visual system seems to be isotropic (that is, sensitivity seems to be equivalent for contours of any orientation) (Teller, Morse, Borton, & Regal, 1974). For another, the immature visual system may not violate the assumptions of linearity as seriously because the range of contrasts to which infants are sensitive is so small. In any event, the inaccuracies that might arise from violations of these four conditions can be minimized by measuring CSFs under certain conditions and by restricting the application of linear systems analysis to those situations in which the violations are small. The primary restrictions are (1) use of stimuli in which contrast is not significantly above threshold; (2) use of stimuli in which average luminances are within a restricted range; and (3) caution concerning which segment of the visual field is actually being studied. These points are discussed in greater detail by Banks and Salapatek (1981, pp. 28–29) and by Cornsweet (1970, pp. 324–339). If these restrictions are heeded, the CSF and linear systems analysis should be quite useful to the study of infant pattern vision.

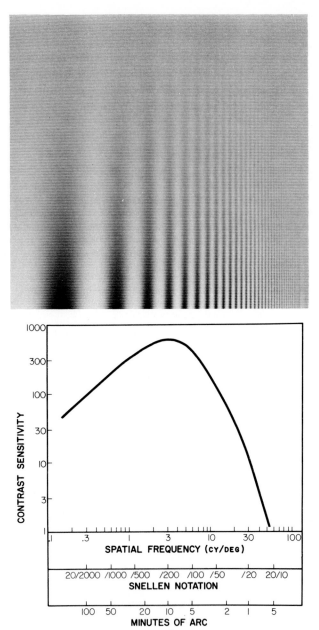

Fig. 4. A sine wave grating and a typical adult contrast sensitivity function (CSF). The upper part of the figure displays a sine wave grating in which spatial frequency increases from left to right and contrast increases from top to bottom. The lower part of the figure shows a typical adult CSF. Contrast sensitivity, the reciprocal of contrast at threshold, is plotted as a function of spatial frequency. Scales relating spatial frequency to Snellen equivalents and stripe width in minutes of arc are shown for comparison. If the figure is viewed from a distance of 1.5 m, the scales at the bottom indicate the actual frequency values of the grating in the upper part of the figure. (Adapted from Banks and Salapatek, 1981.)

III. Infant Contrast Sensitivity and Related Topics

The CSFs of young infants have been measured by three laboratories. Two of the groups, Atkinson *et al.* (1977a) and Banks and Salapatek (1978), have used preferential looking techniques primarily while the other, Pirchio, Spinelli, Fiorentini, and Maffei (1978), has used the visual evoked potential. The CSF data from these studies have been reviewed elsewhere, so we refer the interested reader to those sources for details (Banks & Dannemiller, 1985; Banks & Salapatek, 1983).

Atkinson *et al.* (1977a) and Banks and Salapatek (1978) used versions of the forced-choice preferential looking technique to test 1, 2, and 3 month olds. The contrast of sine wave gratings was varied systematically in order to determine the least contrast necessary to elicit 70 or 75% correct responding. The results from Banks and Salapatek are shown in Fig. 5. Contrast sensitivity increased significantly from 1 to 3 months, particularly at high spatial frequencies. Indeed, estimates of the highest detectable spatial frequency (the acuity cutoff) increased from 2 to 4 c/deg. The low-frequency falloff in sensitivity that is characteristic of adult CSFs is not observed at 1 month, but is at 2 and 3 months. The Banks and Salapatek data and the Atkinson *et al.* data agree remarkably well on the shape and height of the CSF at 2 and 3 months of age. They disagree concerning overall contrast sensitivity at 1 month, but agree on the shape of the CSF at that age.

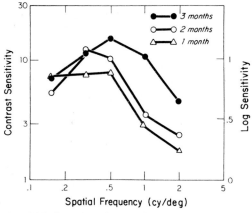

Fig. 5.   The average CSFs for 1, 2, and 3 month olds as reported by Banks and Salapatek. The average contrast sensitivity for each age group is plotted as a function of spatial frequency. (From Banks and Salapatek, 1978.)

A comparison of the adult CSF in Fig. 4 and the infant functions in Fig. 5 reveals distinct differences. Clearly, infant CSFs are shifted to a lower band of spatial frequencies. Moreover, all infants appear to have a substantial deficit in overall contrast sensitivity relative to adults. Such comparisons motivate an important question: To what extent are these early deficits the result of nonvisual factors such as motivation?

Evoked potential measurements can answer this question to some extent because they are presumably less susceptible to motivational effects than are behavioral techniques. Using visual evoked potentials, Pirchio *et al.* (1978) measured CSFs in one infant from $2\frac{1}{2}$ to 6 months of age. They also measured two points on the CSF in a number of infants from 2 to 10 months. The results for the infant tested longitudinally revealed a steady increase in contrast sensitivity, particularly at high frequencies, from $2\frac{1}{2}$ to 6 months. The $2\frac{1}{2}$-month data were quite similar to the 2- and 3-month results of Atkinson *et al.* and Banks and Salapatek. The results from the infants tested cross-sectionally by Pirchio *et al.* confirmed this. Harris, Atkinson, and Braddick (1976) measured the CSF in one 6 month old, using both the visual evoked potential and preferential looking. In spite of differences in some of the stimulus parameters and the obvious differences in response measures, the two techniques yielded similar estimates of the CSF. Their data suggest that adult contrast sensitivity is only two times higher than that of 6 month olds.

The similarity of visual evoked potential and behavioral results suggests that the poor contrast sensitivity reported for young infants reflects mostly visual rather than nonvisual motivational factors. Thus, the pattern information to which young infants are sensitive is probably a small fraction of the information available to adults.

These developmental CSF data have been used to predict sensitivity (that is, detection thresholds) to a variety of patterns. These demonstrations include quantitative predictions of "face acuity" (Atkinson *et al.*, 1977b), qualitative predictions of acuity for irregular versus regular gratings (Banks and Salapatek, 1981), quantitative predictions of acuity for square wave gratings versus rectangular wave gratings (Banks and Salapatek, 1981), and quantitative predictions of contrast sensitivity for rectangular wave gratings of different duty cycles (Banks and Stephens, 1982). The accuracy of these predictions illustrates the utility of the CSF and linear systems analysis for characterizing the sensitivity of the developing visual system to different sorts of patterns.

Up to this point, we have simply presented a technique that allows one to predict input–output relationships, without pinpointing the types of processing that actually occur in the visual system. In order to develop a plausible preference model, however, one must consider processing mechanisms as well. Therefore, in the next section we describe recent work on the development of feature-selective visual mechanisms. Results from this work determine some of the characteristics of the preference model presented later on.

All mature sensory systems seem to possess many parallel pathways, each specialized to convey information about a particular set of stimuli. In the visual system, different sorts of pattern information from the same location in the visual field are signaled by different neurons. For instance, different cells in the primary visual cortex of cats and monkeys respond exclusively to stimuli of particular orientations (Hubel & Wiesel, 1962, 1968). Such cells also respond selectively to different bands of spatial frequency, one cell responding to low spatial frequencies and another to high frequencies (Campbell, Cooper, & Enroth-Cugell, 1969; Albrecht, DeValois, & Thorell, 1980). A number of psychophysical demonstrations have suggested that human adults process pattern information in parallel with mechanisms that are analogous to these cortical cells. Different mechanisms appear to be tuned to different orientations and spatial frequencies (Braddick, Campbell, & Atkinson, 1978). These mechanisms have been called orientation channels and spatial-frequency channels even though any given mechanism probably responds selectively to both orientation and spatial frequency.

Several investigators have argued the importance of these channels to pattern recognition and identification (e.g., Ginsburg, 1978; Marr, 1982; Pollen, Lee, & Taylor, 1971). Nonetheless, their development has only recently been investigated. Derrington and Fuchs (1981) reported that the spatial-frequency specificity of kitten cortical cells increases postnatally. Blakemore and Van Sluyters (1975) and Bonds (1979) reported a similar finding for orientation specificity.

Banks, Stephens, and Hartmann (1985) used a masking paradigm to measure the spatial-frequency selectivity of channels in human infants and adults. Detection thresholds were measured for sine wave gratings presented in either the presence or absence of a narrow-band noise masker. (The masker was a stimulus, continuously present, that was intended to render the grating less detectable when it was presented.) At all ages the masker caused an increase in the threshold for detecting the grating when the spatial frequencies of the masker and sine wave grating were similar. However, when the masker and grating differed in frequency by two octaves (a factor of four), the grating's threshold was unaffected by the masker in 3 month olds and adults. This result indicates that pattern information whose frequency content differs by two octaves is processed by separate channels and, therefore, constitutes evidence for multiple spatial-frequency channels with narrow bandwidths. In $1\frac{1}{2}$ month olds, however, the masker increased the grating's threshold even when the grating and masker differed by two octaves. Consequently, separate, narrow-band channels were not demonstrated at that age. Banks *et al.* used these data to estimate channel bandwidths at different ages. The estimates were slightly less than ± 1.3 octaves for 3 month olds and adults. A bandwidth could not be estimated at $1\frac{1}{2}$ months because no frequency-selective masking was observed. These results imply that spatial-frequency channels are quite unselective early in life but acquire adult-like specificity by 3 months. Banks *et al.* (1985) conducted a second experiment, using a different paradigm, to test the reliability of this age-related shift. The results corroborated those of the first experiment.

To date, the development of orientation selectivity has not been investigated in humans. In cats, spatial frequency and orientation selectivity develop at similar rates. We assume, therefore, that spatial frequency and orientation selectivity develop at similar rates in humans, too. Thus, in our preference model we assume that no spatial frequency- or orientation-selective channels operate before 2 months of age. After that age, we assume the presence of ± 1.0-octave spatial-frequency channels and ± 15-degree orientation channels.

Another important feature of our preference model concerns the shape of the filtering function $A_h(f,g)$ that should be used for different ages and stimulus contrasts. Banks and Salapatek (1981) assumed that the CSF of the appropriate age should be used at all stimulus contrasts. Recent evidence suggests, however, that this assumption should be questioned. The adult psychophysical literature illuminates important differences between threshold and suprathreshold processing. Georgeson and Sullivan (1975), for example, examined the perception of spatial contrast near threshold and above. They asked adults to adjust the contrast of a sine wave grating of one spatial frequency (the "comparison" grating) until it appeared to match the contrast of a sine wave grating of a different frequency (the "standard" grating). The standard was a grating of 5 c/deg, a value near the peak of the adult CSF. When the contrast of the standard was near threshold, adults set the contrast of the comparison gratings to higher values that were predictable from the CSF. This result is expected since the CSF is a threshold function that describes the minimum contrast required to detect gratings of different frequencies. The most interesting result in this experiment, however, occurred when the contrast of the standard was set to a value well above threshold. Adults in this situation adjusted the contrast of the comparison to the same physical value as the contrast of the standard. This is an unexpected result because the optical imperfections of the eye cause two gratings of equal contrast but different spatial frequencies to produce different retinal image contrasts. In other words, when adults set 5 and 20 c/deg gratings to equal physical contrasts, they were accepting as equal in perceived contrast two gratings with retinal image contrasts differing by a factor of 4.7 (Campbell & Gubisch, 1966). Georgeson and Sullivan called this phenomenon "contrast constancy." The phenomenon implies that the adult CSF does not describe the relative perceived contrasts of suprathreshold gratings. The function that does is much flatter than the CSF.

According to current theory, multiple spatial-frequency channels are needed to achieve contrast constancy (Hess, 1983; Georgeson & Sullivan, 1975). Because such channels appear to develop by 3 months, Stephens and Banks (1985) examined the development of contrast constancy in young infants. Two sine wave gratings, differing in spatial frequency by a factor of 3, were presented simultaneously to $1\frac{1}{2}$ and 3 month olds. The contrast of one grating was varied in order to estimate the contrasts at which fixation preference for the two gratings was equal. The equal preference points for $1\frac{1}{2}$ month olds were predictable from their CSFs. The 3 month olds' equal preference points were also predictable from CSFs but only for low-contrast stimuli. At high contrasts, equal preference occurred when the gratings were of the same physical contrast. Thus, if one accepts the assumption that equal preference in infants is analogous to perceived contrast matches in adults, Stephens and Banks' data imply that contrast constancy is observed at 3 months but not $1\frac{1}{2}$ months. In other words, the CSF is an adequate description of the relative perceived contrast of gratings among $1\frac{1}{2}$ month olds for both near-threshold and suprathreshold stimuli. Things are more complicated for 3 month olds: The CSF adequately describes the relative perceived contrast of gratings at low contrasts, but the function needed for high contrasts is flatter than the CSF. For this reason, we assume in our preference model that the CSF is the appropriate filter to use for infants less than 2 months of age regardless of stimulus contrast. We assume further that the CSF is the appropriate filter to use for older infants so long as near-threshold stimuli are involved; a flatter function is required for suprathreshold contrasts.

We should discuss one final point before describing the details of the linear systems preference model. One might not expect the linear systems approach to yield accurate predictions of infants' preferences among suprathreshold patterns. For one thing, the assumptions of linear systems analysis are more likely to be violated when applied to suprathreshold rather than threshold stimuli. Specifically, the assumption of linearity is probably violated. We do not know how seriously this assumption is violated, so we use a practical approach to the problem. We assume that the assumption is not seriously violated and use the linear systems equations to predict infants' preferences among suprathreshold patterns. If the predictions turn out to be accurate, our assumption must have been correct that the violations of the linearity assumption were not serious.

IV. Linear Systems Preference Model

With the background from Sections II and III, we now describe the linear systems preference model. This model is an elaboration of the one presented by Banks and Salapatek in 1981. Its domain is the visual preferences of infants from birth to 3 months of age, though it could be extended to older infants once more is known about their contrast sensitivity and frequency/orientation channels. By visual preference we mean the tendency to look longer at one pattern over another when given the choice. Unfortunately, this definition of preference obscures many telling features of infants' looking behavior, such as the particular eye movements used and the lower probability of looking with repeated presentations (Haith, 1980), but the definition is consistent with the majority of experiments that were suitable for reanalysis. The model does not incorporate the effect of repeated stimulus presentations as in habituation experiments. The interested reader should refer to Dannemiller and Banks (1983, 1985), Slater, Earle, Morison, and Rose (1985), and Slater and Morison (1985) for discussions of this topic. We should also emphasize that a clear distinction between preference and discrimination is necessary. The model presented here only concerns preferences, that is, infants' tendency to fixate one pattern over another. When the model predicts that two patterns are equally preferred, it does not imply that they are indiscriminable. Thus, the model does not yield predictions concerning discrimination per se. The reasons for drawing this distinction between preference and discrimination are described by Banks and Salapatek (1981, pp. 38–39).

The linear systems preference model assumes that infant pattern preferences are governed by the pattern information available to decision centers in the central nervous system. There are three facets to this assumption.

1. The pattern information available to central decision centers is a small fraction of the information impinging on the infant's eye; considerable information is lost in processing by the optic media, retina, and central visual pathways. This loss of information can be thought of as filtering.

2. The CSF is assumed to be a good description of the filtering characteristics of the visual system before 2 months of age. Thus, from birth to 2 months, our model uses the CSF to filter stimuli of all contrasts. For older infants, the model uses the CSF to filter stimuli with near-threshold contrasts and a flatter function to filter suprathreshold stimuli. These filtering functions are displayed in Fig. 6. Data obtained by Banks and Salapatek (1978) and Stephens and Banks (1985) were chosen to derive these functions because their stimulus conditions (field size and average luminance) were similar to those in most preference experiments.

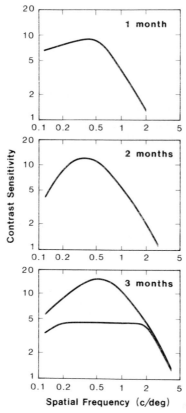

Fig. 6. *The filtering functions used in the linear systems preference model. The functions were derived from the CSFs of Banks and Salapatek (1978) and the contrast matching data of Stephens and Banks (1985). Each function is represented by a smooth curve. The lower curve for the 3 month olds is the flat filtering function used for high contrasts.*

3. The model assumes that infants tend to direct their eyes toward and hold fixation on or near the most "salient" pattern, once filtered by the appropriate filtering function. Salience has been defined in a variety of ways in the preference literature. The linear systems model presented here uses an explicit decision rule to determine the salience, or preference value, of any two-dimensional, time-invariant pattern. The rule, which we call the square root of sums rule, makes some physiological and psychophysical sense. It assumes that each stimulus is filtered by the appropriate filtering function and then channeled into spatial-frequency and orientation channels. In the case of infants less than 2 months of age, we have assumed that only one frequency/orientation channel exists (Banks *et al.*, 1985), so all the information is channeled into it. The output of that channel is deter-

mined by integrating the absolute values of the amplitude spectrum. In the case of infants older than 2 months, we assume that several frequency/orientation channels exist (Banks *et al.*, 1985), so the information is channeled into several ±1-octave, ±15-degree channels. This channeling is portrayed in Fig. 7. The output of each channel is determined by integration. The resultant is then squared and added to the squared output of the other channels. Finally, the square root of this sum is computed and this number is the predicted preference value. The square root of sums rule is similar to one used by Ginsburg (1978) in adult work, and can be used to compute a preference value for any two-dimensional, time-invariant pattern.

Let us summarize how the linear systems model works before describing the results of our reanalyses of preference experiments. A preference value is computed for each stimulus in an experiment by presenting the stimulus to a computer version of the model. Let us trace one stimulus through the steps involved. The Fourier transform of the stimulus is computed first, yielding an amplitude spectrum (see Figs. 2 and 3), which is simply the magnitude, spatial frequency, and orientation of each of the stimulus' constituent sine wave gratings. The amplitude spectrum is then multiplied by the appropriate filtering function (Fig. 6). The result is that components to which the infants are quite sensitive are transmitted and those to which infants are insensitive are attenuated. This filtered spectrum is then presented to the decision rule. For infants younger than 2 months, the filtered amplitude spectrum is integrated and the resultant is the predicted prefer-

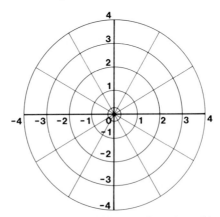

Fig. 7.   *Schematic of the frequency/orientation channels used in the linear systems preference model. The coordinates of the figure are the same as those in Figs. 2 and 3. The thin lines represent the boundaries of different frequency/orientation channels. The frequency bandwidths are ± 1.0 octave and the orientation bandwidths are ± 15 degrees. All components falling within a given channel are integrated.*

ence value. For infants older than 2 months, the filtered amplitude spectrum is channeled into spatial-frequency/orientation channels (Fig. 7), and the spectrum within each channel is integrated. The resultant is squared and added to the squared outputs of all the other channels. Finally, the square root of the sum is computed and that number is the predicted preference value. We compute predicted preference values for each stimulus in a preference experiment and can use those numbers to predict the pattern of results.

V. Reanalyses of Preference Experiments

We have used the linear systems model to reanalyze several well-known preference experiments. The experiments are (1) the checkerboard studies conducted by several investigators, (2) the size and number studies of Fantz and Fagan (1975), (3) the contour density studies of Maisel and Karmel (1978), and (4) the matrix studies of Salapatek (1975). We chose these particular experiments for reanalysis because the experiments were reasonably well known, the observed preferences were robust, and the stimuli were fairly easy to analyze with the computation facilities we had at the time. We also describe reports by Gayl, Roberts, and Werner (1983) and Slater *et al.* (1985), who used linear system techniques to predict preferences.

As it turns out, the contour density model of Karmel (1969) bears some resemblance to the linear systems model, so we consider contour density predictions in several sections, too. Simply stated, the similarity between the contour density and linear systems models is the following. The contour density of a pattern is generally increased by adding more elements with shorter interelement distances, a process roughly equivalent to increasing the dominant spatial frequencies. Generally, then, the contour density of a pattern is roughly proportional to the spatial frequencies of the dominant Fourier components. This relationship is by no means perfect, however, so there are ways to contrast the predictions of contour density and linear systems models, as we will see.

A. CHECKERBOARDS

As mentioned in Section I, several researchers have presented checkerboards of various check sizes to infants and found that the most preferred check size decreases with age. The results of these experiments are summarized in Fig. 8, which is based on Fig. 2.3 of Karmel and Maisel (1975). The solid symbols represent the most preferred check size as a function of age. The consistency of these results is remarkable in view of the fact that they were drawn from different experiments using different procedures.

Martin S. Banks and Arthur P. Ginsburg

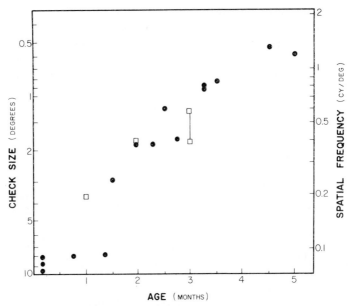

Fig. 8.   Preferences for checkerboards with different check sizes as a function of age. The most preferred check size is plotted on the left ordinate and the corresponding spatial frequency of the fundamental component on the right ordinate. The filled symbols represent the results of different experiments as analyzed by Karmel and Maisel (1975). The open squares represent the predictions of the linear systems model. The two squares for 3 month olds represent the prediction when the CSF serves as the filtering function (top square) and the prediction when a flatter function (see Fig. 6) is used (bottom square).

We presented checkerboards of different check sizes to our computer implementation of the model and computed a predicted preference value for each. The resulting predictions are displayed as open symbols in Fig. 8. Notice that a range of predictions is indicated for the 3 month olds. The upper end of the range is the prediction if one assumes that the CSF is the appropriate filtering function; the lower end is the prediction if one assumes a flatter filtering function (see Fig. 6). The predictions match the observed preferences faithfully. Thus, the linear systems model seems to predict age-related changes in checkerboard preferences rather well.

As mentioned above, Karmel (1969) used a post hoc analysis to determine hypothetical functions that best described the relationship between checkerboard preferences and contour density at different ages. Obviously, the resulting agreement between observed and predicted preferences was good. Consequently, Karmel and colleagues used the derived hypothetical functions to predict preferences for patterns other than checkerboards. We will describe those analyses for each set of stimuli considered below.

B. SIZE AND NUMBER

We have also reanalyzed the size and number study of Fantz and Fagan (1975). These investigators had proposed that the size and number of pattern elements in a checkerboard were the primary determinants of checkerboard preferences. They argued that a model that combined the effects of size and number of elements would predict preferences better than either complexity or contour density alone. To examine this, they used the set of stimuli shown in Fig. 9. The size and number of pattern elements were varied independently in these stimuli. The relative preferences of 5, 10, 15, 20, and 25 week olds were measured by presenting all possible pairings of the stimuli. When the number of elements was equated (e.g., 2–2 vs 2–1 in Fig. 9), the member with larger elements was preferred. When element size was equated (e.g., 2–1 vs 8–1), the member with more elements was preferred. There were, however, some interesting developmental trends. The size variable was a better predictor of preference than the number variable at 5 weeks, and the reverse was true from 10 to 25 weeks.

We used the 1-month filtering function to reanalyze Fantz and Fagan's 5-week data and the 3-month functions to reanalyze their 10-week data. Using the curvilinear function of Fig. 6, we obtained correlations between the predicted and observed preferences of 0.92 and 0.95 for the 5-week and 10-week data, respectively. The correlation was 0.97 for 10 week olds when the flat filtering function of Fig. 6 was used. Obviously, the model provided an excellent fit between predicted and observed preferences. Figure 10 summarizes this relationship. The left panel represents the 5-week data and predictions, and the right panel the 10-week data and predictions. The predicted preference value for each stimulus is indicated by the abscissa and the observed looking time by the ordinate. The agreement between predicted and observed preferences was very good. Thus, the linear systems model predicts preferences among size and number stimuli quite well.

We also computed predictions for Karmel's (1969) contour density model. The correlations between the observed looking times and the predicted preferences based on contour density were 0.98 and 0.69 for the 5 and 10 week olds, respectively. Thus, the contour density model also predicts preferences among size and number stimuli accurately for younger but not older infants.

C. MAISEL AND KARMEL STUDY

The experiments we have discussed thus far involved only linear, nonconcentric patterns. To broaden our survey, we next examined the model's ability to predict preferences among different sorts of patterns. We chose

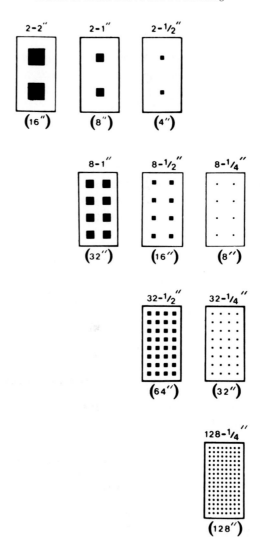

Fig. 9. *Stimuli used in the size and number experiment of Fantz and Fagan. The numbers at the top of each stimulus indicate the number and size of elements. The numbers at the bottom are the total length of contour. (From Fantz and Fagan, 1975.)*

Maisel and Karmel's (1978) data on preferences of 5 and 9 week olds for bull's-eyes varying in the size and number of concentric rings, concentric squares varying in the size and number of squares, and checkerboards varying in size and number. Maisel and Karmel presented three versions of each of these stimuli. (They actually presented a fourth type of pattern, a propeller pattern, but we did not analyze these data because at the time we did

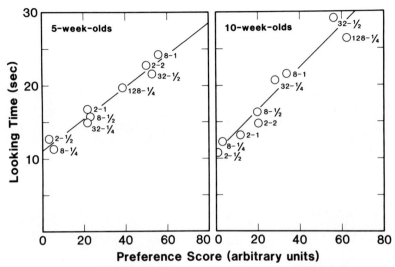

Fig. 10. *The observed and predicted preferences among size and number stimuli for 5 and 10 week olds. Observed looking time for each stimulus is plotted as a function of the preference value predicted by our model. Each data point is labeled as in Fig. 9.*

not have the facilities to compute the Fourier transform of these stimuli accurately.) Each trial consisted of a simultaneous presentation of one of the patterns paired with an unpatterned stimulus. Maisel and Karmel found that the younger infants preferred the bull's-eye, checkerboard, and concentric squares of lowest contour density. The older infants preferred those of intermediate density. The only obvious effect of configuration, when contour density was equated, was a preference for checkerboards over the other patterns. We used the 1-month and 2-month filtering functions of Fig. 6 to reanalyze the 5-week-old and 9-week-old data, respectively. We did not compute separate correlations for each age because of the small number of stimuli presented. The predictions were again quite good; the correlation between the observed and predicted most preferred stimulus was 0.96. The contour density correlation was 0.80.

D. MATRIX STUDIES

Finally, we examined some of Salapatek's (1975) matrix studies. Specifically, we reanalyzed his matrix studies 3 and 4, which were conducted with 2 month olds.

The matrix studies were developed to examine young infants' abilities to discriminate patterns and shapes. The stimuli presented in matrix study 3 are shown in Fig. 11. Notice that each stimulus had a uniform half com-

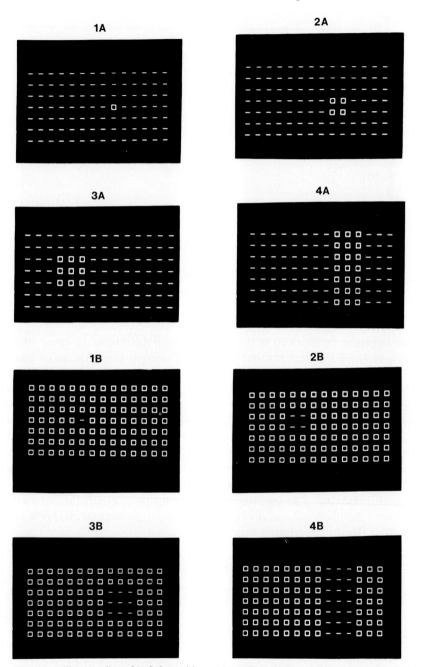

Fig. 11.   The stimuli used in Salapatek's matrix study 3. (Adapted from Salapatek, 1975.)

posed of line segments (1A, 2A, 3A, and 4A) or squares (1B, 2B, 3B, and 4B) and a half with a discrepant embedded matrix. Salapatek hoped that infants would preferentially fixate the side with the discrepancy whenever they could discriminate the discrepant and background elements. The size of the discrepant matrix varied from one to 7 × 3. Prior to the presentation of each matrix stimulus, the infant's line of sight was centered with a fixation stimulus. Then the fixation stimulus was replaced by one of the matrix stimuli and the direction of first fixation was scored. The 2 month olds did not preferentially fixate either half when the discrepant matrix was a single or 2 × 2 matrix embedded in a field of lines or squares (1A, 2A, 1B, and 2B). However, differential looking was observed with the 3 × 3 and 3 × 7 matrices. Infants looked *toward* the embedded square matrix (numbers 3A and 4A) and *away from* the embedded line matrices (3B and 4B). Stated another way, the infants always preferred the side with more squares whether they were discrepant or not. This behavior is distinctly different from that of older subjects. Three year olds and adults looked toward the discrepant matrices whether they were composed of squares or lines.

Salapatek asked what stimulus properties determined the 2 month olds' unexpected preferences. He explored two hypotheses: (1) the infants may simply have chosen the brighter of the two sides since the side with more squares was always brighter than the side with more lines; and (2) the infants may have chosen the side with greater contour density since squares have more contour than lines. Matrix study 4 was conducted to test the first hypothesis. The stimuli used are shown in Fig. 12. Note that stimuli 3A and 3B were identical to two of the stimuli in study 3. Stimuli 3AR and 3BR in

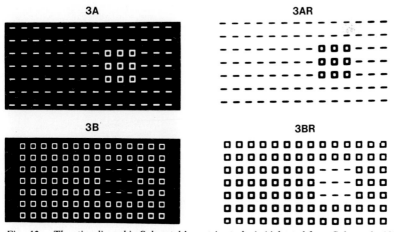

Fig. 12. The stimuli used in Salapatek's matrix study 4. (Adapted from Salapatek, 1975.)

study 4 were also similar to 3A and 3B in study 3, but they were reversed
in brightness. Salapatek reasoned that if infants were simply looking to the
brighter of the two sides, they should look toward the side with more squares
in stimuli 3A and 3B and toward the side with more lines in 3AR and 3BR.
The results clearly disconfirmed this hypothesis. Infants preferentially fixated the side with more squares in all of the stimuli. Salapatek concluded
that infants simply preferred to fixate the side with greater contour density.

We reanalyzed these experiments in the following fashion. The stimuli in
Figs. 11 and 12 were divided at midline. Each of those half stimuli was then
presented to our preference model. We assumed that the infants' tendency
to fixate one half over the other was determined solely by the difference in
preference values for the two halves. The predictions and observed data are
summarized in Fig. 13. The ordinate plots the percentage of first fixations
toward the side with the discrepant matrix. The abscissa plots the predicted
preference value for the side with the discrepancy; positive values mean that
fixation should be toward the discrepant matrix, and negative values mean
they should be away from the discrepancy. Notice that the model predicts
that infants should prefer the halves with more squares in all of the 3 × 3

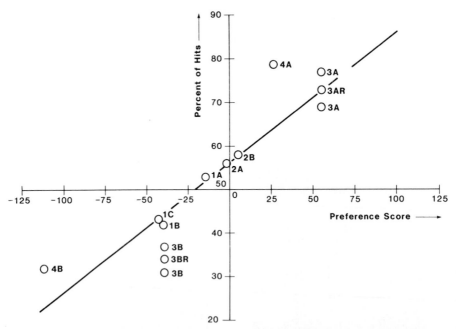

Fig. 13.   The observed and predicted preferences among the stimuli of matrix studies 3
and 4. The percentage of hits is plotted as a function of the difference of preference values
for the two sides of the stimulus. The percentage of hits is the percentage of first looks to the
side with the discrepant embedded matrix. Each data point is labeled as in Figs. 11 and 12.

and 3 × 7 stimuli even when that reflects a preference for the nondiscrepant side. Once again the agreement between the predicted and observed preferences was rather good; the correlation between the predictions and the data was 0.90. We also calculated the contour density predictions; they too were quite accurate, yielding a correlation of 0.93.

E. OTHER REANALYSES

As mentioned above, Gayl *et al.* (1983) and Slater *et al.* (1985) have also used linear systems techniques to examine infants' preferences among suprathreshold patterns. Gayl *et al.* reanalyzed Karmel's (1969) data. In that experiment, Karmel presented two types of checkerboards, regular and random, to 13 and 20 week olds. Each type was presented with four different check sizes. Karmel presented the stimuli in all possible pairings and measured infants' mean looking time for each. The results are summarized in Fig. 14. Interestingly, the most preferred check size among regular checkerboards was considerably larger than the optimal check size among random check patterns.

To reanalyze these data, Gayl *et al.* used a linear systems approach very

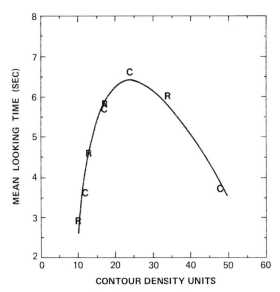

Fig. 14. The looking times observed by Karmel (1969) for regular and random checkerboards. Mean looking time for each stimulus is plotted as a function of contour density. The symbols C and R represent checkerboards and random check patterns, respectively. The line through the data points indicates Karmel's (1969) best-fitting function. (From Gayl et al., 1983.)

similar to the one described here and by Banks and Salapatek (1981). The similarity is illustrated by the following quotation: "the amount of time an infant spends looking at a complex pattern is some function of how well the infant sees the pattern, and . . . how well the infant sees the pattern can be estimated by considering the spatial frequency components of the pattern in relationship to the infant's spatial frequency sensitivity" (p. 34). Gayl *et al.* chose the 3-month CSF of Banks and Salapatek (1978) as the filtering function for Karmel's 13 week olds. Once the various stimuli were filtered, three different decision rules were employed to compute preference values. The first rule was identical to a rule considered by Banks and Salapatek (1981) and the second was identical to our square root of sums rule assuming no frequency/orientation channels. The third rule was similar to our square root of sums rule assuming the presence of multiple frequency/orientation channels. The first two rules simply did not predict Karmel's preference data very well. The third rule was much more successful, yielding a correlation of 0.95 between the predicted and observed looking times. This close relationship is illustrated in Fig. 15.

As mentioned above, Karmel (1969) derived his estimates of the optimal contour density at 13 and 20 weeks by analyzing these regular and random

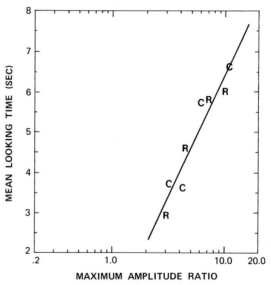

Fig. 15.   The observed and predicted preferences among regular and random checkerboards as reported by Gayl et al. Mean looking time for each stimulus is plotted as a function of the preference value predicted by their model. The symbols C and R represent checkerboards and random check patterns, respectively. (From Gayl et al., 1983.)

checkerboard data in a post hoc fashion. Thus, it is not meaningful to ask whether the contour density model can adequately account for these data. How similar is the Gayl *et al.* model to ours? It appears to be quite similar. As we mentioned, the decision rule they chose for 3 month olds is very similar to our rule for infants of that age. Unfortunately, one cannot ascertain the bandwidths of the frequency/orientation channels from their report, so we are not certain that our rules are similar in detail. One obvious difference between our model and theirs is the choice of filtering functions. They chose the 3-month CSF of Banks and Salapatek (1978), and we chose functions ranging from Banks and Salapatek's 3-month CSF to the flatter function of Stephens and Banks (1985). Our experience, howeveŕ, is that the curvilinear CSF and the flattened function yield reasonably similar predictions of *relative* preferences among stimuli, so this difference between our model and theirs may not be significant.

Slater *et al.* (1985) directly compared a linear systems model with Karmel's contour density model. To newborns they presented five pairs of stimuli that were identical in contour density but dissimilar in the distribution of spatial frequency components. These stimuli were patterns of stripes with different widths and spacings. The number of stripes was held constant, so the contour densities of the stimuli were identical. Slater *et al.* used a simple version of Banks and Salapatek's (1981) model to compute linear systems predictions. For all five pairings, infants preferentially fixated the stimulus predicted by the linear systems model. Consequently, Slater *et al.* concluded that the linear systems model provided a better account of newborns' preferences than the contour density model did.

VI. Evaluation of Preference Models

Most of the older preference models—discrepancy, complexity, and size and number—were not able to predict young infants' preferential looking for a reasonably diverse set of patterns. The contour density model was somewhat more successful. Nonetheless, the generic linear systems model predicted preferences more accurately than any of the older models for all of the stimuli considered. In this sense, linear systems models provide a better account of early preferences. Let us consider some of the reasons for this. As we noted in Section I, the discrepancy and complexity models were simply not explicit enough to test rigorously. The proponents of these models never stated clear definitions of stimulus complexity or discrepancy. They also never pinpointed measurable changes in infants' processing capabilities that caused age-related shifts in preference. The size and number model of Fantz and Fagan (1975) was more explicit but very limited in scope; they never stated how their model could be extended to stimuli other than check patterns. The contour density model of Karmel (1969) was commendably explicit and, as we have shown, able to account for an impressive array of preference data. In general, however, the predictions of the contour density model have not been as accurate as those of the linear systems model. Indeed, when Slater *et al.* (1985) constructed stimuli to oppose the predictions of the two models, their version of the linear systems model was clearly superior.

Although three versions now exist, the differences among the linear systems models do not appear to be important. The version presented here is the most explicit (and recent) of the three, however, so we will not discuss the others henceforth.

The linear systems model presented here offers several advantages over other previous preference models. (1) It utilizes a rich description of visual stimuli based on Fourier's theorem. It also puts to use powerful engineering techniques that allow one, in principle, to relate any two-dimensional, time-invariant stimulus to its response. (2) It uses empirical data (such as CSFs and channel bandwidths) to determine the age-related changes in processing that underlie shifts in preference. Almost all of the model's parameters have been set by empirical observations of the age changes in basic visual mechanisms. The only exceptions are the orientation bandwidths of channels in infants older than 2 months (there are no data, so we assumed adult-like bandwidths), and the choice of decision rule (in the absence of relevant data, we have chosen a simple and plausible one). (3) Most importantly, the model has proven so far to provide quite accurate predictions of actual preference data from birth to 3 months of age.

The linear systems model might share important features with the neural substrate models of Fantz *et al.* (1975), Karmel and Maisel (1975), and Haith (1980). It proposes, just as the neural models do, that infants' tendency to look at one pattern over another is governed by how well the pattern passes through the infant's filtering function. The linear systems view uses the CSF and contrast matching data to describe this filtering function. The neural substrate models use the size and shape of hypothetical receptive fields. Presumably, the size and shape of the CSF (and the suprathreshold filtering function) are dependent on receptive field size and shape at various levels in the visual system. Thus, the filtering functions of the linear systems model could be manifestations of the visual cortical receptive fields proposed by Haith and others.

The success of the linear systems model to date is surprising in some ways. For one thing, one might expect predictions based on linear systems equations to break down under suprathreshold conditions due to violations of the assumption of linearity. Our results, and those of Gayl *et al.* and Slater *et al.,* imply that the violations are simply not serious enough to affect the predictions greatly. Another surprise stems from the types of analyses used to test the model. All of the analyses that Gayl *et al.,* Slater *et al.,* and we have presented were based on between-subjects comparisons. Clear individual differences exist among infant preferences (Thomas & Jones-Molfese, 1977) and CSFs (Atkinson *et al.,* 1977a; Banks & Salapatek, 1981), so one might not expect between-subjects analyses to yield such high correlations. As Gayl *et al.* pointed out, within-subject experiments would presumably improve the accuracy of predictions even further.

Our results suggest an interesting research question: To what extent are "cognitive" variables such as stimulus significance, meaningfulness, or familiarity required to explain early preferences? This question could not be pursued rigorously in the past because "sensory" variables could not be controlled effectively. An example will clarify this point. Suppose one wanted to know when infants first exhibit a preference for faces because of their social significance. Showing that infants of a certain age preferred facelike over nonfacelike stimuli would not be convincing because critics could argue that the facelike stimuli simply passed better through the peripheral stages of visual processing (perhaps because they were high in contrast, the features were somewhat regularly spaced, etc.). To examine such a question experimentally, one would have to construct two stimuli, one facelike and one not, that passed equally well through peripheral processing. But one would not know how to construct such stimuli without a clear, quantitative model of the sensory aspects of pattern processing. The linear systems model might be useful in this regard. Its development has been based on empirical observations of the development of basic mechanisms of pattern vision. It has been tested with abstract, nonrepresentational patterns. It postulates nothing about the significance, meaningfulness, or familiarity of a visual stimulus. Thus, the model would not predict a strong preference for a face over a similar, but nonfacelike, stimulus except to the degree that the face provided spatial frequency information that fit the infant's filtering function better. One could use the linear systems model as a guide in constructing stimuli that minimized differences in how well they were transmitted in peripheral processing. Such stimuli would allow one to investigate infants' perceptions of faces as social objects more rigorously. Our argument here assumes, of course, that the linear systems model provides an accurate characterization of filtering in peripheral stages of processing. This assumption is at least plausible given how well linear systems techniques portray sensitivity to various sorts of patterns (Atkinson *et al.,* 1977b; Banks & Salapatek, 1981; Banks & Stephens, 1982).

As Banks and Salapatek (1981) have pointed out, simple sensory-based models, like the one described here, cannot adequately account for preferences in older infants: their preferences are assuredly influenced by the significance of a stimulus since certain stimulus configurations, such as Mom's face, acquire particular significance. It will be of particular interest to delimit the ages for which the linear systems model does and does not work. A clear failure to predict preferences at a certain age will imply that processes other than simple optical and neural filtering by the peripheral visual system have become significant to the infant's perceptual world.

VII.   Some Final Thoughts about the Rules for Preferences

The success of the linear systems model in predicting infant pattern preferences suggests an intriguing question: Why should young infants' visual behavior obey such simple rules? In other words, why should infants look at patterns they can see well rather than patterns they cannot? There is no obvious way to explore this question experimentally, but we would like to offer two related hypotheses.

The first hypothesis was stated originally by Fantz (1961). He put it this way: "It is . . . reasonable to suppose that the early interest of infants in form and pattern in general, as well as in particular kinds of pattern, play an important role in the development of behavior by focusing attention on stimuli that will later have adaptive significance" (p. 72). This hypothesis is attractive because patterned regions in the visual field are in fact much more likely than unpatterned regions to contain information that will become significant to the infant (e.g., faces, drop-offs, furniture). We would like to extend Fantz' hypothesis to incorporate our finding that infants prefer to fixate high-contrast, low-frequency contours over anything else. What does such pattern information normally correspond to in the infant's environment? Most objects are seen because of the contrast between their surface and the background. So a preference for high-contrast contours should generally correspond to a tendency to fixate object boundaries. What about the preference for low spatial frequencies? As Banks and Salapatek (1981) observed, the spatial frequencies contained within an object change systematically with the distance between the infant and the object. As an object is brought closer, its angular size increases and its constituent sine wave components shift toward lower frequencies. Thus, a preference for low spatial frequencies corresponds to a tendency to fixate near rather than distant objects. Such a behavioral strategy is reasonable because young infants cannot direct effective action toward objects more than a meter away.

Furthermore, objects of concern, such as the face of a parent interacting with them, are generally presented at close range.

The second hypothesis about the teleology of early visual preferences is different from, but not contradictory to, the first. Briefly stated, the hypothesis is that preferential looking toward highly visible patterns is a useful strategy for providing visual stimulation that is needed to guide the development of the central visual system.

This hypothesis evolved from recent observations of how visual experience influences the development of central visual structures. The microstructure of the human visual cortex is strikingly immature at birth (e.g., Conel, 1939–1959). We do not know, of course, what the physiological properties of the cortex are at this age, but one suspects that they are quite immature, too. Indirect evidence from other species supports this claim. For example, the visual cortex of kittens is anatomically immature at birth and so are the physiological properties of individual cortical cells. Among physiological properties, the orientation (Blakemore and Van Sluyters, 1975), disparity (Pettigrew, 1974), and spatial-frequency (Derrington and Fuchs, 1981) selectivities of single cells are ill defined until 5–7 weeks after birth.

There is overwhelming evidence that particular types of visual experience are required for adultlike definition to emerge. Blakemore and Van Sluyters (1975), for example, traced the development of orientation selectivity in kittens reared with normal visual experience and with no visual experience. Before 4 weeks, the cortical cells of normally reared and binocularly deprived kittens were essentially indistinguishable. After 4 weeks, the cells in deprived animals became less and less responsive and selective compared to cells in normal animals. Blakemore and Van Sluyters next reared kittens in a variety of restricted environments in order to determine what sorts of visual experience were necessary to keep cortical development on its normal course. The necessary ingredients for normal binocularity and orientation selectivity were high-contrast, elongated contours presented to both eyes simultaneously. In support of this conclusion, Blakemore (1976) reported that reducing the illumination into one eye had no discernible effect on cortical development so long as both eyes experienced the same contour information.

Blakemore and Van Sluyters (1975) proposed a model of innate and experiential influences on the development of single cortical cells. They noted that most cortical cells in young kittens are not as selective as they are in adults. Those that are reasonably selective tend to be monocular. Blakemore and Van Sluyters argued that cortical cells must eventually acquire strict, adultlike preferences for similar environmental features presented to the two eyes. In other words, a given cortical cell must ultimately prefer similar orientations, spatial frequencies, and directions of motion for both eyes. Their model proposed that binocular visual experience with elongated contours provides vigorous, correlated neuronal activity, and that this activity is required for the acquisition of similar stimulus preferences for a narrow range of features.

If experience with patterned visual stimulation, correlated between the eyes, is a necessary condition for normal cortical development, how can an immature organism ensure that it receives an adequate diet of such stimulation? A few sensorimotor strategies come to mind. For one, it would be beneficial to focus or accommodate the eyes to provide sharp images to the retina; apparently, even young infants are capable of focusing with moderate accuracy (Banks, 1980; Braddick, Atkinson, French, & Howland, 1979). Second, it would be important to orient the two eyes toward roughly the same position in space in order to guarantee that a given feature falls on nearly corresponding regions on the two retinas, something neonates are equipped to do (Slater & Findlay, 1975). Finally, it would be useful to fixate (i.e., direct the foveas toward) regions in the visual environment that contain large, high-contrast contours. But the reader might raise questions about this claim. Why does the infant profit from orienting the *foveas* toward pattern stimulation? Such a fixation strategy would tend to maximize the amount of pattern information to which the foveal and parafoveal retina was exposed. But why might that be important? First, as Haith (1978) emphasized, the majority of the visual cortex is devoted to foveal and parafoveal processing, so this fixation strategy would ensure that most of the cortex would be exposed to patterned stimulation. Second, the requirements for spatial resolution and for the acquisition of similar feature preferences are probably greater for cortical cells subserving the fovea as opposed to the eccentric retina. For these reasons, we speculate that patterned stimulation of the central retina is important to the guidance of cortical development.

How would one determine which regions of the visual field provide the most adequate stimulation? It seems reasonable that measures of visual sensitivity could tell us which regions should be stimulating and which should not. If the filtering functions presented in Fig. 6 are valid estimates of how sensitive infants are to various sorts of information, then infants, when given a choice, should prefer to fixate pattern information that passes easily through those filtering functions. In other words, they should follow the rules the linear systems model claims they do.

In summary, our second hypothesis is that young infants' looking behavior reflects a fixation strategy that tends to expose the central retina to quite visible pattern information in order to provide the stimulation required for normal cortical development.

ACKNOWLEDGMENTS

This research was supported by NIH Research Grant HD–12572 and NIMH Research Scientist Development Award MH–00318 to MSB. The authors thank the late Philip Salapatek for many helpful discussions and Pat Bennett, Les Cohen, and Al Yonas for comments on an earlier draft.

REFERENCES

Albrecht, D. G., DeValois, R. L., & Thorell, L. G. (1980). Visual cortical neurons: Are bars or gratings the optimal stimuli? *Science, 207,* 88–90.

Aslin, R. N. (1985). Motor aspects of visual development in infancy. In P. Salapatek & L. B. Cohen (Eds.), *Handbook of infant perception.* New York: Academic Press.

Atkinson, J., Braddick, O., & Moar, K. (1977a). Development of contrast sensitivity over the first 3 months of life. *Vision Research, 17,* 1037–1044.

Atkinson, J., Braddick, O., & Moar, K. (1977b). Infants' detection of image defocus. *Vision Research, 17,* 1125–1126.

Banks, M. S. (1980). The development of visual accommodation during early infancy. *Child Development, 51,* 646–666.

Banks, M. S., & Dannemiller, J. L. (1985). Visual psychophysics. In P. Salapatek & L. B. Cohen (Eds.), *Handbook of infant perception,* New York: Academic Press.

Banks, M. S., & Salapatek, P. (1978). Acuity and contrast sensitivity in 1-, 2-, and 3-month old human infants. *Investigative Ophthalmology and Visual Science, 17,* 361–365.

Banks, M. S., & Salapatek, P. (1981). Infant pattern vision: A new approach based on the contrast sensitivity function. *Journal of Experimental Child Psychology, 31,* 1–45.

Banks, M. S., & Salapatek, P. (1983). Infant visual perception. In P. Mussen (Ed.), *Handbook of child psychology* (Vol. 2). New York: Wiley.

Banks, M. S., & Stephens, B. R. (1982). The contrast sensitivity of human infants to gratings differing in duty cycle. *Vision Research, 22,* 739–744.

Banks, M. S., Stephens, B. R., & Hartmann, E. E. (1985). The development of basic mechanisms of pattern vision. Spatial frequency channels. *Journal of Experimental Child Psychology,* in press.

Berlyne, D. E. (1960). *Conflict, arousal, and curiosity,* New York: McGraw-Hill.

Blakemore, C. (1976). The conditions required for the maintenance of binocularity in the kitten's visual cortex. *Journal of Physiology, 261,* 423–444.

Blakemore, C., & Van Sluyters, R. C. (1975). Innate and environmental factors in the development of the kitten's visual cortex. *Journal of Physiology, 248,* 663–716.

Bonds, A. B. (1979). Development of orientation tuning in the visual cortex of kittens. In R. D. Freeman (Ed.), *Developmental neurobiology of vision.* New York: Plenum.

Braddick, O., Atkinson, J., French, J., & Howland, H. C. (1979). A photorefractive study of infant accommodation. *Vision Research, 19,* 1319–1330.

Braddick, O., Campbell, F. W., & Atkinson, J. (1978). Channels in vision: Basic aspects. In R. Held, H. W. Leibowitz, & H.-L. Teuber (Eds.), *Handbook of sensory physiology. Perception* (Vol. 8). New York: Springer-Verlag.

Brennan, W. M., Ames, E. W., & Moore, R. W. (1966). Age differences in infants' attention to patterns of different complexity. *Science, 151,* 354–356.

Campbell, F. W., Cooper, G. F., & Enroth-Cugell, C. (1969). The spatial selectivity of the visual cells of the cat. *Journal of Physiology, 203,* 223–235.

Campbell, F. W., & Gubisch, R. W. (1966). Optical quality of the human eye. *Journal of Physiology,* **186,** 558-578.

Cohen, L. B. (1972). Attention-getting and attention-holding processes in infant visual preferences. *Child Development,* **43,** 869-879.

Conel, J. L. (1939-1959). *The postnatal development of the human cerebral cortex* (Vols. 1-7). Cambridge: Harvard Univ. Press.

Cornsweet, T. N. (1970). *Visual perception.* New York: Academic Press.

Dannemiller, J. L., & Banks, M. S. (1983). Can selective adaptation account for early infant habituation? *Merrill-Palmer Quarterly,* **29,** 151-158.

Dannemiller, J. L., & Banks, M. S. (1985). Selective adaptation and infant habituation: A reply to Slater and Morison. *Merrill-Palmer Quarterly,* in press.

Dember, W. N., & Earl, R. W. (1957). Analysis of exploratory, manipulatory, and curiosity behaviors. *Psychological Review,* **64,** 91-96.

Derrington, A. M., & Fuchs, A. F. (1981). The development of spatial-frequency selectivity in kitten striate cortex. *Journal of Physiology,* **316,** 1-10.

Dobson, V., & Teller, D. Y. (1978). Visual acuity in human infants: A review and comparison of behavioral and electrophysiological studies. *Vision Research,* **18.**

Fantz, R. L. (1958). Pattern vision in young infants. *Psychological Record,* **8,** 43-47.

Fantz, R. L. (1961). The origin of form perception. *Scientific American,* **204,** 66-72.

Fantz, R. L. (1963). Pattern vision in newborn infants. *Science,* **140,** 296-297.

Fantz, R. L., & Fagan, J. F., III. (1975). Visual attention to size and number of pattern details by term and preterm infants during the first six months. *Child Development,* **16,** 3-18.

Fantz, R. L., Fagan, J. F., III, & Miranda, S. B. (1975). Early visual selectivity as a function of pattern variables, previous exposure, age from birth and conception, and expected cognitive deficit. In L. B. Cohen & P. Salapatek (Eds.), *Infant perception: From sensation to cognition. Basic visual processes* (Vol. 1). New York: Academic Press.

Fantz, R. L., & Nevis, S. (1967). Pattern preferences and perceptual-cognitive development in early infancy. *Merrill-Palmer Quarterly,* **13,** 77-108.

Fox, R., Aslin, R. N., Shea, S. L., & Dumais, S. T. (1980). Stereopsis in human infants. *Science,* **207,** 323-324.

Gaskill, J. D. (1978). *Linear systems, Fourier transforms, and optics.* New York: Wiley.

Gayl, I. E., Roberts, J. O., & Werner, J. S. (1983). Linear systems analysis of infant visual pattern preferences. *Journal of Experimental Child Psychology,* **35,** 30-45.

Georgeson, M. (1979). Spatial fourier analysis and human vision. *Tutorial Essays in Psychology,* **2,** 39-88.

Georgeson, M. A., & Sullivan, G. D. (1975). Contrast constancy: Deblurring in human vision by spatial frequency channels. *Journal of Physiology,* **252,** 627-656.

Ginsburg, A. P. (1978). *Visual information processing based on spatial filters constrained by biological data.* Doctoral dissertation, University of Cambridge.

Greenberg, D. J., & Blue, S. Z. (1975). Visual complexity in infancy: Contour or numerosity? *Child Development,* **46,** 357-363.

Haith, M. M. (1978). Visual competence in early infancy. In R. Held, H. Leibowitz, & H. L. Tenber (Eds.), *Handbook of sensory physiology.* Berlin: Springer-Verlag.

Haith, M. M. (1980). *Rules that babies look by.* Hillsdale, NJ: Erlbaum.

Haith, M. M., Kessen, W., & Collins, D. (1969). Response of the human infant to level of complexity of intermittent visual movement. *Journal of Experimental Child Psychology,* **7,** 52-69.

Harris, L., Atkinson, J. L., & Braddick, O. (1976). Visual contrast sensitivity of a 6-month-old infant measured by the evoked potential. *Nature (London),* **264,** 570-571.

Hess, R. F. (1983). Contrast coding in amblyopia. II. On the physiological basis of contrast recruitment. *Proceedings of the Royal Society of London,* **217,** 331-340.

Hubel, D. H., & Wiesel, T. N. (1962). Receptive fields, binocular interaction and functional architecture in the cat's visual cortex. *Journal of Physiology,* **160,** 106-154.

Hubel, D. H., & Wiesel, T. N. (1968). Receptive fields and functional architecture of monkey striate cortex. *Journal of Physiology,* **195,** 215-243.

Kagan, J. (1970). Attention and psychological change in the young child. *Science,* **170,** 826-832.

Karmel, B. Z. (1969). The effect of age, complexity, and amount of contour density on pattern preferences in human infants. *Journal of Experimental Child Psychology,* **7,** 339-354.

Karmel, B. Z., & Maisel, E. B. (1975). A neuronal activity model for infant visual attention. In L. B. Cohen & P. Salapatek (Eds.), *Infant perception: From sensation to cognition. Basic visual processes* (Vol. 1). New York: Academic Press.

Kelly, D. H. (1976). Pattern detection and the two-dimensional Fourier transform: Flickering checkerboards and chromatic mechanisms. *Vision Research,* **16,** 277-287.

Maisel, E. B., & Karmel, B. Z. (1978). Contour density and pattern configuration in visual preferences in infants. *Infant Behavior and Development,* **1,** 127-140.

Marr, D. (1982). *Vision: A computational investigation into the human representation and processing of visual information.* San Francisco: Freeman.

McCall, R. B., & Melson, W. H. (1970). Complexity, contour, and area as determinants of attention in infants. *Developmental Psychology,* **3,** 343-349.

Miranda, S. B. (1970). Visual abilities and pattern preferences of premature infants and full-term neonates. *Journal of Experimental Child Psychology,* **10,** 189-205.

Miranda, S. B., & Fantz, R. L. (1971). Distribution of visual attention by newborn infants among patterns varying in size and number of details. *Proceedings of the Annual Convention of the American Psychological Association,* **6,** 181-182.

Munsinger, H., & Weir, M. W. (1967). Infants' and young children's preference for complexity. *Journal of Experimental Child Psychology,* **5,** 69-73.

Peeples, D. R., & Teller, D. Y. Color vision and brightness discrimination in two-month-old human infants. *Science,* **189,** 1102-1103.

Pettigrew, J. D. (1974). The effect of visual experience on the development of stimulus specificity by kitten cortical neurones. *Journal of Physiology,* **237,** 49-74.

Pirchio, M., Spinelli, D., Fiorentini, A., & Maffei, L. (1978). Infant contrast sensitivity evaluated by evoked potentials. *Brain Research,* **141,** 179-184.

Pollen, D., Lee, J. R., & Taylor, J. H. (1971). How does the striate cortex begin the reconstruction of the visual world. *Science,* **173,** 74-77.

Ratliff, F. (1965). *Mach bands: Quantative studies on neural networks in the retina.* San Francisco: Holden-Day.

Ruff, H. A., & Birch, H. G. (1974). Infant visual fixation: The effect of concentricity, curvilinearity, and the number of directions. *Journal of Experimental Child Psychology,* **17,** 460-473.

Ruff, H. A., & Turkewitz, G. (1975). Developmental changes in the effectiveness of stimulus intensity on infant visual attention. *Developmental Psychology,* **11,** 705-710.

Salapatek, P. (1975). Pattern perception in early infancy. In L. B. Cohen & P. Salapatek (Eds.), *Infant perception: From sensation to cognition. Basic visual processes* (Vol. 1). New York: Academic Press.

Slater, A., & Morison, V. (1985). Selective adaptation cannot account for early infant habituation: A response to Dannemiller and Banks (1983), *Merrill-Palmer Quarterly,* **31,** 99-103.

Slater, A., Earle, D. C., Morison, V., & Rose, D. (1985). Pattern preferences at birth and their interaction with habituation-induced novelty preferences. *Journal of Experimental Child Psychology,* in press.

Slater, A. M., & Findlay, J. M. (1975). Binocular fixation in the newborn baby. *Journal of Experimental Child Psychology,* **20,** 248–273.

Spelke, E. (1976). Infants' intermodal perception of events. *Cognitive Psychology,* **8,** 553–560.

Stephens, B. R., & Banks, M. S. (1985). The development of contrast constancy. *Journal of Experimental Child Psychology,* in press.

Teller, D. Y., & Bornstein, M. H. (1985). Infant color vision and color perception. In P. Salapatek & L. B. Cohen (Eds.) *Handbook of infant perception,* New York: Academic Press.

Teller, D. Y., Morse, R., Borton, R., & Regal, D. (1974). Visual acuity for vertical and diagonal gratings in human infants. *Vision Research,* **14,** 1433–1439.

Thomas, H. (1971). Discrepancy hypotheses: Methodological and theoretical considerations. *Psychological Review,* **78,** 249–259.

Thomas, H., & Jones-Molfese, V. (1977). Infants and I scales: Inferring change from the ordinal stimulus selections of infants for configural stimuli. *Journal of Experimental Child Psychology,* **23,** 329–339.

Welch, M. J. (1974). Infants' visual attention to varying degrees of novelty. *Child Development,* **45,** 344–350.

Yonas, A., & Owsley, C. (1985). Development of visual space perception. In P. Salapatek & L. B. Cohen (Eds.), *Handbook of infant perception,* New York: Academic Press.

AUTHOR INDEX

Numbers in italics refer to pages on which the complete references are listed.

Reynolds, R. E., 51, 61, 63, 64, 71, 72, *80,*
81
Reznick, J. S., 97, *111*
Ribble, M. A., *204*
Richards, I. A., 66, 71, *80*
Richer, S., *204*
Richman, C. L., 121, 122, 129, 130, *145,*
147
Ricks, D. P., *204*
Rim, Y., 158, *202*
Rips, L. J., 74, *80*
Rittenhouse, R. K., 58, 59, 64, *79*
Roberts, J., 167, *204*
Roberts, J. O., 227, 235, 236, 237, 239, *244*
Robbins, L. C., 172, *205*
Robinson, S., 52, 53, 55, 68, *79*
Robinson, W. A., 175, *200*
Rodrigue, J. R., 35, *42*
Roe, A., 164, *204*
Roff, M., *204*
Rollins, H. A., 127, 128, 139, *145*
Romanoff, J. S., 160, *204*
Rosch, E. H., 74, *80,* 85, 94, 95, *111,* 121,
133, *146, 148*
Rose, D., 224, 227, 235, 237, 238, 239, *245*
Rose, S. A., 97, *111*
Rosenbaum, A. L., 191, *201*
Rosenberg, B. G., 151, 152, 157, 163, *204*
Rosenstiel, A. K., 72, *81*
Rosenthal, R., 153, 164, *204*
Rosnow, R. L., 153, 164, *204*
Ross, B. M., 6, *46*
Ross, J. M., 156, 157, 168, *199*
Rosser, M., 84, *110*
Rossi, E. L., 127, *148*
Rossi, S. I., 127, *148*
Rothbart, M. K., 17, *46*
Ruddy, M., 9, 12, *42, 46*
Ruff, H. A., 208, *245*
Rumelhart, D. E., 118, *147*
Rundus, D., 115, *148*
Russell, M., 194, *204*

S

Salapatek, P. H., 11, 12, 21, *44,* 211, 217,
218, 219, 220, 222, 224, 225, 227, 231,
232, 236, 237, 239, 240, *243*
Sampson, E. E., 152, *204*

Santrock, J., 177, *202*
Scarr, S., 167, *200*
Schalter, W. M., *204*
Schank, R. C., *46*
Scheinfeld, D., 175, *204*
Schneider, H., 118, 129, *148*
Schneider, W., 39, *46,* 124, 139, *148*
Schoonover, S. M., 161, 162, 168, *204*
Schubert, D. S. P., 150, 151, 156, 188, 190,
204, 205
Schubert, H. J. P., 150, 151, 188, *204, 205*
Schubert, M. R., *201*
Schüller, V., 166, 167, 197, *202*
Seider, R. A., 189, *200*
Selvin, S., 191, *204*
Sewell, M., *204*
Shafer, J. W., 194, *199*
Shepard, R. N., 87, *111*
Shea, S. L., 210, *244*
Shepp, B. E., 61, 69, *80,* 85, 88, 90, 91,
100, 107, 108, *110, 111, 112*
Sherick, I., 172, *202*
Sherman, T., 11, *45*
Shiffrin, R. M., 39, *46,* 118, 124, *148*
Shobin, E. J., 74, *80*
Siegel, I. E., 175, *198*
Siegel, L. S., 6, 8, 9, *46,* 123, *146*
Siegler, R. S., 22, 39, *46,* 118, *146, 148*
Siladi, D., 116, *144*
Silberstein, L., 53, 54, 70, 72, *80*
Simon, H. A., 119, *145*
Simpson, H. R., 156, 157, 168, *199*
Singer, L. T., 2, 15, *43*
Slater, A., 224, 227, 235, 237, 238, 239,
242, *245, 246*
Slobin, D. I., 50, *80*
Smalley, R. E., *204*
Smith, E. E., 74, *80*
Smith, J. D., 91, *112*
Smith, J. R., 156, *199*
Smith, L. B., 85, 88, 91, 92, 95, *111, 112*
Sokolov, E. N., 21, *46*
Sowry, B. M., 59, 62, *78*
Spelke, E. S., 88, *110,* 210, *246*
Sperber, R. D., 71, 74, *79,* 124, *146*
Spiers, P. S., 192, 195, *204*
Spilich, G. J., 123, *145, 148*
Spinelli, D., 219, 220, *245*
Spitz, R. A., 173, *204*
Spock, B., 184, *204*

Stabeneau, J. R., *204*
Stein, B. S., 26, *43*
Stein, Z., 152, 161, 166, *198*
Steinberg, E. R., 71, *80*
Stenberg, C., *42*
Stendler, C. B., 172, *204*
Stephens, B. R., 220, 221, 222, 224, 225, 226, 239, *243, 246*
Stern, W., 2, *46*
Sternberg, R. J., 2, 3, 9, 10, 17, 18, 22, 23, 24, 26, 27, 28, 31, 32, 34, 38, 39, *42, 43, 45, 46, 47,* 51, 53, *80, 81*
Sterner, G. A., 182, *204*
Stone, B. P., 117, 141, *147*
Stone, L. J., 184, *205*
Strauss, M. S., 11, *42,* 84, 95, 97, 102, *110, 112*
Strude, M. J., 153, *205*
Strumpfer, D. J., 181, *205*
Sturge, C., 177, *199*
Suchindran, C. M., 152, *205*
Sullivan, G. D., 222, 223, *244*
Suomi, S. J., 176, 178, *205*
Sutton-Smith, B., 151, 152, 157, 163, 186, *204, 205*
Svenson, O., 102, *111*
Swartz, K. B., 91, *111*

T

Tarkin, B., 129, 131, 141, *148*
Taylor, J. H., 221, *245*
Teller, D. Y., 210, 211, 217, *244, 245, 246*
Templer, J., 189, *205*
Terman, L. M., 9, *46*
Tesser, A., 177, *205*
Tetewsky, S., 32, *46*
Teyber, E. C., 184, *201*
Thomas, A., 172, *205*
Thomas, C. B., 194, *199*
Thomas, H., 209, 239, *246*
Thompson, B. E., 121, 133, 134, *144*
Thorell, L. G., 221, *243*
Tighe, T. J., 100, *112*
Timberlake, J., 187, *200*
Toman, W., 178, *205*
Tourangeau, R., 51, 53, *80, 81*
Trause, M. A., 172, *205*
Tsukada, G. K., 178, *205*

Tulving, E., 114, *148*
Turkewitz, G., 208, *245*
Tversky, A., *81*

U

Ulvund, S. E., 9, 40, *46*
Uzgiris, I., 8, 9, *46*

V

Vandell, D. L., 177, *202*
VanHorn, H., *206*
Van Sluyters, R. C., 221, 241, *243*
Velandia, W., 161, 162, *205*
Ventis, L., 156, 166, 183, 188, *202*
Verbrugge, R. R., 55, 56, 65, *81*
Vernon, P. E., 3, *46*
Vesonder, G. T., 123, *148*
Vietze, P. M., 36, *47*
Visher, S. S., 166, *205*
Voegtle, K., 59, 62, *78*
Vosniadou, S., 61, 63, 64, 65, 66, 70, 71, 72, *81*
Voss, J. F., 123, *145, 148*
Vye, N. J., 26, *43*
Vygotsky, L. S., 77, *81*

W

Wadland, W., 172, *202*
Wagner, M. E., 150, 151, 188, *204, 205*
Wagner, R. K., 26, *47*
Waldrop, M. F., 6, *44,* 158, 188, 193, *205*
Walker, L. V., 189, *205*
Wang, L., 192, 195, *204*
Weil, C. M., 71, 74, *79,* 124, *146*
Weinberg, R. A., 167, *200*
Weiner-Erlich, W. K., 107, 108, *110*
Weir, M. W., 209, *245*
Welch, M. J., 209, *246*
Wellman, H. M., 95, *110,* 117, 142, *145, 148*
Werner, H., 6, *47,* 57, *81*
Werner, J. S., 11, 23, 38, *47,* 227, 235, 236, 237, 239, *244*
West, S. A., 57, 58, 59, 67, 72, 73, *79*

SUBJECT INDEX